POLITY AND ECONOMY OF THE PUNJAB DURING THE LATE EIGHTEENTH CENTURY

Polity and Economy of the Punjab during the Late Eighteenth Century

VEENA SACHDEVA

MANOHAR
2026

The publication of this book was financially supported by the Indian Council of Historical Research. The responsibility for the facts stated or opinions expressed is entirely of the author and not of the Council.

First published 1993
Reprinted 2026

ISBN 978-81-7304-033-7

Published by
Ajay Kumar Jain *for*
Manohar Publishers & Distributors
4753/23 Ansari Road, Daryaganj
New Delhi 110 002

Printed at
Replika Press Pvt. Ltd.

To

Jai Aditaya, Shanaya and Aveer Singh

Preface

In a country ruled by 'seventy thousand sovereigns', it would be wrong to assume that 'any class could find happiness, contentment or rest'. This was Henry T. Prinsep's comment on Sikh polity during the late eighteenth century. His reference to the number of Sikh rulers cannot be taken literally. But there is hardly any doubt that their number was much larger than the number of new rulers in any other area of equal size in the former empire of the Mughals. What Prinsep does not mention, and perhaps did not know, is the fact that the number of non-Sikh rulers who supplanted the Mughals in the Punjab was equally large. The present study deals with all the new rulers in the area between the rivers Satlej and Indus, besides the hill principalities formerly attached to the province of Lahore.

Prinsep's assumption that the condition of the subject people could not be happy under 'seventy thousand sovereigns' raises the question of the effect of political change on the life of the people in the Punjab. This assumption can be examined with reference to the political organization, administrative arrangements, land revenue, patterns of state patronage and the main features of urban as well as agrarian economy in the territories of the numerous chiefs who came to rule over the Punjab in place of the Mughals. Since the conclusions drawn are not only new but also radically different from what has been said on the subject by most of the historians, it becomes almost obligatory to set forth all the relevant evidence in detail. In addition to the source material in Persian and Punjabi and the contemporary accounts of the European and native travellers, this study is based substantially on the unpublished records available at the National Archives of India, New Delhi.

This book is a revised version of the doctoral thesis submitted to Guru Nanak Dev University in 1987 under the title 'Polity and Economy in the Late Eighteenth-Century Punjab'. I take this opportunity to express my deep sense of gratitude to Professor J.S. Grewal who supervised my research with great interest. I am thankful to Professor Indu Banga who took interest in this study at all stages. Among other individuals and institutions, I acknowledge with pleasure the help received from Mr. T.K. Majumdar and Mr. L.K. Dass of Shimla, and S. Gianinder Singh and S. Jaswinder Singh Marwaha of Amritsar. Among the libraries which I found most helpful I must mention the Department of History, Guru Nanak Dev University, Amritsar; Sikh History Research Department, Khalsa College, Amritsar; the Deputy Commissioner's office, Amritsar; Central Library, Patiala; Punjab State Archives, Patiala and the National Archives of India, New Delhi. It would have been difficult for me to complete this study without a Research Fellowship and a Research Associateship from Guru Nanak Dev University, Amritsar. The Indian Council of Historical Research gave financial assistance for this publication, and the publishers have done their work with great care and patience.

Mr. N.K. Maini has been extremely helpful to the author in seeing this book through the press.

VEENA SACHDEVA

Contents

Glossary

Akāli	:	also called *nihang* : the militant followers of Guru Gobind Singh who regarded themselves to be the guardians of the faith.
'Āmil	:	a revenue collector, interchangeable with *kārdār* as the administrator of a *ta'alluqa.*
Bairāgī	:	a member of the Vaishnava order of ascetics.
Batāī	:	division of produce between the cultivator and the state.
Begār	:	a cess in lieu of unpaid labour.
Bet	:	the flood plain of a river.
Bhet	:	an offering to a deity; land given in charity.
Bigha	:	a measure of land generally considered equal to 20 *biswas* or 2 *kanals*; also 1/4 of a *ghumāon.*
Chahār Mahāl	:	the four *mahāl* of Aurangabad, Pasrur, Sialkot and Eminabad ceded to Nadir Shah by the Mughal emperor and later claimed by Ahmad Shah Abdali.
Chahāram	:	literally, one fourth; the fourth share generally of the produce, and sometimes of the revenues; *chahāramī*: a holder of the *chahāram.*
Dal Khālsa	:	the combined forces of a number of Sikh leaders for a specific purpose.
Deg	:	literally a cauldron, signifying bounty.
Dhādi	:	a musician who used to sing in praise of the Sikh Gurus and recount the heroic deeds of the Sikhs.
Dharmarth	:	literally by way of religious duty; land revenue alienated in favour of a religious personage or institution.
Dharmsāla	:	synonymous with *gurdwāra* as a place of Sikh worship; also a resting place for travellers.
Dīwān	:	the head of the finance department at headquarters.
Doāb	:	a region lying between two rivers.
Faqīr	:	used generally for a Muslim mendicant.
Fateh	:	victory.
Faujdār	:	the official who maintained troops for law and order.

Ghee : clarified butter.

Ghumāon : a measure of land, varying in different parts of the Panjab and consisting of 8 *kanals*; also, equal to 4 *bighas*.

Ghurcharha : a horse-rider; a cavalry man.

Granthī : professional reader of the Granth.

Gurmata : a decision taken by the Sikhs before the Guru Granth Sāhib.

Har Mandar : the Golden Temple at Amritsar.

Hundī : a bill of exchange.

Ijāra : an arrangement in which a certain source of income was placed in the charge of a person on the condition that he would pay a certain stipulated sum to the state in return.

In'ām : literally, a reward; an assignment of revenue distinct from *jāgīr* and *dharmarth*, and implying the idea of reward; *in'ām-i- zamīndarī* : the revenue-free lands given to *chaudharīs* and *muqaddams* in addition to their customary commission (generally called *pachotra*).

Jāgīr : an assignment of land revenue in lieu of salary.

Kanāl : a measure of land consisting of 20 *marlas* and equal to one-half of a *bigha* or 1/8th of a *ghumāon*.

Kankūt : a method of assessment based on the appraisement of the standing crop by measurement of the land and inspection of the crop.

Kārdār : a revenue collector of a *ta'alluqa* or a *pargana*.

Katra : a market-cum-residential quarter, with its own entrance and internal management.

Khālisa : lands from which revenues were collected directly by the state in contrast with the land alienated in *jāgīr, dharmarth, in'ām* or any other kind of alienation of revenue.

Khālsa : an epithet used for the followers of Guru Gobind Singh, derived from the idea of a direct link between the Sikh and the Guru; used for an individual Sikh as well as for the collective body.

Khānqah : a religious establishment, generally of the *sufi* recluses.

Kharīf	:	the autumnal harvest, sown in April-May before the commencement of the rains and reaped in October-November.
Khatri	:	from the Sanskrit *kshaṭriya*; a caste to which most of the Hindu revenue officials and other administrators belonged in the Punjab.
Khidmatgār	:	a servant; an attendant.
Lambardār	:	a village headman.
Lāngarī	:	the person in charge of the kitchen (*langar*) of a chief.
Lungī	:	a piece of cloth worn tied to the waist and flowing down to ankles.
Madad-i-ma'āsh	:	literally, aid for subsistence; it was the term most commonly used in the Mughal times for land revenue alienated in favour of a religious personage or institution.
Mahant	:	the head of a religious order or establishment among the Hindus and *udāsī* Sikhs.
Mansab	:	literally, office, position or rank; indicating under the Mughals the status, obligations and remuneration of its holder in the official hierarchy.
Mansabdār	:	the holder of a rank carrying certain fixed remuneration and obligations.
Marla	:	a measure of land consisting of 9 *sarsais* and equal to 1/20th of a *kanāl* or 1/160th part of a *ghumāon*.
Maund	:	a unit of weight consisting of 40 *sers*.
Mauza'	:	a village.
Mirāsī	:	a caste of Muslims generally employed as musicians, bards and genealogists.
Muhalla	:	a quarter in a town.
Mulla	:	a Muslim priest and teacher, generally in charge of the mosque in a village.
Munshī	:	a writer or a scribe.
Muqaddam	:	a village headman.
Mutasaddi	:	an accountant, an official.
Nāzim	:	the governor of a province; an administrator.
Nazrāna	:	the tribute paid by a vassal.
Nirmala sādhs	:	the ascetics and renunciants belonging to the *nirmala* order among the Sikhs.

Pachotra : a commission of 5 per cent on the revenues collected, received by *chaudharīs* and *muqaddams* as remuneration for their services.

Panch : a member of the *panchāyat*; the headman of a village or of one of its sub-divisions.

Pandit : a Brāhman, whether learned or not.

Pargana : an administrative unit next to *suba*; synonymous with a *ta'alluqa*.

Parwāna : a written order under the seal of a person in power.

Pattīdār : literally, the holder of a share; used for autonomous co-sharer of a chief.

Patwāri : the village accountant.

Qānūngo : a hereditary keeper of the revenue records at the *pargana* or the ta'alluqa level; *qānūngoi* : the office of the *qānūngo*; the perquisites and remuneration related to it, also called *rasūm-i- qānūngoī*.

Qāzī : an official appointed by the government to administer civil and criminal justice according to the Islamic Law.

Rabī' : the spring crop generally sown in October-November and reaped in April-May.

Rāgī : a singer, particularly of the verses in the Sikh Scripture.

Rākhī : literally protection; a transitional arrangement signifying essentially the Sikh chief's claim to a part of the produce from land in return for protection afforded against all other claimants.

Sādh : a person devoted to religious pursuits.

Samādh : a memorial raised on the place of cremation, generally for persons prominent in one sphere or another.

Sammat : an era; the Bikramī Era.

Sanad : royal ordinance or any deed or grant or certificate from one in authority.

Sarbat Khālsa : the entire body of the Khālsa; the Sikh Panth.

Sardār : a leader; a Sikh ruler.

Sawār : a horseman.

Sayyad : a descendant of Prophet Muhammad, especially one of his grandson, Hussain, and held in veneration by the rulers and the people alike.

Ser : a measure of weight varying in different parts of the Punjab, and for different articles but generally reckoned as 1/40th of a *maund;* a seer.

Shaikh : the head of a religious fraternity; the title taken by the descendants of Prophet Muhammad.

Sharī'at : the Islamic Law.

Sūba : a province or the primary division of an empire; *sūbadār* : the governor of a province.

Takya : a place of repose or the dwelling place of a *faqīr*.

Tegh : the sword, signifying physical force.

Thākurdwāra : a temple dedicated to Lord Vishnu or one of His incarnations.

Thāna : a garrison stationed usually in a newly conquered territory; a garrison in a fort; *thānadār* : the commandant of a garrison or of a fort; *thānadārī* : literally, the office of the thānadār; also a cess for him.

Tirnī : the grazing tax.

Toshākhāna : the royal treasury.

Udāsī : literally, a renunciant; viewed traditionally as a follower of Guru Nanak through his son Sri Chand who founded an ascetical order of Sikhs; *udāsī akhara*: a religious establishment of the *udāsī* order.

Vakīl : an agent or a deputy; an envoy.

Vaishnava : relating to the worshipers of Lord Vishnu, in His incarnations of Rama and Krishna in particular.

Zabt : a method of assessment based on measurement and applied commonly to perishable and superior crops.

Zamīndār : literally, the possessor of land; a peasant proprietor; also the holder of a right over a certain share in the produce from land.

1

CHIEFS OF THE HILLS

I

J. Hutchison and J.Ph. Vogel in their *History of the Punjab Hill States* divide the Punjab hills into three groups: the western, between the rivers Indus and Jehlam; the central, between the rivers Jehlam and Ravi; and the eastern, between the rivers Ravi and Satlej. In the western group, according to them, there were twelve principalities, all associated with the province of Kashmir. These principalities were Gingal, Muzaffarabad, Khagan, Garhi, Rash, Dhamtaur (Dhantawar), Gandgarh, Darband, Tarbela, Pharwala, Sultanpur and Khanpur.[1]

A careful analysis of the available evidence suggests, however, that some of these principalities were attached to the province of Lahore during the Mughal times. Darband, for instance, is mentioned in the *Ā'in-i-Akbarī* under the province of Lahore.[2] It may be safe to infer that the principalities to the south of Darband were also under the province of Lahore. The principalities of Khanpur, Sultanpur and Tarbela lay between Darband and Rawalpindi. Pharwala or Prahla, which was under the Gakkhars during the reign of Akbar, was situated in the south of Rawalpindi.[3]

---

[1] J. Hutchison & J.Ph. Vogel, *History of the Punjab Hill States*, Department of Languages and Culture, Simla, 1982 (reprint, first published in 1933), I, 41 (cited hereafter as *Hill States*).

[2] Abu'l-Fazl Allami, *Ā'īn-i-Akbarī* (tr. into English by Colonel H.S. Jarrett), Oriental Books Reprint Corporation, New Delhi, 1978 (3rd ed., first published in 1891), II, 327.

[3] Irfan Habib, *Atlas of the Mughal Empire*, Oxford University Press, New Delhi ,1982, 4A. *Gazetteer of the District Hazara (*1907), Map No.2 (all the subsequent references to the District Gazetteers would be prefixed hereafter by *DG*). Ahsan Raza Khan, *Chieftains in the Mughal Empire During the Reign of Akbar*, Indian Institute of Advanced Study, Simla, 1977, Plate No. 2.

Darband was wrested from the Qarlugh Turks by the Tanaoli Afghans around 1700. During the early eighteenth century, the new chiefs of Darband actually established two principalities: the Hindwal chiefs ruling over upper Darband and the Pallal chiefs ruling over lower Darband (Sarai Niamat Khan). The Gujjar Chiefs of Tarbela were displaced by the Utmanzais in the early eighteenth century. In Sultanpur, the Karral and Dhund tribes became independent of the Gakkhars under their own chiefs at Nara and Mari. In Khanpur, however, the Gakkhars continued to enjoy power during the eighteenth century.[4] When Ahmad Shah Abdali took over the provinces of Lahore and Kashmir, he asserted his suzerain claims over all the principalities formerly attached to these provinces. Whereas, the control of Ahmad Shah and his successors over the principalities of the central and the eastern group was nominal, their control over upper and lower Darband, Tarbela, Nara, Mari and Khanpur was more effective throughout the late eighteenth century.[5] These principalities were finally liquidated by Maharaja Ranjit Singh in the nineteenth century.[6]

According to Hutchison and Vogel, there were twentytwo principalities in the central group: Jammu, Mankot (Ramkot), Jasrota, Lakhanpur, Samba, Tirikot, Akhnur, Riasi, Dalpatpur, Bhau, Kirmchi (Bhoti), Chenini, Bandralta (Ramnagar), Basohli, Bhadarwah, Bhadu, Bhimber, Khari Khariali, Kashtwar, Punch, Kotli and Rajauri.[7] However, all these principalities were not attached to the province of Lahore. Kashtwar, Punch, Kotli and Rajauri remained subject to the governor of Kashmir during the Mughal period and also when Kashmir was taken over by the Afghans.[8] One more principality included by Hutchison and Vogel in the central group, namely Lakhanpur, had been taken over by the chiefs of Jasrota sometime in the early eighteenth century.[9] Of the remaining seventeen principalities, closest to the plains were Khari Khariali, Bhimber and Akhnur between the rivers Jehlam and Chenab, and Jammu, Dalpatpur, Bhau, Samba, Tirikot and Jasrota

---

[4] *DG Hazara* (1907), 24, 28-29, 36, 123-24. George Forster, *A Journey from Bengal to England*, Punjab Languages Department, Patiala, 1970 (reprint, first published in 1808), II, 49.

[5] Mountstuart Elphinstone, *An Account of the Kingdom of Caubul*, Oxford University Press, London, 1972 (reprint, first published in 1815), II, 235-36 & 256.

[6] *DG Hazara* (1907), 128-31, 190-91.

[7] Hutchison & Vogel, *Hill States*, I, 45-46.

[8] Ahsan Raza Khan, *Chieftains in the Mughal Empire*, 20-22.

[9] *Hill States*, II, 574.

between the Chenab and the Ravi. In the middle were Riasi, Kirmchi, Bandralta, Mankot, Bhadu and Basohli. Beyond Riasi, along the Chenab was Chenini, and beyond Bandralta was the principality of Bhadarwah, between Kashtwar and Chamba.

According to Hutchison and Vogel, there were fourteen principalities in the eastern group: Kangra, Guler, Jaswan, Siba, Datarpur, Nurpur, Chamba, Suket, Mandi, Kulu, Kutlehr, Bangahal, Shahpur, and Kotla.[10] The last of these, however, was established after 1750 and Kahlur (Bilaspur), which is not included in their list, was very much there even in the reign of Akbar.[11] Closest to the plains were Siba, Datarpur, Jaswan and Kutlehr between the Satlej and the Beas, and Nurpur between the Beas and the Ravi. On both sides of the river Satlej was Kahlur. Beyond Siba, on both sides of the river Beas, was Kangra. The principality of Guler, on the right of the Beas, lay between Kangra and Siba and that of Shahpur, between Nurpur and Kangra. Beyond Kangra, between the rivers Beas and Satlej, were the principalities of Mandi and Suket. Still deeper in the Himalayas were the principalities of Chamba and Kulu, the former between the Pir Panjal and Dhaula Dhar ranges and the latter between the Dhaula Dhar and the Satlej. Between Chamba and Kulu was the small principality of Bangahal.

Around 1750, thus, there were over thirty contiguous principalities between the rivers Jehlam and Satlej, attached to the province of Lahore. The chiefs of these principalities had started paying tribute to the Mughal emperors during the sixteenth century. They had also to send their own contingents during the time of war. They accepted the political control of the Mughal suzerain, with the implication that they could not enter into political relations with one another or with an outside power. Succession to the throne of a vassal was also controlled by the suzerain.[12]

Even in the heyday of the Mughal empire, the hill chiefs had tried at times to re-assert their independence by refusing to send tribute or contingents. The aspiration of the hill chiefs to be independent became more pronounced with the decline of the Mughal power in the early eighteenth century. When Ahmad Shah Abdali replaced the Mughals in the Punjab, he tried to assert his suzerain claims over all the hill

---

[10] Ibid., I, 50.

[11] *Ā'īn-i-Akbarī* (Eng. tr.), II, 328.

[12] Indu Banga, *Agrarian System of the Sikhs: Late Eighteenth and Early Nineteenth Century*, Manohar Publications, Delhi, 1978, 29-60. Ahsan Raza Khan, *Chieftains in the Mughal Empire*, 28-53.

chiefs.[13] Similarly, when the Sikh rulers replaced Ahmad Shah Abdali's rule in the Punjab, they tried to collect tribute from the hill chiefs.[14] A few of the hill chiefs themselves tried to assert political control over their neighbours. In the process, the Punjab hills witnessed a changing pattern of political relationships. The Afghan and Sikh rulers could not exercise the kind of control that had been exercised by the Mughals. Consequently, during the late eighteenth century, a considerable number of the hill chiefs became independent of outside control. The emergence of independent rulers in the hills was in itself a significant development.

As already indicated, a new principality came into existence in 1785 when Kotla under Dhian Singh became independent of Guler.[15] However, the principalities of Kutlehr, Bangahal and Shahpur were obliterated between 1750 and 1800.[16] The decrease in the number of principalities signified a notable change in the political situation. More significant was the change in the relative positions of the chiefs during this period. In order to understand the nature of political change in the hills during the late eighteenth century, we may turn to the earlier background of these principalities.

II

Some of the oldest principalities were in the eastern group. Kangra was the most ancient, over two thousand years old. Of its four offshoots, Jaswan was founded in the twelfth century and Guler in the early fifteenth. Siba was founded around 1450 as an offshoot of Guler. Datarpur, was established around 1550 as an offshoot of Siba. Another ancient principality in the eastern group was Kulu, founded in the second century A.D. There were five other principalities older than the

---

[13] *Tārīkh-i-Ālamgīr Sānī* (tr. into English by Jadunath Sarkar, seen in typescript), Punjab State Archives, Patiala, 88b. J.Ph. Vogel, *Catalogue of Bhuri Singh Museum at Chamba*, Baptist Mission Press, Calcutta, 1909, 56-61. Ganda Singh, *Ahmad Shah Durrani*, Asia Publishing House, Bombay, 1959, 52-55.

[14] Frederic Drew, *The Jummoo and Kashmir Territories*, Oriental Publishers, Delhi, 1971 (reprint, first published in 1875), 11. George Forster, *A Journey from Bengal to England*, I, 262-63, 271, 286-87, 324-25.

[15] Hutchison & Vogel, *Hill States*, I, 206.

[16] Ibid., I, 262; II, 489-90, 492-93.

first offshoot of Kangra. Chamba was established in the sixth century; Suket in the eighth century; Kahlur in the tenth; and Nurpur and Kutlehr were founded in the eleventh century. By the beginning of the sixteenth century, Mandi and Bangahal had also become well established. All these thirteen principalities were made tributary by Akbar. The principality of Shahpur was carved out by a prince of Nurpur as a *mansabdār* of Shah Jahan.[17]

Jammu was the oldest principality of the central group. It was in existence in the first century A.D. Of its ten offshoots, Jasrota was founded in the beginning of the thirteenth century and Mankot around 1300. Lakhanpur was founded in the early fourteenth century as an offshoot of Jasrota. Samba and Tirikot were established towards the end of the century as offshoots of Lakhanpur. Riasi, Bhau, Dalpatpur, Akhnur and Kirmchi, were founded after the thirteenth century as offshoots of Jammu. There were four other principalities which were older than the first offshoot of Jammu. Basohli was founded in the seventh century; Chenini in the ninth and Bandralta in the eleventh century. Bhadu was founded in the eleventh century as an offshoot of Basohli. Another offshoot of Basohli was Bhadarwah, founded in the fifteenth century. By this time, Bhimber and Khari Khariali had also come into existence.[18]

Only a few of the vassal chiefs rose in revolt after the death of Akbar. The Nurpur chief Jagat Singh, with his son Rajrup Singh, refused to send the tribute collected from the hill chiefs of the eastern group in 1641. He defended himself for about six months in the forts of Mau, Nurpur and Taragarh but had to surrender in the end.[19] Dhruv Dev of Jammu refused to pay tribute early in the eighteenth century when Abdus Samad Khan was the Mughal governor of Lahore. His son and successor, Zakariya Khan, led an expedition against Jammu and obliged

---

[17] Ibid., I, 110-11, 210, 212, 273, 341-43; II, 52, 376, 425, 491 & 496. *DG Kangra* (1883-84), 257. G.C. Barnes & J.B. Lyall, *Report of the Land Revenue Settlement of the Kangra District*, Lahore, 1889, 9 (all subsequent references to Settlement Reports would be prefixed by *SR*). *DG Gurdaspur* (1883-84), 13.

[18] Hutchison & Vogel, *Hill States*, I, 47, 48; II, 515, 565, 567, 573-74, 579, 585 & 725. Ahsan Raza Khan, *Chieftains in the Mughal Empire*, 39.

[19] Samsām-ud-Daula Shāh Nawāz Khan, *Maāthir-ul-Umara* (tr. into English by H. Beveridge), II, Part 1, Janaki Prakashan, Patna, 1979, 574-75.

Dhruv Dev to send regular tribute.[20] Ranjit Dev, who succeeded Dhruv Dev, appears to have refused to send tribute. He was imprisoned at Lahore in 1735 and released only in 1746 presumably on the assurance that he would not repeat the offence.[21]

Some of the chiefs tried to resolve their disputes by resorting to arms rather than referring them to the suzerain. Kalian Chand of Kahlur, for instance, invaded Suket in 1645 with the help of Suraj Sen of Mandi. Kalian Chand was killed in the battle, and Suraj Sen fled from the field. Sidh Sen, a grandson of Suraj Sen, attacked Suket in 1688 with the aid of Bhim Chand of Kahlur. They were successful against the chief of Suket and obliged him to cede some of his territory which they divided among themselves. When Sidh Sen attacked Bangahal in the beginning of the eighteenth century, the chief of Bangahal invited Man Singh of Kulu to his aid. Sidh Sen was repulsed but Man Singh retained most of the territories of Bangahal under his control. Dhruv Dev of Jammu invaded Guler in the first decade of the eighteenth century with the help of the chiefs of Bhadu and Basohli. Udai Singh of Chamba came to assist Dalip Singh, the minor chief of Guler, and drove out the invaders with the help of the chiefs of Siba, Kahlur and Mandi.[22]

In a few cases, disputes were referred to the suzerain by the contending chiefs. Shah Jahan, for instance, settled a dispute between Prithi Singh of Chamba and Sangram Pal of Basohli about the *pargana* of Bhalai. It was made over to Prithi Singh by an order of Shah Jahan in 1648.[23] The grant of Bhalai to Chamba had to be confirmed by Aurangzeb in 1666.[24]

Some of the hill chiefs accepted service with the Mughal empire. Raja Basu, the chief of Nurpur, for instance, held the *mansab* of 1,500 under Akbar which was raised to 3,500 by Jahangir. Suraj Mal, who succeeded Basu, received the *mansab* of 2,000 from Jahangir. Jagat Singh, who succeeded Suraj Mal in 1619, was given the rank of 1,000 *zāt* (personal) and 500 *sawar* (horse), later raised to 3,000 personal and

---

[20] *Asrar-i-Samadi* (tr. into Punjabi by Janak Raj & Gurbakhsh Singh), Punjabi University, Patiala, 1972, 40-48.

[21] Shahamat Ali, *The Sikhs and the Afghans*, Punjab Languages Department, Patiala, 1970 (reprint, first published in 1847), 81-82.

[22] Hutchison & Vogel, *Hill States*, I, 205, 354, 358; II, 492.

[23] Vogel, *Catalogue of Bhuri Singh Museum*, 52-54. Hutchison & Vogel, *Hill States*, I, 293; II, 601- 06.

[24] Vogel, *Catalogue of Bhuri Singh Museum*, C.4.

2,000 horse by Jahangir himself.[25] The successors of Jagat Sigh held high ranks under Shah Jahan and Aurangzeb.[26] As *mansabdārs* of the Mughal empire, these chiefs were asked to perform services like other *mansabdārs*. Jagat Singh, for instance, was appointed a *faujdār* in the province of Kabul. Shah Jahan appointed Rajrup as the *faujdār* of Kangra to collect the yearly tribute from the hill chiefs of the region.[27] Sarang Dev of Jammu held the *mansab* of 1,500 with 600 horse under Jahangir.[28] Prithvi Singh of Chamba held the *mansab* of 1,000 personal and 400 horse under Shah Jahan. Bikram Singh of Guler was given the *mansab* of 2,500 by Aurangzeb and appointed as the *faujdār* of Kangra.[29]

Several of the vassal chiefs lost a part of their territories during the Mughal period. Jai Chand of Kangra, for instance, had to surrender the *pargana* of Pathiyar in the reign of Akbar.[30] The fort of Kangra was occupied by Jahangir in 1620.[31] Partap Chand of Chamba lost Rihlu, Chari and Gharoh in 1575. Pathankot was taken away from Raja Basu, the chief of Nurpur, in 1594-95.[32] The principalities of Jammu, Mankot and Jasrota were occupied by Akbar in 1602 but restored to their chiefs by Jahangir in 1620.[33] The chiefs of Lakhanpur and Samba were less fortunate. Their principalities were taken over by Akbar and

---

[25] Hutchison & Vogel, *Hill States*, I, 227. *Tuzuk-i-Jahāngīrī* (tr. into English by Alexander Rogers), II, Munshiram Manoharlal, Delhi, 1968 (2nd ed.), 75 & 182. *Maāthir-ul- Umara* (Eng. tr.), I, 394 & 726.

[26] After Jagat Singh's death, his son Raja Rajrup received a rank of 1,500 personal and 1,000 horse from Shah Jahan. Under Aurangzeb, Rajrup's rank was increased to 3,500 foot and horse. On Rajrup's death in 1661, his son Raja Mandhata was created a *mansabdār* of 2,000. *Maāthir-ul-Umara* (Eng. tr.), II, Part 1, 574-76; I, 726. *SR Kangra (*1889), 9.

[27] *Maāthir-ul-Umara*, I, 726; II, Part 2, 574-75. Hutchison & Vogel, *Hill States*, I, 235-36.

[28] *Tuzuk-i-Jahāngīrī* (Eng. tr.), II, 182 & 250.

[29] Hutchison & Vogel, *Hill States*, I, 205 & 305.

[30] Al-Badaoni, *Muntakhab-ut-Tawārīkh* (tr. into English by W.H. Lowe), II, Academica Asiatica, Patna, 1973, 166. Hutchison & Vogel, *Hill States*, I, 298.

[31] *Tuzuk-i-Jahāngīrī* (Eng. tr.), II, 25, 183-85. *Maāthir-ul-Umara* (Eng. tr.), I, 414-15.

[32] Hutchison & Vogel, *Hill States*, I, 225-26 & 298.

[33] Abu'l Fazl, *Akbarnāma* (tr. into English by H. Beveridge), III, Rare Books, Delhi, 1973 (reprint), 1206-07 & 1213. *Tuzuk-i-Jahāngīrī* (Eng. tr.), II, 154.

never restored.[34] The chief of Nurpur lost a large chunk of his territory when Shahpur was carved out as a separate principality in 1650.[35] The only chief to gain in territory was Udai Singh of Chamba who was given Pathiyar by Muhammad Shah in 1744.[36]

III

During the late eighteenth century, three of the principalities of the eastern group went down under pressure from the neighbouring chiefs. One of these was Bangahal which had been much reduced in size before 1750. Its remnant was taken over by Raja Ghamand Chand of Kangra in the 1760s. The entire territory of Kutlehr was taken over by the chiefs of Kangra in two stages. The Chauki area, that is the northern half, was seized by Ghamand Chand in 1758, and the area of Kutlehr proper was annexed by Raja Sansar Chand in 1786.[37] The third principality to be obliterated was that of Shahpur. After the death of its chief, Saeed Khan, in 1781, Raja Prithi Singh of Nurpur thought of regaining the areas lost by his predecessors in the seventeenth century.[38] The widow of Saeed Khan was keen to protect the patrimony of her minor son and invited the Sikh chiefs of Pathankot and Sujanpur for assistance. They did mobilize their troops but only to take over the tracts of Kandi and Palahi which belonged to Saeed Khan. Shahpur proper was annexed by Prithi Singh.[39]

There were about half a dozen principalities which lost part of their territory during the late eighteenth century, and remained subordinate to one or another ruler for most of the time. One of these was Basohli. Its chief, Raja Amrit Pal, was obliged by Raja Ranjit Dev of Jammu to surrender his right to collect tribute from Bhadu.[40] Raja Ugar Singh of Chamba took over the *parganas* of Bhalai and Jund in 1758.[41] The Raja of Basohli was able to recover these *parganas* in 1774 with the help of Raja Ranjit Dev who by now was exercising suzerain

---

[34] Hutchison & Vogel, *Hill States*, II, 573-75.

[35] *Lahore Political Diaries: Punjab Government Records, 1846-49*, Pioneer Press, Allahabad, 1911, IV, 7. *DG Gurdaspur* (1883-84), 13.

[36] Vogel, *Catalogue of Bhuri Singh Museum*, 54-56.

[37] Hutchison & Vogel, *Hill States*, II, 489 & 493.

[38] *Punjab Government Records, 1846-49*, IV, 7-8.

[39] *DG Gurdaspur* (1883-84), 13. Hutchison & Vogel, *Hill States*, I, 262.

[40] Hutchison & Vogel, *Hill States*, II, 604-07.

[41] Vogel, *Catalogue of Bhuri Singh Museum*, c.11, 67-68.

control over the chief of Basohli.[42] In 1782, Raja Raj Singh of Chamba was able to annex these *parganas* once again. The Raja of Basohli had to pay war indemnity as well.[43] At this time, the Raja of Basohli had sought help from Jai Singh Kanhiya; his men decided to linger on in Basohli.[44] In 1785, Raja Prithi Singh of Nurpur took over the area of Lakhanpur which had belonged to Basohli for half a century.[45] The chiefs of Basohli, thus, lost much in territory and resources and consequently in prestige during the late eighteenth century.

Another principality in the central group to shrink was Bhimber. Its chief was obliged to pay tribute to Gujjar Singh Bhangi of Gujrat in 1770 when his submontane territories were taken over by the chief of Gujrat. The principality of Guler was also shorn of a large chunk of its territory. Raja Parkash Chand of Guler had appointed Wazir Dhian Singh to look after the administration of the Kotla area. He became independent of the chief of Guler in 1785.[46]

Mahan Chand, the chief of Kahlur, lost territories on both sides of the river Satlej during the last decade of the eighteenth century.[47] The petty chiefs of Simla hills, known as Bara Thakurian, stopped paying tribute to the chief of Kahlur.[48] The chief of Hindur (Nalagarh) occupied the adjoining territory of Kahlur before he invaded the principality to capture more of its area.[49] Raja Sansar Chand of Kangra took over some of the Kahlur territory close to his fort of Mahal Morian.[50]

---

[42] Hutchison & Vogel, *Hill States*, II, 610.

[43] Vogel, *Catalogue of Bhuri Singh Museum*, c.25, 70. Hutchison & Vogel, *Hill States*, I, 316.

[44] George Forster, *A Journey from Bengal to England*, I, 270-71. Mohinder Singh Randhawa, *Basohli Paintings*, Publication Division, Government of India, Delhi, 1954, 49.

[45] Hutchison & Vogel, *Hill States*, I, 262-63; II, 573-74.

[46] Ganesh Das, *Chār Bāgh-i-Panjab* (tr. into Punjabi by Amarwant Singh, seen in typescript), Guru Nanak Dev University, Amritsar, 133. Sohan Lal, *Umdat-ut-Tawārīkh* (tr. into Punjabi by Amarwant Singh, ed. J.S. Grewal & Indu Banga), Guru Nanak Dev University, Amritsar 1985, Daftar II, 132 & 149. *SR Kangra, 1889*, 10-11.

[47] Hutchison & Vogel, *Hill States*, II, 497. George Forster, *A Journey from Bengal to England*, I, 241.

[48] These Bara Thakurian were Baghal, Kunhiar, Beja, Dhami, Keonthal, Kothar, Jubbal, Baghat, Bajji, Mailog, Mangal and Balsan.

[49] Hutchison & Vogel, *Hill States*, II, 506.

[50] *SR Kangra (*1889), 10. G.T. Vigne, *A Personal Narrative of a Visit to Ghuzni, Kabul and Afghanistan*, London, 1840, I, 138. Hutchison & Vogel, *Hill States*, II, 505-06.

Another principality in the eastern group to lose some territory during the last decade of the eighteenth century was Mandi. It was invaded by the joint forces of Raja Sansar Chand of Kangra, Raja Pritam Singh of Kulu and Raja Bikram Sen of Suket. The chief of Mandi at this time was a minor. The allies were able to annex several forts and the surrounding areas to their own dominions.[51]

The dissolution of Mughal authority in the province of Lahore did not bring independence to all the principalities in the Punjab hills. For a large number of principalities, the political change meant only the change in their suzerains. When Ahmad Shah Abdali occupied the province of Lahore and asserted his suzerain rights over the hill chiefs, many of the principalities in the central and eastern group started paying tribute to him. Notable among these were Jasrota, Bandralta, Mankot, Bhadarwah, Bhadu, Chenini, Khari Khariali, Akhnur, Samba, Riasi, Kirmchi, Bhau, Dalpatpur, Tirikot, Jaswan, Datarpur and Siba.[52] The first fourteen of these principalities were in the central group and subsequently, they all became subordinate to Ranjit Dev.[53] The three principalities of the eastern group appear to have become independent for a few years in the time of Ahmad Shah Abdali but they were made tributary by Jassa Singh Ramgarhia even before the death of Ahmad Shah.[54] When Jai Singh Kanhiya defeated Jassa Singh Ramgarhia in 1775, he asserted his political control over these principalities. When Jai Singh was expelled from Kangra in 1786, the chiefs of these principalities were obliged to acknowledge the suzerainty of Sansar Chand of Kangra.[55] In the central group, the chiefs of Bhadarwah had to pay regular tribute to the chiefs of Chamba after the death of Raja Ranjit Dev.[56] The chiefs of Bhadu, Basohli and Bandralta paid tribute to the chiefs of Chamba though not every year.[57]

---

[51] Hutchison & Vogel, *Hill States*, II, 362, 393-94.

[52] *DG Kangra* (1883-84), 38.

[53] George Forster, *A Journey from Bengal to England*, I, 272-73. Frederic Drew, *The Jummoo and Kashmir Territories*, 9. Kirpa Ram, *Gulabnāma* (tr. into English by Sukhdev Singh Charak), Light & Life Publishers, New Delhi, 1977, 39-42.

[54] Hutchison & Vogel, *Hill States*, I, 177. Indu Banga, *Agrarian System of the Sikhs*, 41.

[55] *DG Kangra* (1883-84), 39. *SR Kangra* (1874), 113.

[56] Vogel, *Catalogue of Bhuri Singh Museum*, CC.22, 33, 34, 35, 36, 37, 42 & 48.

[57] Hutchison & Vogel, *Hill States*, I, 318.

On the whole, the chiefs of the hills did not lose much of their territory to the new rulers of the plains; nor did all the hill chiefs pay tribute to them. In other words, the chiefs who established their suzerain claims over the hill principalities, or who added to their territories, belonged to the hills. Raja Bikram Sen of Suket was able to recover all the territory which his predecessors had lost to the chief of Mandi in the late seventeenth century. The chief of Kulu was able to add a *pargana* to his dominions at the cost of the chief of Mandi. As already mentioned, the chief of Nurpur was able to recover Shahpur after the death of Saeed Khan in 1781, and to take over the area of Lakhanpur from the chief of Basohli in 1785.[58]

The chiefs who dominated much of the politics of the hills during the late eighteenth century were Ranjit Dev of Jammu in the beginning of the period, Raj Singh of Chamba in the middle and Sansar Chand of Kangra towards the end of the period. Ranjit Dev was quick to acknowledge the political supremacy of Ahmad Shah Abdali and to help him in his campaigns. As a reward, he was able to occupy considerable territories in the plains. At one stroke, he got the *parganas* of Zafarwal, Sankhtara and Aurangabad. At a later stage, he occupied the submontane area of Chawinda, Chaubara, Gangowal, Daulatabad, Kathua and Hamidgarh in the districts of Sialkot and Gujrat. It is generally agreed that for some time at least Ranjit Dev was able to receive tribute from all the chiefs of the central group and from some of the chiefs of eastern group. Notable among those who paid tribute to Ranjit Dev, or sent contingents for service, were the chiefs of Bhadarwah, Chenini, Kirmchi, Bandralta, Mankot, Basohli, Bhadu, Akhnur, Bhimber, Khari Khariali, Chamba and even Kashtwar.[59]

In the early 1770s, Ranjit Dev was probably at the height of his power. Jammu at this time was a flourishing city and a very important centre of trade and commerce. This probably was a source of his strength. Subsequently, however, the wealth of Jammu became a source of temptation for others. In 1774, when Brij Raj Dev, the elder son of Ranjit Dev, rebelled against him, the Sikh chiefs of the plains were prepared to help both the parties. In the process, Ranjit Dev was

---

[58] Ibid, II, 394 & 468.

[59] Kirpa Ram, *Gulabnāma* (Eng. tr.), 34-35, 37-38 & 42-43. Hutchison & Vogel, *Hill States*, II, 541 & 581. *SR Sialkot* (1865), 44. Ganda Singh, *Ahmad Shah Durrani*, 52-55. Amin Chand, *A History of the Sialkot District* (tr. Charles A. Roe), Central Jail Press, Lahore, 1874, 16.

obliged to pay tribute to the Bhangi chiefs and after his death in 1781, Jammu was sacked by Mahan Singh Sukarchakia.[60]

In fact, the power of Ranjit Dev was on the decline already before his death, and the power of Chamba was on the increase. Raja Umed Singh of Chamba had recovered the territories to the south of the Dhaula Dhar range which his ancestors had lost to the Mughals in the reign of Akbar. In 1758, he occupied the *parganas* of Bhalai and Jund which had been taken over by the chief of Basohli in the 1730s. He was able to get confirmation for the *pargana* of Pathiyar from Ahmad Shah Abdali in 1762. On the death of Umed Singh in 1764, his son Raj Singh was a minor, and for some time he came under the influence of Ranjit Dev whose sister was married to Umed Singh. Raj Singh lost Bhalai and Jund to Raja Amrit Pal of Basohli in 1775 when Ranjit Dev too was hostile to Raj Singh because he had started asserting himself against the Jammu chief.[61]

Soon after Ranjit Dev's death, Raj Singh recovered Bhalai and Jund and imposed a heavy indemnity on the chief of Basohli. In 1783, he obliged Fateh Pal of Bhadarwah to shift his allegiance from the chief of Jammu to himself. Three years later, Raj Singh also obliged the chief of Kashtwar to become his vassal. In the last decade of the century, Sansar Chand of Kangra tried to occupy the area of Rihlu near Palampur but he was thwarted in his attempt by Raj Singh. However, Raj Singh lost his life in the battle. His son and successor, Raja Jit Singh improved upon the legacy left to him. He imposed tribute on the chiefs of Basohli, Bhadu and Bandralta.[62]

More spectacular than the rise of Ranjit Dev and Raj Singh was that of Sansar Chand of Kangra. His grandfather, Raja Ghamand Chand, had been quick to offer his services to Ahmad Shah Abdali, and to gain from this diplomatic submission. At the cost of the chief of Kutlehr, Ghamand Chand added Chauki to his own dominions. He obliged the chief of Bangahal to cede some of his possessions. However, Ghamand

---

60 George Forster, *A Journey from Bengal to England,* I, 283-85 & 286-87. Henry T. Prinsep, *Origin of the Sikh Power in the Panjab and Political Life of Maharaja Ranjit Singh,* Punjab Languages Department, Patiala, 1970 (reprint, first published in 1834), 245-47.

61 Vogel, *Catalogue of Bhuri Singh Museum,* 59-61, 67 & c.11. Hutchison & Vogel, *Hill States,* I, 315; II, 542.

62 Hutchison & Vogel, *Hill States,* I, 316-18. Vogel, *Catalogue of Bhuri Singh Museum,* c.22; cc. 32-38, 40, 42, 48 & 50. *SR Kangra* (1889), 13. G.T. Vigne, *Travels into Kashmir,* I, 142.

Chand did not succeed in recovering the fort of Kangra which had remained a prize possession of his ancestors for many centuries.[63]

Sansar Chand had the honour of recovering the Kangra fort from Jai Singh Kanhiya in 1786. This great achievement was actually his first. When he came to the throne in 1775, he was only ten years old, and the occupation of Kangra was his cherished aspiration. After the occupation of his ancestral fort, he started looking around for territorial aggrandizement. He took over the remaining territory of the chief of Kutlehr. He obliged the chiefs of Mandi and Kulu to pay five lacs of rupees as the price of retaining the Bangahal territories they had taken over. In 1792, he invaded Mandi with the support of the chiefs of Kulu and Suket. The fort of Anantpur was taken over and the minor chief of Mandi was obliged to pay one lac of rupees as annual tribute. By the end of the eighteenth century, Sansar Chand was literally a Maharaja, exercising suzerain rights over a number of chiefs. Those who paid tribute to him included Prakash Chand of Guler, Dhian Singh of Kotla, Sher Singh of Siba, Gobind Chand of Datarpur, Surma Sen of Mandi, Ranjit Sen of Suket, Bir Singh of Nurpur, Pritam Singh of Kulu, Umed Singh of Jaswan and Mahan Chand of Kahlur.[64]

IV

The first striking aspect of the hill principalities is their survival for a very long time. Kangra and Jammu had come into existence as early as the first century after Christ. Six more principalities came into existence before the tenth century. It is interesting to find a score of new principalities being founded from the eleventh to the fifteenth century. This was a period of important political changes in northern India.

---

[63] Ganda Singh, *Ahmad Shah Durrani*, 152 & 274. *DG Kangra (*1883-84), 38. *SR Kangra (*1889), 12. Hutchison & Vogel, *Hill States*, I, 175; II, 493.

[64] Sohan Lal, *Umdat-ut-Tawārīkh* (Pbi. tr.), II, 28-29 & 31. Aliuddin, *Ibratnāma* (tr. into Punjabi by Gurbakhsh Singh, seen in typescript), Punjabi University, Patiala, 301. *SR Kangra* (1889), 10. Hutchison & Vogel, *Hill States*, I, 176, 180-82 & 361-62; II, 467-68, 483 & 489. Khushwaqt Rai, *Tawārīkh-i-Sikhan* (tr. into Punjabi by Milkhi Ram, seen in typescript), Punjabi University, Patiala, 208. *SR Hoshiarpur* (1885), 22 & 116. G.T. Vigne, *Travels into Kashmir*, I, 137-38. Foreign/Secret Consultation, 21 November 1809, National Archives of India, New Delhi, Nos. 15 & 51.

However, most of the new principalities during this period were not founded by outsiders; they were mostly offshoots of offshoots. On the whole, the hill principalities leave the dominant impression of stability. This was chiefly due to the inaccessibility of the hills and their relative lack of resources. Moreover, the limited resources of the hill principalities and their ties of kinship, coupled with the local physical conditions, stood in the way of any one of them annexing large territories at the cost of others.

The chiefs of the hills had learnt to adapt themselves to aggressive pressure from outside. They were generally not unwilling to acknowledge the political supremacy of the more powerful rulers. For this purpose the long tradition of suzerain-vassal relationship enabled them to retain the substance of power and the bulk of their resources by acknowledging a powerful ruler as their suzerain. Several of the hill principalities were subordinate to the Sultans of Delhi. In the time of Akbar, nearly all the hill chiefs accepted his suzerainty. Some of them accepted service under the Mughal empire. The imposition of suzerain's political control over the hills made for stability. Only a couple of principalities went out of existence and one new principality was founded during the Mughal period. Apart from this, there were some changes in the relative position of the different chiefs.

With this background, we can appreciate the political change in the Punjab hills during the late eighteenth century. Ahmad Shah Abdali and the Sikh chiefs who established their power in the Punjab plains during the second half of the eighteenth century tried to get into the shoes of the Mughal rulers. However, the success of the new suzerains was only partial. They could subdue some of the hill chiefs for some time but not all of them throughout the period. Furthermore, there was not one but several suzerains in the plains. In this situation, the well established framework of the suzerain-vassal relationship of the Mughal times was no longer operative. If the rulers of the plains filled a part of the vacuum, some of the hill chiefs themselves tried to assert suzerain rights over their neighbours. It was in this context that Ranjit Dev of Jammu, Raj Singh of Chamba and Sansar Chand of Kangra became dominant in large parts of the hills at one time or another during the late eighteenth century.

Considering the background of stability in the hills, the changes in the fortunes of the principalities of Jammu, Chamba and Kangra in a period of about fifty years were significant. An obvious factor that can account for this change was the removal of the political control of the Mughals. Secondly, the resources of the principalities of Jammu,

Chamba and Kangra were relatively large, and their rulers possessed rather exceptional abilities. In the general process of turmoil in the hills during the late eighteenth century, three principalities went out of existence and one new principality was established. This may not appear to be much of a change, but even this kind of a change had not been witnessed during the previous two hundred years.

2

CHIEFS OF THE UPPER DOABS

In the upper Doabs of the Punjab plains, it is possible to identify about seventy principalities during the late eighteenth century. Twentysix of these were in the upper Bari and seventeen each in the Jalandhar and the Rachna Doab. In the Chaj Doab, there was only one principality; in the Sindh Sagar Doab, there were ten. In terms of religious affiliation, fiftythree of these chiefs were Sikh and eighteen were Muslim. The number of Jat chiefs was much larger than that of the Rajputs, the former accounting for fortytwo and the latter for only twelve.

I

The city of Lahore had served as the capital of the province under the Mughals for a few centuries before it was taken over by Ahmad Shah Abdali in 1752. In 1765, it was occupied by three Sikh chiefs. One of them was Gujjar Singh who occupied much larger territories in the Chaj Doab with his headquarters at Gujrat. Another was Lehna Singh, the adopted son of Gujjar Singh's maternal grandfather, Gurbakhsh Singh. The third was Sobha Singh of Niazbeg who occupied the territory in the south of Lahore.[1] The fort of Lahore fell to the share of Lehna Singh who possessed a few villages in Atari and a small chunk of territory across the river Ravi.[2] He did not add to his territories after 1765 but he does figure in the negotiations of Ahmad Shah Abdali and of his grandson Zaman Shah with the Sikh chiefs during their invasions

---

[1] Lepel Griffin, *The Panjab Chiefs*, 391. Aliuddin, *Ibratnāma* (Pbi. tr.), 324-25.

[2] Maulvi Abdul Qadir, 'Memorandum of the Route between Delhi and Cabul', *Asiatic Annual Register* (1806), 10. Lepel Griffin, *The Panjab Chiefs*, 311 & 392.

of the Punjab.[3] After his death in 1797, Sobha Singh was succeeded by his son Chait Singh who became unpopular among the citizens of Lahore. This was one reason why the prominent persons of Lahore were keen to help Ranjit Singh in his occupation of the city in 1799. After a brief resistance, Chait Singh surrendered the fort. He was allowed to retain Wainki near Atari in *jāgīr* for service.[4]

Before he occupied a part of Lahore, Sobha Singh had occupied over a score of villages in the south of Eminabad in the Rachna Doab, and several villages in the south of Lahore, including Niazbeg.[5] He did not add to his territories after 1765. Nor did he take any prominent interest in the politics of the late eighteenth century. On his death in 1797, he was succeeded by his son Mohar Singh. When Ranjit Singh besieged Lahore in 1799, Mohar Singh left the city without offering any resistance.[6] He was heard of no more.

The city of Amritsar did not belong to any single chief but it was adopted as headquarters only by Hari Singh Bhangi, a Dhillon Jat from the village Panjwar near Amritsar. He appears to have occupied some territory close to Amritsar in the 1750s.[7] In 1760, he was able to subjugate the Sial chief of Jhang. Chiniot was taken over at this time and given to Karam Singh Dulu.[8] An expedition against Qasur in 1763 was led primarily by Hari Singh Bhangi. He also fought against Ahmad Shah Abdali in the *ghallughāra* near Malerkotla.[9] In 1765, when he led

---

[3] W.S. Setton Karr, *Selections from Calcutta Gazette of the Years 1789 to 1797*, II, 465. Foreign/Secret Proceedings, 23 June 1797, Nos. 5 & 7.

[4] Abstract of a letter of 4 December 1797, *Poona Residency Correspondence, 1774-99* (ed. Jadunath Sarkar), VIII, 63. Sohan Lal, *Umdat-ut-Tawārīkh* (Pbi. tr.), II, 48-52.

[5] Ram Sukh Rao, *Jassa Singh Binod* (ms), f, 260 a. H.R. Goulding & T.H. Thornton, *Old Lahore*, Civil and Military Gazette Press, Lahore, 1924, 76.

[6] Sohan Lal, *Umdat-ut-Tawārīkh* (Pbi. tr.), II, 48-51.

[7] Ahmad Shah, *Tārīkh-i-Panjab* (Pbi. tr.), 39. Ratan Singh Bhangu, *Prāchīn Panth Parkāsh*, 385. Ganesh Das, *Chār Bāgh-i-Punjab* (Pbi. tr.), 128.

[8] Qazi Nur Muhammad, *Jangnāmāh* (tr. into English by Ganda Singh), Sikh History Research Centre, Amritsar, 1939, 59-60. *DG Jhang* (1883-84), 32.

[9] Ratan Singh Bhangu, *Prāchīn Panth Parkāsh*, 368, 385-90. Giani Gian Singh, *Raj Khalsa* (Vol. III of *Tawārīkh Guru Khalsa*), Punjab Languages Department, Patiala, 1970 (reprint), 3.

an expedition against Ala Singh of Patiala because of his submission to Ahmad Shah Abdali, Hari Singh was killed in the battle.[10]

Hari Singh's elder son, Jhanda Singh, succeeded him at Amritsar. For nine years, he fought battles and made conquests on a considerable scale. He conquered the Sialkot region above Gujranwala in association with a number of chiefs in 1770, but retained only a portion of the conquest along the river Chenab to the west of Sialkot.[11] Ranjit Dev of Jammu was made tributary at this time.[12] In the year following, the Baloch chief of Bhera was ousted from some of his territory and Dhanna Singh Kalalwala was installed there as a ruler.[13] The most striking achievement of Jhanda Singh was the conquest of Multan in 1772. He appointed Diwan Singh as its *subadār*.[14] In 1774, Jhanda Singh fought in support of Ranjit Dev against his son Brij Raj Dev who was supported by Charhat Singh Sukarchakia and Jai Singh Kanhiya. Both Charhat Singh and Jhanda Singh died during this conflict.[15]

The death of Jhanda Singh may be regarded as the beginning of the decline of what Ganesh Das refers to as the 'royal house of Bhanga Singh Bahadur'.[16] Jhanda Singh's younger brother Ganda Singh succeeded him but only to die of illness in 1775. During this one year, Pathankot was taken over by an associate of Jai Singh Kanhiya from a collateral of Jhanda Singh Bhangi. Ganda Singh was succeeded by Jhanda Singh's son Charhat Singh and then by his own son Desa Singh in 1775 itself.[17] The Sial chief of Jhang refused to pay tribute in

---

[10] Ganda Singh, *Ahmad Shah Durrani*, 308. Kirpal Singh, *Life of Maharaja Ala Singh of Patiala and His Times*, 125-26. Karam Singh 'Historian', *Baba Ala Singh*, 173.

[11] *SR Sialkot* (1865), 46.

[12] George Forster, *A Journey from Bengal to England*, I, 286-87. Giani Gian Singh, *Raj Khalsa*, 4.

[13] *SR Shahpur* (1866), 37.

[14] R. Maclagan, 'Fragments of the History of Mooltan, the Derajat and Buhawulpoor from Persian MSS', *Journal of the Asiatic Society of Bengal*, 13 (1848), 565-67 & 571. *DG Multan*, (1883-84), 27. Ganesh Das, *Chār Bāgh-i-Panjab* (Pbi. tr.), 132.

[15] Sohan Lal, *Umdat-ut-Tawārīkh* (Pbi. tr.), II, 13. Aliuddin, *Ibratnāma* (Pbi. tr.), 304.

[16] Ganesh Das, *Early Nineteenth Century Panjab*, (a part of *Chār Bāgh-i-Panjab*, tr. into English by J.S. Grewal & Indu Banga), Guru Nanak University, Amritsar 1975, 17.

[17] Ahmad Shah, *Tārīkh-i- Panjab* (a part of *Tārīkh-i-Hind*, tr. into Punjabi by Gurbakhsh Singh), Punjabi University, Patiala, 1972, 41-42.

1778.[18] Two years later, Desa Singh lost Multan to Timur Shah, the son and successor of Ahmad Shah Abdali. He himself died in 1782 and was succeeded by his son Gulab Singh.[19]

None of the successors of Ganda Singh was an experienced ruler. Most of the time in fact, they were in minority and the affairs of the principality were presumably looked after by the widows of the former chiefs. Gulab Singh added Tarn Taran to his possessions before he conquered Qasur in 1790. It remained under his control for four years. The Afghan chief of Qasur was able to recover his territories in 1795, a little before or at the time of the first invasion of the Punjab by Zaman Shah.[20] In 1800, Gulab Singh joined some other chiefs against Ranjit Singh and died at Bhasin near Lahore where the armies of the allies were facing Ranjit Singh.[21] Gulab Singh was succeeded by his minor son Gurdit Singh who was dislodged from Amritsar by Ranjit Singh in 1805. He was given a *jāgīr* for subsistence.[22]

Much of the upper Bari Doab was conquered and occupied by the Kanhiyas. About half a dozen Sikh chiefs are traditionally associated with the Kanhiya *misl*.[23] The most important of them was Jai Singh, a Sandhu Jat from the village Kanha Kachha in the south of Lahore. He appears to have started occupying pockets of territory as early as 1750.[24] He made conquests in the Bari Doab jointly with some of his associates and Jassa Singh Ramgarhia. He came into possession of Batala, Dera Baba Nanak and Kahnuwan with a large number of villages

---

[18] *SR Jhang* (1882), 37.

[19] Abstract of a letter of 24 April 1780, *Calender of Persian Correspondence*, V, No. 1843.

[20] Giani Gian Singh, *Raj Khalsa*, 622. Lepel Griffin, *The Panjab Chiefs*, 53-54.

[21] Extract from a letter of 20 May 1800, *Poona Residency Correspondence, 1800-03*, IX, 19. Sohan Lal, *Umdat-ut-Tawārīkh* (Pbi. tr.), II, 55. Ganesh Das, *Chār Bāgh-i-Panjab* (Pbi. tr.), 142.

[22] There is a controversy regarding the date of the occupation of Amritsar. Prinsep, Latif and Cunningham place it in 1802. Ganesh Das and Giani Gian Singh place it in 1803. Sohan Lal, the court chronicler of the Maharaja, who should be more reliable on the point, places it in 1805.

[23] The 'Kanhiya' chiefs were Jai Singh Sandhu, Haqiqat Singh Sandhu and his nephew Tara Singh Sandhu, Amar Singh Bagga, Gulab Singh Khaira and Majja Singh Randhawa.

[24] For the seal of Jai Singh used on his order since A.D. 1750, B.N. Goswamy and J.S. Grewal, *The Mughal and Sikh Rulers and the Vaishnavas of Pindori*, Documents XXIV & XXV.

around these towns. A large chunk of territory around Hajipur and Mukerian in the Jalandhar Doab adjoined his possessions in the Bari.[25] In 1774, he sided with Charhat Singh Sukarchakia against Jhanda Singh Bhangi who was supporting Ranjit Dev of Jammu.[26] Two years later, he made a common cause with Jassa Singh Ahluwalia against the Ramgarhia chief and ousted him from his possessions. The hill chiefs who were tributary to Jassa Singh Ramgarhia became subordinate to Jai Singh Kanhiya.[27] His greatest achievement against the hill chiefs was the occupation of Kangra in 1783.[28] In the year following, he expressed his annoyance with Mahan Singh Sukarchakia who had sacked Jammu as an ally but kept all the booty to himself. Mahan Singh encouraged Jassa Singh Ramgarhia to take back his possessions. Consequently, in a battle fought at Achal near Batala in 1785, Jai Singh's eldest son Gurbakhsh Singh was killed. The Ramgarhia chief occupied Batala and nearly all his former possessions except Kalanaur.[29] Jai Singh succeeded in recovering Batala in 1789. Before his death in 1793, his grand daughter Mehtab Kaur was betrothed to Mahan Singh's son Ranjit Singh.[30]

The affairs of the principality were managed by Sada Kaur, the widow of Gurbakhsh Singh. She became a staunch supporter of Ranjit Singh after his marriage to Mehtab Kaur in 1795. She was supporting Ranjit Singh with her forces when he occupied Lahore in 1799.[31] The prestige of Sada Kaur increased with the rise of Ranjit Singh into undisputed power during the first decade of the nineteenth century. As an ally of Ranjit Singh, she gained some territories.[32] After 1809, however, Ranjit Singh gradually started treating his allies as subordinate chiefs and Sada Kaur was no exception. On her death in 1821, all

[25] Aliuddin, *Ibratnāma* (Pbi. tr.), 310. *SR Amritsar* (1860), 3. *DG Gurdaspur* (1883-84), 17 & 20.

[26] Ram Sukh Rao, *Jassa Singh Binod*, (ms), f. 318b.

[27] Ahmad Shah, *Tārīkh-i-Panjab* (Pbi. tr.), 50. Hutchison & Vogel, *Hill States*, I, 261.

[28] Ahmad Shah, *Tārīkh-i- Panjab* (Pbi. tr.), 57.

[29] Ibid., 51. Prinsep, *Origin of the Sikh Power*, 36.

[30] Ahmad Shah, *Tārīkh-i-Panjab* (Pbi. tr.), 51. J.S. Grewal, *Maharaja Ranjit Singh*, Guru Nanak Dev University, Amritsar, 1983, 21.

[31] Fakir Syed Waheeduddin, *The Real Ranjit Singh*, 133 & 137.

[32] Indu Banga, *Agrarian System of the Sikhs*, 61.

her territories around Batala were taken over by the Maharaja.[33] The territories in the Jalandhar Doab had been taken over already in 1812 on the death of Jai Singh's younger sons, Bhag Singh and Nidhan Singh.[34]

The most prominent of Jai Singh's associates in conquest was Haqiqat Singh who too belonged to the village Kanha Kachha. With his headquarters at Fatehgarh Churian, he ruled over a number of villages, largely in a rough circle formed by Fatehgarh Churian, Batala, Kalanaur and Dera Baba Nanak. Another chunk of territory that belonged to Haqiqat Singh was around Narot Jaimal Singh on the left of the river Beas below Kathua and Lakhanpur. He had a number of villages also near Sambrial in the Sialkot region.[35] Haqiqat Singh remained aligned with Jai Singh Kanhiya in most of his campaigns. In 1776, when the Ramgarhia chief was ousted from the Bari Doab, Kalanaur and the surrounding villages fell to the share of Haqiqat Singh. These possessions were retained by his son and successor Jaimal Singh even when the Ramgarhias returned to the Bari Doab in 1785.[36] In the first decade of the nineteenth century, however, he became subordinate to Ranjit Singh like many of his contemporary chiefs. His daughter Chand Kaur was married to Prince Kharak Singh early in 1812.[37] Jaimal Singh died before the year ended and his territories were taken over by Ranjit Singh.[38]

In the upper most part of the Bari Doab, there were three Sikh chiefs: one at Dinanagar, another at Pathankot and the third at Sujanpur. The area around Dinanagar was occupied by Gulab Singh Khaira probably in 1760 as an associate of Jai Singh Kanhiya. He also possessed a small pocket of territory around Khadur.[39] Nothing much is known

---

[33] Ram Sukh Rao, *Sri Fateh Singh Partap Prabhakar* (ed. Joginder Kaur), Published by Editor, Patiala, 1980, 426-27. Ahmad Shah, *Tārīkh-i-Panjab* (Pbi. tr.), 64. *SR Hoshiarpur* (1885), 120.

[34] Sohan Lal, *Umdat-ut-Tawārīkh* (Pbi. tr.), II, 147. Aliuddin, *Ibratnāma* (Pbi. tr.), 313.

[35] Ganesh Das, *Chār Bāgh-i-Panjab* (Pbi. tr.), 128. Giani Gian Singh, *Raj Khalsa*, 557. *SR Sialkot* (1865), 47.

[36] Ahmad Shah, *Tārīkh-i-Panjab* (Pbi. tr.), 50, 56 & 57. Lepel Griffin, *The Panjab Chiefs*, 316-17.

[37] Lepel Griffin, *The Panjab Chiefs*, 322.

[38] Ram Sukh Rao, *Sri Fateh Singh Partap Prabhakar*, 127. Lepel Griffin, *The Panjab Chiefs*, 316.

[39] Ram Sukh Rao, *Sri Fateh Singh Partap Prabhakar*, 127. Lepel Griffin, *The Panjab Chiefs*, 316.

about Gulab Singh's activity in the late eighteenth century. In 1803, he was obliged to pay tribute to Ranjit Singh. In 1809, his territories were taken over and he was given a small *jāgīr* but not Khadur which he wished to have.[40]

Pathankot, with its surrounding area, was occupied by Nand Singh around 1760. After Nand Singh's death in 1774, Pathankot was taken over by Tara Singh, a nephew of Haqiqat Singh of Fatehgarh Churian and the son-in-law of Nand Singh.[41] In 1781, he conquered some area in Shahpur Kandi jointly with the chief of Sujanpur and added twentysix villages to his possessions. In 1807, his territory was taken over by Ranjit Singh who left ten villages to him for subsistence.[42]

Amar Singh Bagga, a Man Jat of Dharmkot Bagga, joined hands with Nand Singh in conquest and got Sujanpur with its surrounding area as his share.[43] Several villages near Dharmkot also belonged to him. In 1781, he added eighteen villages in the Palahi area of Shahpur to his possessions. Four years later, he joined Jassa Singh Ramgarhia to fight the Kanhiya chief Jai Singh.[44] On his death in 1805, his elder son Bhag Singh had to pay *nazrāna* to Ranjit Singh. Bhag Singh died in 1808 and his brother Buddh Singh was allowed to succeed him. However, when he refused to pay a larger tribute in the year following, Sujanpur was taken over and Buddh Singh was given a service *jāgīr*.[45]

Between the territories of the chiefs of Lahore and Haqiqat Singh, there was a small principality under Jodh Singh who was not an associate of Jai Singh. Jodh Singh appears to have occupied only a single pocket of territory around Saurian.[46] He was married to Gujjar Singh's

---

[40] Ahmad Shah, *Tārīkh-i-Panjab* (Pbi. tr.), 63. Ram Sukh Rao, *Sri Fateh Singh Partap Prabhakar*, 127. *DG Gurdaspur* (1883-84), 14.

[41] Ram Sukh Rao, *Jassa Singh Binod* (ms), f. 320 b. W.L. M'Gregor, *History of the Sikhs*, I, 123-24. *DG Gurdaspur* (1883-84), 13 & 14.

[42] Ahmad Shah, *Tārīkh-i-Panjab* (Pbi. tr.), 76.

[43] Amar Singh and Nand Singh had taken over the territory of Ajaib Rai, a *qānūngo* under the Mughals. They divided it between themselves and Nand Singh got Pathankot as his share: *DG Gurdaspur* (1883-84), 14. Foreign/Political Proceedings, 8 April 1859, No. 65.

[44] Sohan Lal, *Umdat-ut-Tawārīkh* (Pbi. tr.), II, 27. Prinsep, *Origin of the Sikh Power*, 35. *DG Gurdaspur* (1883-84), 13.

[45] Ram Sukh Rao, *Sri Fateh Singh Partap Prabhakar*, 129-30. Ahmad Shah, *Tārīkh-i-Panjab* (Pbi. tr.), 63 & 73. *DG Gurdaspur* (1883-84), 12-14.

[46] *SR Amritsar* (1860), 3.

daughter, but he is believed to have supported Ranjit Singh in his occupation of Lahore. The time of his death is not known. His son Amir Singh started serving Ranjit Singh during the second decade of the nineteenth century. He appears to have held Saurian till his death in 1825.[47]

Jassa Singh Ramgarhia and his brothers who were associated with Jai Singh Kanhiya for a short time, occupied territories on both sides of the Beas with their headquarters at Sri Hargobindpur on the right bank of the river. In the Bari Doab, their possessions were around Batala and Kalanaur.[48] Jassa Singh's brother Tara Singh wrested Qadian from its Sayyad chief.[49] In the Jalandhar Doab, they possessed a considerable territory around Dasuya, Garhdiwala, Miani, Urmar, Tanda, Begowal and Bhogpur.[50] According to Ahmad Shah of Batala, Mali Singh was particularly an obnoxious administrator. In any case, Jassa Singh Ahluwalia and Jai Singh Kanhiya and his associates ousted the Ramgarhia brothers from all their territories in 1780.[51] As stated earlier, they were able to come back only in 1785 with the help of Mahan Singh Sukarchakia. Mali Singh and Tara Singh died before the occupation of Lahore by Ranjit Singh in 1799. Jassa Singh alone joined the allies against Ranjit Singh in 1800.[52] He died in 1803 to be succeeded by his elder son Jodh Singh who died in 1816 as a tributary of Ranjit Singh.[53] The claims of his younger brother Vir Singh and his cousin Diwan Singh, the son of Tara Singh, were set aside by Ranjit Singh and the Ramgarhia territory with the scores of its fortresses was taken

---

[47] H.L.O. Garrett & G.L. Chopra (tr. & ed.), *Events at the Court of Ranjit Singh (1810-17)*, 203. Lepel Griffin, *The Panjab Chiefs*, 429-30.

[48] Ahmad Shah, *Tārīkh-i-Panjab* (Pbi. tr.), 46, 49, 53 & 248. Ganda Singh, *Sardar Jassa Singh Ahluwalia*, 70.

[49] Ahmad Shah, *Tārīkh-i-Panjab* (Pbi. tr.), 51-52. Lepel Griffin, *The Panjab Chiefs*, 175 & 380-81.

[50] In all, Jassa Singh possessed territory yielding revenues worth seven lacs of rupees per annum: Foreign/Secret Proceedings, 24 June 1809, No. 7.

[51] Ahmad Shah, *Tārīkh-i-Panjab* (Pbi. tr.), 49-50 & 51. *DG Jullundur* (1904), 32.

[52] Sohan Lal, *Umdat-ut-Tawārīkh* (Pbi. tr.), II, 46. Fakir Syed Waheeduddin, *The Real Ranjit Singh*, 137.

[53] Jodh Singh accompanied Ranjit Singh with his contingents in the expeditions of Kangra, Multan, Bhimber and Rajauri: *Events at the Court of Ranjit Singh (1810-17)*, 40 & 203.

over by the Maharaja. Like the widow of Jodh Singh, Vir Singh and Diwan Singh were given *jāgīrs* for subsistence. Subsequently, Diwan Singh and his sons were taken into service.[54]

The territory along the river Beas from the present Grand Trunk Road to the confluence of the Beas with the Satlej near Harike was occupied by Jassa Singh Ahluwalia. He was one of the most eminent leaders of the Khalsa and on many occasions commanded their combined forces. He occupied Fatehabad in 1753 and it served as his headquarters for thirty years.[55] Before 1765, he occupied Tarn Taran and Sarhali. He also held some territory on the other side of the river Beas and across the river Satlej. After 1765, he increased his territories in the Jalandhar Doab and in the Satlej-Jamuna divide.[56] He subjugated several chiefs of the hills and the plains and obliged them to pay tribute.[57] We have already referred to his alliance with Jai Singh for ousting the Ramgarhias from the Bari Doab. At the time of his death in 1783, he is said to have possessed territories worth eight lacs of rupees a year and commanded about 7,500 horsemen and 2,500 foot.[58]

In the absence of a male heir, Jassa Singh was succeeded by Bhag Singh, the grandson of his cousin-brother. Bhag Singh had to contend with the claims of Jassa Singh's son-in-law, Mohar Singh, but he established his power without much difficulty.[59] With the help of Jai Singh Kanhiya, he succeeded in wresting Sharaqpur from the Nakkai chief Bhagwan Singh.[60] He succeeded also in recovering Tarn Taran from Gulab Singh Bhangi.[61] However, he failed to stop the Ramgarhias from recovering their former territories in the Bari Doab. Till Bhag

---

[54] Ahmad Shah, *Tārīkh-i-Panjab* (Pbi. tr.), 52-53. Sohan Lal, *Umdat-ut-Tawārīkh* (Pbi. tr.), II, 195 & 236-37.

[55] *DG Kapurthala State* (1904), 4.

[56] Foreign/Secret Consultation, 26 December 1846, No. 65. *DG Firozpur* (1883-84), 20-21 & 47. Ram Sukh Rao, *Jassa Singh Binod* (ms), ff 76 a, 206b, 225a,b.

[57] Ram Sukh Rao, *Jassa Singh Binod* (ms), ff 76a, 93a, 95b, 96a,b, 119a, 125b, 135b, 140b, 152b, 159b, 177b, 187b, 195b, 206a, 225a,b & 230b. Lepel Griffin, *The Rajas of the Punjab*, 503-4, 511-12.

[58] Foreign/Secret Proceedings, 24 June 1809, No. 7. Ganda Singh (ed.), *Early European Accounts of the Sikhs*, 43.

[59] *Revised Pedigree-Tables of the Families Mentioned in the Revised edition of Chiefs and Families of Note in the Punjab*, 238.

[60] Ram Sukh Rao, *Jassa Singh Binod* (ms), f, 173b.

[61] Giani Gian Singh, *Raj Khalsa*, 622.

Singh's death in 1801, the Ramgarhia and Ahluwalia chiefs remained on unfriendly terms, trying to encroach upon each other's territory.[62]

Bhag Singh left this legacy to his son Fateh Singh. In 1802, Fateh Singh entered into an alliance with Ranjit Singh which enabled him to increase his territories in his early career.[63] At the time of Jaswant Rao Holkar's appearance in the Punjab in 1805, the British signed a treaty with Fateh Singh and Ranjit Singh together.[64] However, the Treaty of Amritsar in 1809 was signed by the British with Ranjit Singh alone as the sole Sikh sovereign on the west of the Satlej. Ranjit Singh did not take long to reduce Fateh Singh Ahluwalia to the position of a vassal.[65] In 1825, Fateh Singh crossed the river Satlej to seek protection with the British against the alleged designs of Ranjit Singh over his territories. However, he was persuaded by Ranjit Singh as well as by the British political agents to return to his capital at Kapurthala.[66] He was now reconciled to his status of a vassal. But, in the process, he lost his territories in the Bari Doab and his fort and possessions in the city of Amritsar.[67] Nevertheless, Ranjit Singh treated him with great respect and a certain degree of consideration throughout his life, while Fateh Singh Ahluwalia performed extremely useful services for the Maharaja. Upon his death in 1837, his son Nihal Singh succeeded to his position after paying a heavy *nazrāna* to Ranjit Singh. In 1845, Nihal Singh did not support the British against his suzerain at Lahore and his territories on the east of the river Satlej were

---

[62] Ram Sukh Rao, *Sri Fateh Singh Partap Prabhakar*, 75 & n 3.

[63] Sohan Lal, *Umdat-ut-Tawārīkh* (Pbi. tr.), II, 51. Ahmad Shah, *Tārīkh-i-Panjab* (Pbi. tr.), 73. Prinsep, *Origin of the Sikh Power*, 44.

[64] It was Fateh Singh who negotiated the treaty in their joint names. Both of them were termed *sardārs* in the treaty: Foreign/Secret Consultation, 26 December 1846, No. 6. George Campbell, *Memoirs of My Indian Career* (ed. Charles E. Bernard), I, 45.

[65] Fateh Singh was asked to accompany Ranjit Singh with his forces on every expedition. He was also to attend Ranjit Singh at his court: Foreign/Secret Consultation, 30 January 1810, No. 18. Sohan Lal, *Umdat-ut-Tawārīkh* (Pbi. tr.), II, 53, 95, 156, 175-76, 199, 241-42, 269 & 275.

[66] Ahmad Shah, *Tārīkh-i-Panjab* (Pbi. tr.), 67. Ram Sukh Rao, *Sri Fateh Singh Partap Prabhakar*, 461-63. Foreign/ Political Consultation, 7 November 1836, No. 46. Aliuddin, *Ibratnāma* (Pbi. tr.), 353.

[67] Ahmad Shah, *Tārīkh-i-Panjab* (Pbi. tr.), 68. J.S. Grewal, 'Ramdaspur to Amritsar', *Studies in Urban History* (ed. J.S. Grewal & Indu Banga), Guru Nanak Dev University, Amritsar, 1981, 120.

annexed to the British empire. The Kapurthala state during the British rule in the Punjab came to be confined to the Jalandhar Doab.[68]

Neither the Ahluwalias nor the Bhangis were able to dislodge the petty chiefs of Jandiala and Jodhanagri during the late eighteenth century. The founder of the Jandiala principality, Kirpal Das, was a grandson of Baba Handal, regarded as the founder of the Niranjania sect. Kirpal Das had carved out a territory worth 50,000 rupees a year by supporting Ahmad Shah Abdali against the Sikhs.[69] He was succeeded by his brother Dyal Das, who ruled only for a short time. His successor, Saran Das, had to pay *nazrāna* to Jassa Singh Ahluwalia in 1768 as the mark of his submission. Saran Das's son and successor Bishambar Das supported Zaman Shah during his invasions of the Punjab, acknowledging at the same time the superior claims of Fateh Singh Ahluwalia.[70] Jandiala was wrested from Bishambar Das by Ranjit Singh in 1812, and handed over to Fateh Singh Ahluwalia.[71]

A small principality around Jodhanagri was established by Dharam Das whose ancestors were *zamīndārs* of the area during the Mughal times. He submitted to Ahmad Shah Abdali and was allowed to retain all his villages worth about 35,000 rupees a year. He supported Ahmad Shah Abdali in his campaigns against the Sikhs and one of his sons is said to have accepted Islam.[72] Dharm Das was obliged to become a tributary of Jassa Singh Ahluwalia. He tried to become independent after the death of the Ahluwalia chief but Bhag Singh Ahluwalia proved to be too strong for him. Dharm Das's son and successor, Ram Chand was killed in a battle at Nadala while fighting for his suzerain Fateh Singh Ahluwalia in 1804.[73] Ranjit Singh took over Jodhanagri, leaving to the minor son of Ram Chand a village worth 2,000 rupees a year for subsistence.[74]

---

[68] Foreign/Political Consultation, 28 November 1836, No. 22. Lepel Griffin, *The Rajas of the Punjab*, 543-51. *DG Kapurthala State* (1904), 6.

[69] Khushwaqt Rai, *Tawārīkh-i-Sikhān* (Pbi. tr.), 94-95.

[70] Ram Sukh Rao, *Sri Fateh Singh Partap Prabhakar*, 202, 352-53. Lepel Griffin, *The Rajas of the Punjab*, 503.

[71] Sohan Lal, *Umdat-ut-Tawārīkh* (Pbi. tr.), II, 56. Giani Gian Singh, *Raj Khalsa*, 624. *DG Jullundur* (1904), 44.

[72] Ram Sukh Rao, *Sri Fateh Singh Partap Prabhakar*, 84. Foreign/Political Proceedings, 29 December 1849, No. 49A.

[73] Ram Sukh Rao, *Sri Fateh Singh Partap Prabhakar*, 84-85.

[74] Foreign/Political Proceedings, 29 December 1849, No. 49A.

The Afghan principality of Qasur, though surrounded by Sikh dominions on all sides, survived into the early nineteenth century. The Afghans of Qasur had settled there in the sixteenth century. In the early eighteenth century, some of them were serving the Mughal empire as *mansabdārs*. Bayazid Khan, whose father had served under Aurangzeb, was serving as the *faujdār* of Jammu under Bahadur Shah. His nephew Shams Khan at this time was the *faujdār* of Jalandhar.[75] Both of them died fighting against Banda Bahadur. Hussain Khan, the younger brother of Bayazid Khan, was authorized to collect revenues from the area around Qasur. In fact, he was encouraged by the Sayyad brothers to rise in revolt against Abdus Samad Khan, the governor of Lahore, and he died fighting in a battle near Chunian.[76] Closely related to this family was Shahdad Khan who served Abdus Samad Khan with distinction as a *mansabdār* of the Mughal empire. His son Muhiyuddin Khan was the first Mughal *mansabdār* to start acting like a chief in the Qasur region.[77]

In the early 1760s, Qasur was invaded by Hari Singh Bhangi with the support of some other Sikh leaders, but Muhiyuddin Khan maintained his independence. In 1771, Jhanda Singh Bhangi obliged Hamid Khan, a nephew and successor of Muhiyuddin Khan, to pay four lacs of rupees as *nazrāna*.[78] Hamid Khan's nephew Nizamuddin Khan felt obliged around 1790 to accept service with Gulab Singh of Amritsar. A few years later, however, he re-established himself at Qasur and successfully withstood pressure from Gulab Singh.[79] During Zaman Shah's invasions of the Punjab in the late 1790s, Nizamuddin Khan felt encouraged in fact to entertain the idea that he could become the governor of Lahore on behalf of Zaman Shah.[80]

---

[75] *Maāthir-ul-Umarā* (Eng. tr.), I, 642. *DG Lahore* (1883-84), 197.

[76] *Asrar-i-Samadi* (Pbi. tr.), 7, 22-28. *Maāthir-ul-Umarā* (Eng. tr.), I, 73.

[77] *Maāthir-ul-Umarā* (Eng. tr.), II, Part 2, 747 & 750. *Asrar-i-Samadi* (Pbi. tr.), 16-21. Aliuddin, *Ibratnāma* (Pbi. tr.), 375. Giani Gian Singh, *Tawārīkh Guru Khālsa*, II, 177-78.

[78] Ram Sukh Rao, *Jassa Singh Binod* (ms), ff 76 & 314-15. Ratan Singh Bhangu, *Prāchīn Panth Parkāsh*, 385-90.

[79] Aliuddin, *Ibratnāma* (Pbi. tr.), 378-79. *DG Lahore* (1883-84), 197.

[80] Foreign/Secret Consultation, 25 January 1797, No. 9. Foreign/Political Consultation, 25 January 1799, No. 26. Aliuddin, *Ibratnāma* (Pbi. tr.), 455.

However, when Lahore was occupied by Ranjit Singh in 1799, Nizamuddin Khan entered into an alliance with Gulab Singh against Ranjit Singh. The opposing armies faced each other near Bhasin between Lahore and Amritsar but retreated without a battle.[81] Nizamuddin Khan extended his territories to the east of the Satlej, before he was attacked by Ranjit Singh in 1801 and obliged to submit. On his death in the year following, he was succeeded by his minor son Fateh Din Khan, but the affairs of the principality were actually managed by his uncle Qutbuddin Khan. In 1807, Ranjit Singh took over the territories of Qasur, giving large *jāgīrs* to both Qutbuddin Khan and Fateh Din Khan in Mamdot and Maruf respectively on the condition of maintaining 100 horsemen each for service under the Maharaja.[82]

To the south of Qasur were the principalities of Chunian and Kanganpur. The principality of Chunian was founded by a Sandhu Jat, Hira Singh, whose father Hemraj was the *chaudharī* of Bharwal in the Pargana of Chunian. Hira Singh appears to have occupied Chunian, Khudian and Satghara around 1763.[83] He died in 1766 during a campaign against the chief of Pakpatan. His nephew, Nahar Singh, died fighting against the Kharals only two years later.[84]

The most powerful chief of this principality was Nahar Singh's son Ran Singh. He extended his territories mainly at the cost of the Kharals, occupying Faridabad, Bucheke, and Jethpur across the river Ravi. Ran Singh extended his territory upto Sharaqpur in the north and conquered Sayyadwala and Kamalia, both in the Rachna Doab, from the neighbouring Sikh chief of Gogera.[85] He died in 1781 to be succeeded by his son Bhagwan Sigh who lost Sayyadwala to its former chief soon after his accession. His sister was betrothed to Ranjit Singh in the early 1780s, when he succeeded in occupying all the territory of Malka

---

81 Abstract of a letter dated 18 March 1802, *Poona Residency Correspondence, 1800-03*, IX, 47. Sohan Lal, *Umdat-ut-Tawārīkh* (Pbi. tr.), II, 46. Ganesh Das, *Chār Bāgh-i-Panjab* (Pbi. tr.), 142.

82 Amar Nath, *Zafarnāma-i-Ranjit Singh* (tr. into Punjabi by Kirpal Singh), Punjabi University, Patiala, 1983, 33. Foreign/Political Proceedings, 29 December 1849, No. 49A. Lepel Griffin, *The Panjab Chiefs*, 54.

83 Sohan Lal, *Umdat-ut-Tawārīkh* (Pbi. tr.), II, 45 Giani Gian Singh, *Raj Khalsa*, 563.

84 *SR Montgomery* (1878), 32. *DG Montgomery* (1933), 36.

85 Giani Gian Singh, *Raj Khalsa*, 564. *DG Montgomery* (1883-84), 31.

Hans.[86] He died in 1789 to be succeeded by his brother Gian Singh who lost Kamalia to the Kharals in the 1790s. Gian Singh died in 1807 and was succeeded by his son Kahn Singh. Three years later, the terrtories of Kahn Singh were taken over by Ranjit Singh and he was made a *jāgīrdār*.[87]

Kanganpur was adopted as his headquarters by Lal Singh who occupied a number of villages around Kanganpur and Maruf in the north of Dipalpur and south of Chunian.[88] In the 1780s, he conquered a part of the territory of Dipalpur. No other important event of his long life is recorded. His territories were taken over by Ranjit Singh in 1807.[89]

Of the seventeen principalities considered so far, only four were non-Sikh. The chiefs of Qadian were Sayyad and the chiefs of Qasur were Afghan. The chiefs of Jandiala were Jat but not Sikh and this probably was also the position of the chiefs of Jodhanagri. The majority of the founders of the principalities in the Bari Doab were, thus, Sikh. One of them was originally a carpenter (Ramgarhia) and another a *kalāl* (Ahluwalia). The remaining eleven were Jat.

The number of Sikh chiefs in the Bari Doab was in fact larger if we take into account the smaller Sikh chiefs. It has been possible to identify nine chiefs whose resources ranged from 15,000 rupees to 60,000 rupees a year. In the case of Mirza Singh Shergill, the annual revenues were less than 15,000 rupees a year.[90] When he died in 1787, his villages were divided among his minor sons Kahn Singh and Jit Singh. Some of their villages were taken over by Jaimal Singh, son of Haqiqat Singh of Fatehgarh Churian.[91] There were several chiefs in the Bari Doab whose territories yielded more than 25,000 rupees but less than 50,000 rupees a year: Arbel Singh Sidhu, Karam Singh Man, Majja Singh Randhawa, Karam Singh Rangar Nanglia, Charhat Singh Sangatpuria, Sahib Singh Randhawa, for example. Karam Singh Rangar Nanglia held his villages till 1802 when Ranjit Singh took

[86] The marriage ceremony took place in 1798: Sohan Lal, *Umdat-ut-Tawārīkh* (Pbi. tr.), II, 45. Foreign/Political Proceedings, 23 June 1854, No. 205. *SR Montgomery* (1878), 32 & 34.

[87] Aliuddin, *Ibratnāma* (Pbi. tr.), 320-31. Giani Gian Singh, *Raj Khalsa*, 565. Indu Banga, *Agrarian System of the Sikhs*, 140.

[88] *SR Montgomery* (1878), 37. *DG Montgomery* (1933), 41.

[89] *DG Montgomery* (1884), 36.

[90] Griffin & Massy, *Chiefs and Families of Note*, I, 450.

[91] Lepel Griffin, *The Panjab Chiefs*, 230-31.

them over and made him a *jāgīrdār*.[92] Majja Singh Randhawa and Sham Singh, son of Karam Singh Man, lost their territories in the late eighteenth century itself, the former to Sada Kaur and the latter to Mahan Singh Sukarchakia.[93] Arbel Singh Sidhu was succeeded by his son Bhup Singh and the latter by Kahn Singh who lost his territories in the first decade of the nineteenth century to become a *jāgīrdār* of Ranjit Singh.[94] The territories of Charhat Singh Sangatpuria were divided amongst his sons Sardul Singh, Nar Singh and Didar Singh; those of Sahib Singh Randhawa, amongst his sons Jit Singh and Buddh Singh. They all lost their territories to Ranjit Singh to become *jāgīrdārs*.[95] Sahib Singh Veglia possessed territory worth 60,000 rupees a year around Taragarh. On his death in 1803, his villages were divided amongst his four sons who were reduced to the position of *jāgīrdārs* by 1813.[96]

By now we have noticed a few chiefs whose territory upon their death was divided among all their male heirs. They can perhaps be treated as *pattīdārs*. In any case, there were a few others too who belonged to this category like Pardhan Singh Randhawa of Talwandi and Mehtab Singh Sandhu of Wadala in the Rachna Doab. We do not know their resources but their territories were divided equally amongst their sons. When the sons of Pardhan Singh, namely Santokh Singh and Sahib Singh, died in 1802 and 1804 respectively, their possessions were taken over by Ranjit Singh.[97] Sham Singh and Nidhan Singh, the sons of Mehtab Singh, lost a part of their estates to the neighbouring chief, Nidhan Singh of Daska, before Ranjit Singh took them over.[98]

II

In the Jalandhar Doab, the territory along the left bank of the river Beas from Pathankot to Harike, including places like Hajipur, Mukerian,

---

[92] Sohan Lal, *Umdat-ut-Tawārīkh* (Pbi. tr.), II, 58. *DG Gurdaspur* (1883-84), 39.

[93] Foreign/Political Proceedings, 29 December 1849, No. 47A. Lepel Griffin, *The Panjab Chiefs*, 178 & 201.

[94] Griffin & Massy, *Chiefs and Families of Note*, I, 390.

[95] Lepel Griffin, *The Panjab Chiefs*, 215 & 339.

[96] Ibid., 375. *DG Gurdaspur* (1883-84), 17.

[97] Lepel Griffin, *The Panjab Chiefs*, 205. *DG Gurdaspur* (1883-84), 40.

[98] Lepel Griffin, *The Panjab Chiefs*, 418.

Dasuya, Miani, Begowal, Dhilwan and Talwandi Chaudhariān, was occupied by Jai Singh Kanhiya, Jassa Singh Ramgarhia and Jassa Singh Ahluwalia. Along the river Satlej, there were four principalities, those of Talwan, Phillaur, Rahon and Kathgarh. Between the river Satlej and the White Bein, there were three more principalities: Banga, Phagwara and Nakodar. There were three other principalities between the White Bein and the Black Bein: Jalandhar, Kapurthala and Hariana. Besides these ten principalities, it is possible to identify seven other small chiefs. In terms of religious affiliation, thirteen of these seventeen chiefs were Sikh, three were Muslim and one was Hindu. All the three Muslim chiefs were Rajput and of the remaining fourteen chiefs only one was a non-Jat: the Khatri chief of Banga.

In the time of Akbar, the Manj Rajputs of Talwan were holding over two lac *bighas* of land as *zamīndārs* commanding 70 horsemen and 700 infantry. The entire *pargana* yielded more than one and a half lac of rupees.[99] The *zamīndār* of Talwan to submit to Ahmad Shah Abdali was Mahmud Khan. During the last invasion of Ahmad Shah in 1767, he occupied Nur Mahal which was held by a *jāgīrdār* of Jassa Singh Ahluwalia. When Jassa Singh tried to recover Nur Mahal, Mahmud Khan invited Sardar Baghel Singh to his help, promising to pay annual tribute.[100] Mahmud Khan's successor Shahbaz Khan lost all his territories to Ranjit Singh early in the nineteenth century.[101]

The chief of Phillaur, Tara Singh, was a Kang Jat like his namesake Tara Singh Dallewalia, and had made joint conquests with him. His territories were on both sides of the river Satlej with the larger chunk in the Jalandhar Doab. On his death, perhaps around 1790, he was succeeded by his brother Koer Singh. Tara Singh's son Sadda Singh succeeded his uncle around 1795. In the time of his son Megh Singh, Ranjit Singh occupied Phillaur in 1809 and gave him some villages in *jāgīr*.[102]

Rahon was adopted as his headquarters by Tara Singh Dallewalia, known also as Gheba. Tara Singh appears to have been an active participant in the campaigns of the Dal Khalsa. His earlier conquests were in Sarai Dakhni and Nawan Shahr to which he added Rahon and

---

99 *Ā'īn-Akbarī* (Eng. tr.), II, 320.

100 *DG Jullundur* (1904), 33-35.

101 Aliuddin, *Ibratnāma* (Pbi. tr.), 95.

102 Ram Sukh Rao, *Sri Fateh Singh Partap Prabhakar*, 220. *DG Jullundur* (1904), 118.

Nakodar.[103] He possessed some territory across the river Satlej, including Dharmkot.[104] In the early years of the nineteenth century, he joined Ranjit Singh in his campaigns. In the process, he came to be regarded as a subordinate chief. When he died in 1807, he was actually accompanying Ranjit Singh on his campaign across the Satlej. His territories were taken over and his sons Jhanda Singh and Dasaunda Singh were allowed to retain Sarai Dakhni in *jāgīr*.[105]

The chief of Kathgarh, Jhanda Singh, was a resident of Sultanwind near Amritsar. He acquired territory in the Jalandhar Doab worth about a lac of rupees a year. He died in 1797 and was succeeded by his son, Tara Singh, who had to acknowledge the supremacy of Ranjit Singh soon after. He was allowed to retain his villages only as a *jāgīrdār*.[106]

Dharam Singh, a Khatri, conquered the town of Banga with 240 villages around. In 1804, he was obliged to become tributary to Ranjit Singh. On his death in 1806, his territories were taken over and his sons were made *jāgīrdārs*.[107]

The founder of the principality of Phagwara was Chaudharī Churh Mal, a descendant of Dharm Chand who had obtained over a score of villages around Phagwara in *zamīndāri* in the reign of Aurangzeb.[108] Jassa Singh Ahluwalia attacked Churh Mal and he submitted on the condition of paying annual tribute. Churh Mal appears to have paid tribute to Jassa Singh and his successors for the rest of his life.[109] After his death in the first decade of the nineteenth century, Phagwara with all

---

[103] Tara Singh expelled Rai Ahmad Manj from Nakodar and occupied it in 1767: Ganesh Das, *Chār Bāgh-i-Panjab* (Pbi. tr.), 128. *DG Jullundur* (1904), 78.

[104] Mahitpur and Ghungrana near Ludhiana were part of Tara Singh's possessions across the Satlej. In total, he possessed 110 villages in this area. Aliuddin, *Ibratnāma* (Pbi. tr.), 363. *DG Firozpur* (1883-84), 22.

[105] Sohan Lal, *Umdat-ut-Tawārīkh* (Pbi. tr.), II, 71 & 77.

[106] Charles Francis Massy, *Chiefs and Families of Note in the Delhi, Jalandhar, Peshawar and Derajat Divisions of the Punjab*, Pioneer Press, Allahabad, 1890, 344-45. *DG Hoshiarpur* (1883-84), 78-79.

[107] *DG Jullundur* (1904), 112-113 & 283. Sohan Lal, *Umdat-ut-Tawārīkh* (Pbi. tr.), II, 71 & 73.

[108] *DG Jullundur* (1904), 44.

[109] Ram Sukh Rao, *Sri Fateh Singh Partap Prabhakar,* 102 & 143. Giani Gian Singh, *Raj Khalsa*, 621.

its villages was taken over by Ranjit Singh and given to Fateh Singh Ahluwalia to be added to his territories.[110]

The Manj Rajputs of Nakodar were holding 80,000 *bighas* of land, yielding over 90,000 rupees a year in the time of Akbar. They commanded twenty horsemen and about a thousand infantry as *zamīndārs*.[111] Rai Ahmad of Nakodar, who was the first to become a chief during the late eighteenth century, was also the first to lose his territory. Nakodar was occupied by Tara Singh Dallewalia in 1767.[112]

The principality of Jalandhar was the most important principality of the Doab. Its founder Khushal Singh was a nephew of Kapur Singh who is well known as Nawab Kapur Singh.[113] Before his death in 1753, Kapur Singh had come into possession of some villages in the Bari Doab. The city of Jalandhar and the villages around were conquered by Khushal Singh after 1753, jointly with Jassa Singh Ahluwalia who also was an associate of Nawab Kapur Singh.[114] Before he died in 1795, Khushal Singh was in possession of Patti in the Bari Doab, a few dozen villages across the river Satlej, including a part of Banur, and the territory around Jalandhar encircled by Nakodar, Kapurthala, Phagwara and Sham Chaurasi.[115] Khushal Singh's son Buddh Singh succeeded to his territories, but ten years later he was obliged to become a tributary of Ranjit Singh. When Ranjit Singh took over Patti and Jalandhar in 1811, Buddh Singh crossed the river Satlej and started residing at Banur where he died in 1816.[116]

The Bhatti Rajputs of Sultanpur were holding over 1,00,000 *bighas* of land yielding over a lac of rupees a year. They commanded

---

[110] Sohan Lal, *Umdat-ut-Tawārīkh* (Pbi. tr.), II, 65. Prinsep, *Origin of the Sikh Power*, 44.

[111] *Ā'īn-i-Akbarī* (Eng. tr.), II, 321.

[112] Aliuddin, *Ibratnāma* (Pbi. tr.), 363.

[113] Ratan Singh Bhangu, *Prāchīn Panth Parkāsh*, 214. Giani Gian Singh, *Tawārīkh Guru Khālsa*, II, 35-36.

[114] Foreign/Secret Proceedings, 24 June 1809, No. 7. Ahmad Shah, *Tārīkh-i-Panjab* (Pbi. tr.), 45. Khushal Singh is also known as Faizullapuria, from the name of Kapur Singh's ancestral village. Since the village was presumably renamed Singhpura, he is also known as Singhpuria.

[115] *SR Amritsar* (1860), 4. Lepel Griffin, *The Rajas of the Punjab*, 61n.

[116] Sohan Lal, *Umdat-ut-Tawārīkh* (Pbi. tr.), II, 70, 133-35. Giani Gian Singh, *Raj Khalsa*, 627. Prinsep, *Origin of the Sikh Power*, 62 & 68.

200 horsemen and one thousand infantry.[117] They consolidated their hold on the territories by a nominal submission to Ahmad Shah. On Ahmad Shah's withdrawal from the Punjab, Rai Ibrahim Bhatti became independent. He adopted Kapurthala as his headquarters with his territory stretching along the river Beas. Before long, however, he had to submit to Jassa Singh Ahluwalia and to pay tribute. His inability or his refusal to pay resulted in a piecemeal occupation of his villages by Jassa Singh Ahluwalia till Kapurthala was taken over in 1780 and Rai Ibrahim was given a *jāgīr* for subsistence.[118]

The territory along the Shivalik from Hariana to Garh Shankar came into the possession of Baghel Singh, known as Karora Singhia.[119] He was a Dhaliwal Jat of Jhabal near Amritsar and had conquered territories as an associate of Karora Singh who was a Sandhu Jat. All the territory conquered by them came into Baghel Singh's possession after Karora Singh's death in 1761. Probably, Baghel Singh did not reside in the Jalandhar Doab because of his territorial and political interests in the Satlej-Jamuna Divide. Nevertheless, he helped Mahmud Khan of Talwan against Jassa Singh Ahluwalia and obtained possession of some villages near Nur Mahal.[120] Before his death in 1805, his elder wife Rup Kaur had started administering the Hariana territories, which she continued to do till her own death in 1809. All her possessions, including the pocket of territory near Nur Mahal, were taken over by Ranjit Singh.[121]

There were three Sikh chiefs in the Jalandhar Doab whose revenues did not exceed rupees three thousand a year: Waryam Singh, Desu Singh and Karam Singh.[122] A few other chiefs possessed territories worth less than 25,000 rupees a year. Karam Singh of Povind, for instance, left to his son a territory worth only 8,000 rupees a year.[123] Mahan Singh held only ten villages near Phillaur.[124] Sahaj Singh

---

[117] *Ā'īn-Akbarī* (Eng. tr.), II, 321.

[118] Ram Sukh Rao, *Jassa Singh Binod* (ms), ff 206b, 255a,b. Lepel Griffin, *The Rajas of the Punjab*, 504, 511-12.

[119] *DG Jullundur* (1904), 34.

[120] Ratan Singh Bhangu, *Prāchīn Panth Parkāsh*, 436-37. Lepel Griffin, *The Rajas of the Punjab*, 50, 52, 61 & 63.

[121] Foreign/Secret Proceedings, 24 June 1809, No. 7. Sohan Lal, *Umdat-ut-Tawārīkh* (Pbi. tr.), II, 104.

[122] Foreign/Political Consultation, 26 January 1855, No. 156.

[123] Foreign/Political Proceedings, 29 December 1849, No. 49A.

[124] *DG Jullundur and Kapurthala State* (1904), 114.

Bhangu held a territory near Phagwara worth about 20,000 rupees a year.[125] The revenues of Nahar Singh Man near Phillaur are not known but there is no indication that he held territories worth more than 20,000 rupees.[126]

III

In the upper Rachna and Chaj Doabs, there were eighteen principalities. Only one of these was under a Rajput chief. All the remaining chiefs were Jat. The most important chief of the upper Rachna Doab was Charhat Singh Sukarchakia. Much of his territory in the Rachna Doab lay between Lahore and Wazirabad. Two more chiefs of the Doab are traditionally linked with Charhat Singh, namely Gurbakhsh Singh Waraich of Wazirabad and Dal Singh Gill who subsequently came to be known as Akalgarhia. In fact, Gurbakhsh Singh was a cousin of Charhat Singh's wife and Dal Singh was a collateral.[127] Charhat Singh had built a fortress in Gujranwala as the base of his political activity and he was supported by both Dal Singh and Gurbakhsh Singh. Around 1760, he occupied places like Eminabad, Qila Didar Singh, Qila Sahib Singh and Wazirabad.[128] Charhat Sigh was among the prominent leaders of the Khalsa who opposed Ahmad Shah Abdali during his invasions of the Punjab after the battle of Panipat. In collaboration with Gujjar Singh, he conquered the upper portion of the Chaj Doab and got Kunjah, Kalra, Phalia, Kuthala and Miani as his share of the conquest. In 1767, he crossed the river Jehlam in concert with Gujjar Singh and conquered Pind Dadan Khan, Ahmadabad, Jehlam, Rohtas and some other places in the Sindh Sagar Doab.[129] The Ghebas, the Jodrahs and the Awans became tributary to Charhat Singh.[130] On his death in 1774,

---

[125] Ibid., 113.

[126] Ranjit Singh took his son Diwan Singh into service: Griffin & Massy, *Chiefs and Families of Note*, I, 60.

[127] Sohan Lal, *Umdat-ut-Tawārīkh* (Pbi. tr.), II, 4. J.S. Grewal, *Maharaja Ranjit Singh*, 14.

[128] Ahmad Shah, *Tārīkh-i-Panjab* (Pbi. tr.), 70. *SR Gujranwala* (1874), 10. Ratan Singh Bhangu, *Prāchīn Panth Parkāsh*, 368-73.

[129] Sohan Lal, *Umdat-ut-Tawārīkh* (Pbi. tr.), II, 10-11. Ahmad Shah, *Tārīkh-i-Panjab* (Pbi. tr.), 70. Ganesh Das, *Chār Bāgh-i-Panjab* (Pbi. tr.), 132.

[130] Lepel Griffin, *The Panjab Chiefs*, 387-88, 536 & 539.

he left an extensive territory with considerable resources to his son and successor Mahan Singh.

Mahan Singh was only ten years old at the time of his father's death and his first problem was to retain possession of the territories conquered by Charhat Singh. In this connection, the refractory *thānadār* of Rohtas was changed.[131] Only after 1780 did Mahan Singh try to expand his territories. He invaded the neighbouring principality of the Chatthas and first occupied Rasulpur, renamed Ramnagar, and then Manchar and Alipur, renamed Akalgarh.[132] This was the major territorial gain of Mahan Singh's life. However, he obliged a few chiefs to pay tribute to him, among whom were the Janjuas in the Sindh Sagar Doab and the chiefs of Akhnur and Jammu in the hills.[133] Mahan Singh also entered into alliances with Jassa Singh Ramgarhia and Sansar Chand of Kangra to reduce the power and prestige of Jai Singh Kanhiya whose grand-daughter Mehtab Kaur was subsequently betrothed to Mahan Singh's son Ranjit Singh.[134] He wrested Mananwala and the surrounding area from Sham Singh Man and thus obtained a footing in the Bari Doab.[135] Towards the end of his rule he supported Gujjar Singh's youngest son Fateh Singh against his elder brother Sahib Singh to recover Sodhra. In the midst of this contest, he died in 1790, leaving a large almost contiguous territory worth about twelve lacs of rupees and a well trained force of 5,000 cavalry to his son Ranjit Singh.[136]

Ranjit Singh was a minor when he succeeded to the principality. But he was well trained in the arts of war. The invasions of Zaman Shah in the late 1790s, brought the youthful Sukarchakia chief into political activity on a large scale, enabling him to emerge as a prominent chief first and then as the leading Sikh chief of the Punjab plains. His personal traits as well as the legacy left by his father and

---

131 Sohan Lal, *Umdat-ut-Tawārīkh* (Pbi. tr.), II, 18-19.

132 Ibid., 24-25. *SR Gujrat* (1874), vii.

133 Sohan Lal, *Umdat-ut-Tawārīkh* (Pbi. tr.), II, 30. Lepel Griffin, *The Panjab Chiefs*, 605.

134 George Forster, *A Journey from Bengal to England*, II, 336. Lepel Griffin, *The Panjab Chiefs*, 319.

135 Foreign/Political Proceedings, 29 December 1849, No. 47A.

136 Sohan Lal, *Umdat-ut-Tawārīkh* (Pbi. tr.), II, 32-34. J.S. Grewal, *Maharaja Ranjit Singh*, 22.

grandfather enabled him to occupy Lahore in 1799, dislodging the successors of Sobha Singh and Lehna Singh.[137]

As an associate of Charhat Singh, Gurbakhsh Singh had got Wazirabad with about 50 villages. Till his death in 1776, he remained on good terms with Charhat Singh and Mahan Singh.[138] His son Jodh Singh extended his territories in the direction of Daska, occupying Ghirthal, Gojra and Mitranwali. Towards the close of Mahan Singh's reign, however, Jodh Singh was supplying gun powder to Sahib Singh who was besieged by Mahan Singh in support of Sahib Singh's brother Fateh Singh.[139] Jodh Singh was able to rule for about two decades more but probably acknowledging Ranjit Singh as his overlord. On his death in 1809, when his son Ganda Singh succeeded to his position, he had to pay heavy *nazrāna* and tribute to Ranjit Singh. A year later, Wazirabad was taken over by the Maharaja and Ganda Singh was given villages worth 10,000 rupees for subsistence.[140]

As an associate of Charhat Singh, Dal Singh Gill had got Ahmadabad in 1767. When Mahan Singh defeated the Chatthas in 1783, Dal Singh was given Alipur (Akalgarh).[141] That was why he was generally referred to as Dal Singh Akalgarhia. Like Jodh Singh Wazirabadia, Dal Singh helped Sahib Singh when he was besieged in Sodhra by Mahan Singh. In 1797, however, he supported Ranjit Singh in his campaign against Jan Muhammad Chattha who was trying to revive the Chattha principality with the support of Zaman Shah.[142] But in 1800, Dal Singh joined Sahib Singh's coalition against Ranjit Singh. That was why Ranjit Singh besieged Akalgarh. He was unable to occupy the territories of Dal Singh because of the joint opposition from Sahib Singh and Jodh Singh. Akalgarh was taken over by Ranjit

---

[137] Foreign/Secret Proceedings, 30 December 1800, No. 85. Sohan Lal, *Umdat-ut-Tawārīkh* (Pbi. tr.), II, 50-52.

[138] *SR Gujranwala* (1874), 9.

[139] Munshi Amin Chand, *A History of the Sialkot District*, 14. *SR Sialkot* (1865), 47.

[140] Sohan Lal, *Umdat-ut-Tawārīkh* (Pbi. tr.), II, 116. *SR Sialkot* (1865), 48. *DG Gujranwala* (1895), 26.

[141] Sohan Lal, *Umdat-ut-Tawārīkh* (Pbi. tr.), II, 5. *DG Gujranwala* (1895), 25-26.

[142] Sohan Lal, *Umdat-ut-Tawārīkh* (Pbi. tr.), II, 38. J.S. Grewal, *Maharaja Ranjit Singh*, 26.

Singh after Dal Singh's death in 1804 and his widow was given two villages for subsistence.[143]

Between Akalgarh and Wazirabad, there was the principality of Rasulnagar (later known as Ramnagar). It belonged to the Chattha Jats who are mentioned in the *Ā'īn-i-Akbarī* as *zamīndārs* with over 95,000 *bighas* of land yielding one and a half lac of rupees a year. They commanded 100 horsemen and 1,000 foot.[144] In the early eighteenth century, Nur Muhammad Chattha occupied the territory around Sayyadnagar and founded Rasulnagar. Around 1750, the Chatthas became refractory under Nur Muhammad. However, when Ahmad Shah Abdali invaded the Punjab, Nur Muhammad submitted to him to be confirmed in his possessions.[145] He died in the 1760s and he was succeeded by his son Pir Muhammad who consolidated his power by founding new fortresses and towns. In a quarrel with his brother Ahmad Khan, Pir Muhammad lost a son. Two sons of Ahmad Khan were also killed. As the price of support against Ahmad Khan, Pir Muhammad Khan had to acknowledge Gujjar Singh Bhangi as his overlord.[146] On his death in 1774, he was succeeded by his son Ghulam Muhammad.

In the early 1780s, Mahan Singh Sukarchakia invaded the territories of Ghulam Muhammad and demanded tribute. Ghulam Muhammad agreed to pay tribute after some reluctance. He was deprived of Sayyadnagar and Rasulnagar, but allowed to retain the territories around Alipur and Manchar. On his refusal to pay regular tribute, Alipur and Manchar too were taken over and his widow was given subsistence *jāgīr*, while his son Jan Muhammad escaped to Kabul.[147] With the help of Zaman Shah, Jan Muhammad recovered his possessions in 1796. But after Zaman Shah's return to Kabul, Ranjit Singh occupied Rasulnagar and Jan Muhammad was killed in a battle. The resistance of the Chatthas under Azim Khan, the maternal uncle of Jan Muhammad,

---

[143] Sohan Lal, *Umdat-ut-Tawārīkh* (Pbi. tr.), II, 57-58. *DG Gujranwala* (1895), 26 & 181.

[144] *Ā'īn-Akbarī* (Eng. tr.), II, 323. H.A. Rose, *A Glossary of Tribes and Castes*, II, 154.

[145] Lepel Griffin, *The Panjab Chiefs*, 403. *DG Gujranwala* (1935), 18.

[146] Sohan Lal, *Umdat-ut-Tawārīkh* (Pbi. tr.), II, 19. *DG Gujranwala* (1884), 15-16.

[147] Lepel Griffin, *The Panjab Chiefs*, 403. *DG Gujranwala* (1895), 181. Aliuddin, *Ibratnāma* (Pbi. tr.), 439.

proved to be of no avail. Their territories were occupied and Jan Muhammad's son accepted service with the Maharaja.[148]

To the south of Gujranwala, there were two principalities of Virk chiefs: Lal Singh with his headquarters at Miraliwala and Sahib Singh with his headquarters at Shaikhupura. Lal Singh had occupied a small territory between Miraliwala and Shaikhupura probably as an associate of Charhat Singh. His son Bagh Singh succeeded to his territory and added many more villages in the area so that he came to rule over about 150 villages.[149] In 1805, his territory was taken over by Ranjit Singh and he was made a *jāgīrdār*, a position to which he was succeeded by his son Jodh Singh.[150] Sahib Singh, the other Virk chief, had the distinction of being the descendant of a *zamīndār* family from the days of Akbar.[151] In 1780, he ousted Inder Singh Virk from Shaikhupura which probably had been conquered by them jointly.[152] Sahib Singh was succeeded by his son Amir Singh. He was obliged to pay *nazrāna* to Ranjit Singh in 1795. In 1808, Ranjit Singh took over the strong fort of Shaikhupura along with the territories of Amir Singh, giving him a *jāgīr* worth 40,000 rupees a year for service.[153]

To the left of Miraliwala and Shaikhupura was the principality of Pindi Bhattian. The Bhattis had come to the Rachna Doab earlier and settled around Pindi Bhattian in the reign of Akbar. In the *Ā'īn-i-Akbarī*, they are mentioned as *zamīndārs* with 2,50,000 *bighas* of land commanding 30 horsemen and 1,000 infantry.[154] Daim Khan Bhatti was holding a high *mansab* under Shah Jahan and his successors also served the Mughal empire as *mansabdārs*.[155] In the 1740s, Muhammad Yar Bhatti founded Jalalpur Bhattian and came into possession of about 200

---

[148] Sohan Lal, *Umdat-ut-Tawārīkh* (Pbi. tr.), II, 33-36. Foreign/ Political Proceedings, 14 November 1851, No. 56. Lepel Griffin, *The Panjab Chiefs*, 405.

[149] Lepel Griffin, *The Panjab Chiefs*, 439. *DG Gujranwala* (1895), 23.

[150] *DG Gujranwala* (1895), 26-27.

[151] Rai Lala Virk was a *chaudharī* over 30 villages under Akbar: Lepel Griffin, *The Panjab Chiefs*, 441.

[152] *SR Gujranwala* (1874), 5. *DG Gujranwala* (1895), 27.

[153] Sohan Lal, *Umdat-ut-Tawārīkh* (Pbi. tr.), II, 39. Ahmad Shah, *Tārīkh-i-Panjab* (Pbi. tr.), 77.

[154] *Ā'īn-Akbarī* (Eng. tr.), II, 323. *SR Gujranwala* (1874), 5-6.

[155] Aliuddin, *Ibratnāma* (Pbi. tr.), 101.

villages in the area around Pindi Bhattian.[156] He was succeeded by his son Jalal Khan who submitted to Zaman Shah in the late 1790s. In the early years of the nineteenth century, the territories of the Bhattis were invaded by Ranjit Singh and Jalal Khan fled to Jhang to seek protection from Ahmad Khan Sial. Pindi Bhattian and the territory of Jalal Khan came into the Maharaja's possession. Jalal Khan's brother and his son were given *jāgīrs* for service.[157]

The Sialkot area above Gujranwala was conquered by Jhanda Singh Bhangi in association with a number of other leaders in 1770. Jhanda Singh himself retained only a portion of the conquest along the river Chenab on the west of Sialkot. The city of Sialkot with the villages around was occupied by four chiefs: Jiwan Singh Ghumman, Mohar Singh Atariwala, Natha Singh Shahid and Sahib Singh. They all lost their possessions to Ranjit Singh in 1807, and subsistence *jāgīrs* were given to Jiwan Singh, Mohar Singh and Natha Singh.[158]

In the remaining areas of the upper Rachna Doab, the most important chief was Bagh Singh Hallowalia, with his possessions in the Parganas of Aurangabad and Zafarwal and his headquarters at Zafarwal. The forts of Qila Sobha Singh and Qila Suba Singh were built by his sons.[159] In 1800, he joined the allies against Ranjit Singh. Four years later, he was obliged by the Maharaja to pay tribute. Towards the end of 1810, his territories were taken over with the exception of Qila Sobha Singh, Qila Suba Singh and a few other places. These too were annexed to the kingdom of Lahore after Bagh Singh's death.[160]

Another chief, Gurbakhsh Singh had his possessions in the Shakargarh area with his headquarters at Doda. On his death in 1795, he was succeeded by his son Suddh Singh who retained his possessions till his death in 1813, presumably as a tributary of Ranjit Singh. Since he had no male heir, his cousin Gajja Singh approached the Maharaja with a large *nazrāna* to get recognition as a successor but his request was

---

[156] Ganesh Das, *Early Nineteenth Century Panjab* (Eng. tr.), 108. *SR Gujranwala* (1874), 6 & 11.

[157] Ram Sukh Rao, *Sri Fateh Singh Partap Prabhakar*, 72. Ahmad Shah, *Tārīkh-i-Panjab* (Pbi. tr.), 72. *DG Gujranwala* (1895), 25 & 182.

[158] Ram Sukh Rao, *Sri Fateh Singh Partap Prabhakar*, 206-07. *SR Silakot* (1865), 13, 45-46.

[159] *SR Sialkot* (1865), 46.

[160] Ganesh Das, *Chār-Bāgh-i-Panjab* (Pbi. tr.), 147. Munshi Amin Chand, *A History of the Sialkot District*, 21.

rejected; the territories of Suddh Singh were taken over by the Maharaja and Gajja Singh was given 25 villages for serving with 18 horsemen.[161]

In the Pargana of Pasrur, Nar Singh Chamiariwala had most of his possessions with his headquarters at Pasrur. However, he possessed territories on both sides of the river Ravi. In fact, his native place Chamiari was in the Bari Doab and he had received much of his territory from the widow of his cousin Sanwal Singh Randhawa.[162] In 1800 and 1801, he supported Sahib Singh of Gujrat against Ranjit Singh. He was made a tributary in 1804. On his death in 1806, Ranjit Singh took over his territories in both the Doabs. His widow and two minor sons were given a modest *jāgīr*.[163]

In the south of the city of Sialkot were the territories of Karam Singh Gill who belonged to Chhina in the Bari Doab.[164] He was a minor chief. Around 1806, Ranjit Singh made him a *jāgīrdār* over 70 horsemen with a *jāgīr* worth 50,000 rupees. His sons, Buddh Singh and Suddh Singh also took service with the Maharaja.[165]

The chief of Daska, Jassa Singh, was the son of a *chaudharī* in the Bari Doab, but he had occupied Daska in the Rachna Doab during the invasions of Ahmad Shah Abdali.[166] He was able to maintain his position against the neighbouring chiefs like Jodh Singh Wazirabadia, Sahib Singh of Gujrat and even Mahan Singh Sukarchakia. His son and successor, Nidhan Singh did not hesitate to submit to Zaman Shah in 1797. Ten years later, he was made a tributary by Ranjit Singh. In 1810, his territories were taken over, and a large *jāgīr* was given to him for maintaining 100 horsemen.[167]

In the upper Chaj Doab, there was only one chief, Gujjar Singh, the founder of the principality of Gujrat. He had defeated the Gakkhar chief of Gujrat in 1765 in an open battle outside the city wall, occupied

---

[161] Foreign/Political Proceedings, 13 August 1852, No. 49. Lepel Griffin, *The Panjab Chiefs*, 212-14.

[162] Qazi Nur Muhammad, *Jangnāmāh* (Eng. tr.), 59-60. *SR Narowal Pargana of the Amritsar District* (1860), 148.

[163] Ganesh Das, *Chār Bāgh-i-Panjab* (Pbi. tr.), 142-43 & 146. *SR Sialkot* (1865), 48. Prinsep, *Origin of the Sikh Power*, 48.

[164] *DG Sialkot* (1895), 27. Munshi Amin Chand, *A History of the Sialkot District*, 11.

[165] Lepel Griffin, *The Panjab Chiefs*, 373-74.

[166] Ibid., 348-49.

[167] Sohan Lal, *Umdat-ut-Tawārīkh* (Pbi. tr.), II, 390. *SR Sialkot* (1865), 48.

his territory and adopted Gujrat as his headquarters.[168] He occupied Jalalpur, Daulatanagar, Dinga, Bahlolpur, Karianwala and Manawar in the upper Chaj Doab. The contiguous territory between the Chenab and the Jehlam upto the territories of Akhnur and Bhimber also came under his control. The chiefs of Akhnur, Bhimber and Khari Khariali accepted his overlordship and paid tribute to him. He was able to occupy several villages in the Rachna Doab, besides the well known town of Sodhra.[169]

Before his death in 1788, Gujjar Singh had started residing at Lahore, leaving Gujrat in the hands of his eldest son Sahib Singh. His territory in the Rachna Doab was probably placed under his son Sukha Singh. The youngest son Fateh Singh, perhaps, lived with him at Lahore. Sahib Singh wrested the territory entrusted to Sukha Singh, killing him, in fact, in the field of battle. Gujjar Singh was much grieved, but he could do little more than appoint Fateh Singh to the Rachna Doab territories. Fateh Singh was ousted by Sahib Singh after Gujjar Singh's death.[170] Thus, the entire territory of Gujjar Singh Bhangi came into Sahib Singh's possession.

In the last decade of the eighteenth century, Sahib Singh was one of the most powerful Sikh chiefs, particularly after the death of Mahan Singh Sukarchakia. Before the end of the century, however, he lost his possessions in Lahore to Ranjit Singh. The combination of Sikh, Afghan and Rajput chiefs formed by Sahib Singh against the new ruler of Lahore at Bhasin came to nothing. By the beginning of the nineteenth century, Sahib Singh was on the defensive, looking for allies against Ranjit Singh. By 1807, Sahib Singh had to acknowledge Ranjit Singh's supremacy and to pay tribute to him.[171] Within three years more, his territories were taken over by the Maharaja and his son Gulab Singh was given *jāgīr* worth only 4,000 rupees in the Gujranwala area.

---

[168] Gujjar Singh also held a part of the city of Lahore. Ratan Singh Bhangu, *Prāchīn Panth Parkāsh*, 403. *SR Jehlam* (1883), 25. *DG Gujrat* (1883-84), 15-16.

[169] Ganesh Das, *Chār Bāgh-i-Panjab* (Pbi. tr.), 133. Foreign/Political Proceedings, 29 December 1849, No. 47A. *SR Sialkot* (1865), 48. *SR Gujranwala* (1874), 9.

[170] Lepel Griffin, *The Panjab Chiefs*, 295. *DG Gujrat* (1883-84), 16. H.M. Lawrence, *Adventures of an Officer in the Service of Ranjit Singh*, 248.

[171] Ganesh Das, *Chār Bāgh-i-Panjab* (Pbi. tr.), 142-43. Lepel Griffin, *The Panjab Chiefs*, 397.

Subsequently, Sahib Singh was also given Bajwat in the Sialkot area for subsistence till his death in 1814.[172]

IV

In the upper Sindh Sagar Doab, there were ten principalities in all. Eight of these were under Muslim chiefs and two under Sikh chiefs. All the eight Muslim chiefs were Rajput. One of the Sikh chiefs was a Jat and the other a Khatri. Three of these ten principalities were on the north of the river Soan: Rawalpindi, Kot and Pindi Gheb. Between the Soan and the Jehlam, there were five principalities: Talagang, Kusak, Malot, Pind Dadan Khan and Ahmadabad. The small principality of Makhad was between the river Indus and the stream called Sil.

The principality of Rawalpindi may be regarded as founded in 1767 when Gujjar Singh Bhangi, Charhat Singh Sukarchakia and Milkha Singh Thepuria led a joint expedition into the Doab. The territories of the Gakkhars fell to the share of Milkha Singh who adopted Rawalpindi as his headquarters. He kept over 450 villages worth about three lacs of rupees under his direct administration and entrusted nearly 200 villages to the tribal chiefs of the Gakkhars in return for a small tribute.[173] In due course, the Gakkhar chief of Khanpur, the Afghan chief of Sarai Niamat Khan and the Dhund chief of Mari became tributary to Milkha Singh.[174]

Milkha Singh was able to retain his hold over these territories when Zaman Shah led expeditions into the Punjab in the late 1790s.[175] Before his death in 1804, however, he had acknowledged Ranjit Singh's supremacy. His son Jiwan Singh fought in Ranjit Singh's campaigns as a vassal. He died in 1815 to be succeeded by his son Anand Singh. Soon afterwards, however, the territories of Rawalpindi were occupied by Ranjit Singh. Anand Singh was given a *jāgīr* worth 42,000 rupees a

---

172 *Panjab Government Records, 1808-15*, II, 169, 170-72. Foreign/ Secret Consultation, 13 February 1810, No. 3. Ganesh Das, *Chār Bāgh-i-Panjab* (Pbi. tr.), 134.

173 *SR Rawalpindi* (1865), 67-68. Ganesh Das, *Early Nineteenth Century Panjab* (Eng. tr.), 16. Veena Sachdeva, 'The Non-Sikh Chiefs of the Punjab Plains and Maharaja Ranjit Singh', *Journal of Regional History*, II (1981), 8.

174 *DG Rawalpindi* (1895), 52-53.

175 Foreign/ Political Consultation, 24 December 1798, No. 7.

year, in addition to lands worth 8,000 rupees in the former territories of Milkha Singh, to serve with 100 horsemen.[176]

From Rohtas to Rawalpindi, along the hills was the principality of the Gakkhars. They had lived in the upper Sindh Sagar Doab for several centuries and enjoyed a position of distinction under the Mughals.[177] The Gakkhar chief Muazzam Khan was succeeded in 1739 by Muqarrab Khan who brought the area of Gujrat under his control and also received recognition from Ahmad Shah Abdali.[178] However, the power of the Gakkhar chiefs had begun to decline even before the death of Ahmad Shah Abdali. After losing Gujrat to Gujjar Singh Bhangi in 1765, Muqarrab Khan tried to consolidate his position in the Sindh Sagar Doab. But as we mentioned earlier, he was subdued jointly by Charhat Singh Sukarchakia, Gujjar Singh and Milkha Singh Thepuria in 1767. The Gakkhar territory was now confined to the area around Pharwala. This too was taken over by the grandson of Milkha Singh on behalf of Ranjit Singh in the early nineteenth century.[179]

The principality of Kot was under a Gheba chief. The Ghebas are said to be a branch of the Jodrah tribe. After a domestic quarrel, they settled in the western half of Fatehjang and took the name of Gheba. Rai Jalal was the first Gheba chief to pay tribute to Charhat Singh Sukarchakia.[180] He was succeeded by his nephew Muhammad Khan Gheba. Kot was taken over by Ranjit Singh in the first decade of the nineteenth century and its chief was reduced to the status of a *jāgīrdār*.[181]

---

176 Sohan Lal, *Umdat-ut-Tawārikh* (Pbi. tr.), II, 172. Lepel Griffin, *The Panjab Chiefs*, 223. *DG Rawalpindi* (1895), 52.

177 *Akbarnāma* (Eng. tr.), I, 297-300, 398-99, 599 & 622. *Ā'īn-Akbarī* (Eng. tr.), II, 325-28. *Tuzuk-i-Jahāngīrī* (Eng. tr.), II, 161 & 545. Lepel Griffin, *The Panjab Chiefs*, 578-79. *SR Rawalpindi* (1865), 23, 66 & 141.

178 *Tārīkh-i-Ālamgīr Sānī* (Eng. tr.), 191b. *DG Rawalpindi* (1907), 43.

179 Ahmad Shah, *Tārīkh-i-Panjab* (Pbi. tr.), 43. Ratan Singh Bhangu, *Prāchīn Panth Parkāsh*, 403. 'Papers Relating to the Gakkhar Tribe', *Selections From the Records of the Government of the Punjab and its Dependencies*, 11-15. *SR Rawalpindi* (1865), 67-68. Lepel Griffin, *The Panjab Chiefs*, 223 & 580.

180 H.A. Rose, *A Glossary of Tribes and Castes*, II, 285. *SR Rawalpindi* (1865), 75. Lepel Griffin, *The Panjab Chiefs*, 536.

181 Lepel Griffin, *The Panjab Chiefs*, 536.

The Jodrahs had settled in the Sindh Sagar Doab during the sixteenth century. They established their principality around Pindi Gheb.[182] In the beginning of the eighteenth century, Aulia Khan extended his territory to the south-west of Pindi Gheb.[183] His son, Amanat Khan, was obliged by Charhat Singh Sukarchakia to pay tribute. But he stopped paying in the time of Mahan Singh. Eventually, the Jodrah chief submitted to Ranjit Singh and the Pindi Gheb territory was taken over in 1813. Nawab Khan, the successor of Amanat Khan, was allowed to collect one-fourth of the revenues from a part of his former territory.[184]

The area around Attock was under the direct control of the Afghan rulers of Kabul during the late eighteenth century. Between Attock and Malot was the Awan principality on the north of the Salt Range. The Awans had settled in the Sindh Sagar Doab in the late tenth or early eleventh century. In the *Ā'īn-i-Akbarī*, they are mentioned as the *zamīndārs* of three *mahals* with 20,000 *bighas* of culturable land yielding 25,000 rupees. They were commanding 210 horsemen and 4,700 infantry.[185] We find the Awan chiefs paying tribute to Charhat Singh Sukarchakia in the 1760s.[186] They appear to have remained tributary till the early nineteenth century. In 1813, their chief town, Shamsabad was destroyed by Mohkam Chand, who had been sent by Ranjit Singh against the Afghan *faujdār* of Attock. However, the Awan chief Muhammad Nasim Khan was allowed to rebuild the town as a *jāgīrdār* of the Maharaja.[187]

Between Pind Dadan Khan and the stream known as Kahan was the Janjua principality of Kusak along the river Jehlam with Malot on its west above the Salt Range. In the time of Babur, the Janjuas were in possession of the entire country from Attock to Bhera.[188] In the *Ā'īn-i-*

---

182 H.A. Rose, *A Glossary of Tribes and Castes*, II, 388. *SR Rawalpindi* (1865), 154.

183 Lepel Griffin, *The Panjab Chiefs*, 539.

184 *SR Rawalpindi* (1865), 75, 154-55. Lepel Griffin, *The Panjab Chiefs*, 539.

185 *Ā'īn-Akbarī* (Eng. tr.), II, 326-27. H.A. Rose, *A Glossary of Tribes and Castes*, II, 25-26. *DG Jhelam* (1883-84), 77 & 165.

186 Lepel Griffin, *The Panjab Chiefs*, 539.

187 Ibid., 572.

188 Zahiru'ddin-Muhammad Bābur Padshah Ghazi, *Bābur Nāma* (tr. into English by A.S. Beveridge), Oriental Books Reprint Corporation, New

Akbarī, they are mentioned as the *zamīndārs* of ten *mahals* yielding 1,70,000 rupees a year. They were commanding at the time 550 horsemen and more than 7,500 infantry.[189] However, some of the Janjua tribes were driven out from their possessions by the stronger neighbours, notably the Awans, the Gakkhars and the Khokhars. In the middle of the eighteenth century, the Janujas established two principalities: one at Kusak and the other at Malot.[190] The principality of Kusak was important due to the salt mines at Khewra and Makhiala. Its chief, Fateh Muhammad Khan, was able to hold out against his neighbours till he was compelled by Ranjit Singh to become his vassal. In 1810, the territory of Kusak was taken over by the Maharaja and a few villages were left for the subsistence of the Janjua chief.[191] The chief of Malot was obliged to pay tribute to Mahan Singh Sukarchakia in the 1780s. His territories were taken over by Ranjit Singh in the first decade of the nineteenth century.[192]

The chiefs of the principalities of Pind Dadan Khan and Ahmadabad were Khokhars, who are mentioned as *zamīndārs* in possession of about five lacs of *bighas* of land yielding 1,75,000 rupees.[193] The Khokhar *zamīndāri* had flourished under Dadan Khan and his sons during the seventeenth century. One of his grandsons founded Ahmadabad in the late seventeenth century and got recognition from the Mughal government as a *zamīndār* in his own right.[194] By the middle of the eighteenth century, Sahib Khan was ruling over Pind Dadan Khan as a chief and Ruhullah Khan, the grandson of Ahmad Khan, was the chief at Ahmadabad.[195] In the late 1760s, Charhat Singh Sukarchakia invaded the Sindh Sagar Doab and took over the territories of the

---

Delhi, 1970 (reprint), I, 379-80. Ahsan Raza Khan, *Chieftains in the Mughal Empire*, 30-31.

[189] *Ā'īn-Akbarī* (Eng. tr.), II, 327-28.

[190] *SR Jehlam* (1883), 27. *DG Rawalpindi* (1895), 49 & 105. H.A. Rose, *A Glossary of Tribes and Castes*, II, 355.

[191] Sohan Lal, *Umdat-ut-Tawārīkh* (Pbi. tr.), II, 118-127. *DG Jhelam*, (1883-84), 39 & 73.

[192] Lepel Griffin, *The Panjab Chiefs*, 605-06. *DG Jhelam* (1883-84), 38.

[193] *Ā'īn-Akbarī* (Eng. tr.), 325 & 327.

[194] Sohan Lal, *Umdat-ut-Tawārīkh* (Pbi. tr.), II, 11. *DG Jhelam* (1883-84), 74 & 161.

[195] Lepel Griffin, *The Panjab Chiefs*, 589-90. Kali Rai, *Sair-i-Panjab* (tr. into Punjabi by Giani Lal Singh), Punjabi University, Patiala, 1971, 12.

Ḳhokhar chiefs, leaving with them only some of their villages, which were finally annexed by the Maharaja in the early nineteenth century.[196]

The principality of Makhad was not important but it was not insignificant. Tahil Singh Chhachhi was able to conquer the area around Makhad without any outside assistance and ruled over it till his death in 1786. His sons figure as *jāgīrdārs* under Ranjit Singh.[197]

VI

In retrospect we may notice first that the resources of the chiefs of the region under consideration ranged from fifty thousand rupees a year to over ten lacs. However, only four chiefs commanded resources exceeding ten lacs of rupees a year: Hari Singh Bhangi, Jassa Singh Ahluwalia, Charhat Singh Sukarchakia and Gujjar Singh Bhangi. Jassa Singh Ahluwalia had considerable territories on the left of the Satlej also. Even the number of chiefs with resources ranging from five to ten lacs a year was rather small. Among them were Muqarrab Khan Gakkhar, Sahib Khan Khokhar, Jassa Singh Ramgarhia, Buddh Singh Faizullapuria and Baghel Singh Karora Singhia. The last of these had his territories beyond the river Satlej also. About sixteen chiefs commanded resources between one to five lacs of rupees a year. About half a dozen chiefs held territories worth more than 50,000 but less than a lac of rupees. In terms of financial resources, obviously, no chief was very powerful.

Only two of the eighteen Muslim principalities could claim a distant background of political power: the Gakkhars and the Janjuas. The Gakkhars were probably exercising political power before the end of the twelfth century. The majority of the Muslim chiefs were *zamīndārs* and *jāgīrdārs* of the Mughal times: Rai Ibrahim Bhatti, Mahmud Khan and Ahmad Khan Manj, Nur Muhammad Chattha, Muhammad Yar Bhatti, Malik Aulia Khan Jodrah, Rai Jalal Khan Gheba, Sahib Khan Khokhar, Muhiyuddin Khan and Gul Muhammad, for instance. All of them became chiefs by taking advantage largely of the administrative framework of the Mughal empire.

---

196 Lepel Griffin, *The Panjab Chiefs*, 591. Sohan Lal, *Umdat-ut-Tawārīkh* (Pbi. tr.), II, 11.

197 Lepel Griffin, *The Panjab Chiefs*, 197-98.

The Sikh chiefs, by contrast, rose to political power by opposing the politico-administrative framework of the Mughal empire nearly at all levels. Their large number in the upper Doabs of the Punjab justifies a rather detailed comment on the position of the Sikh chiefs as a category. Significantly, nearly all of them established their principalities after the first invasion of Ahmad Shah Abdali in 1748 and before his death in 1772. The first to occupy territories on a more or less permanent basis were the well known chiefs like Hari Singh Bhangi, Jassa Singh Ahluwalia, Jassa Singh Ramgarhia, Jai Singh Kanhiya and Charhat Singh Sukarchakia. Much of the area they occupied was in the Bari Doab, not far from the provincial capital. Besides Charhat Singh who had his territories in the Rachna Doab, Khushal Singh Faizullapuria had come into possession of Jalandhar. In 1765, the provincial capital Lahore, too, was occupied by three Sikh chiefs and a coin was struck to declare Sikh sovereignty. During the five years following, over two dozen principalities were founded covering the Sialkot region of the Rachna Doab, the Gujrat region of the Chaj Doab and the Rawalpindi region of the Sindh Sagar Doab. This pattern lends some support to Ratan Singh Bhangu's statement that there was a tendency among the leaders of the Sikhs to occupy their own villages and the neighbouring territories first.

The majority of the chiefs belonged to the Bari Doab, followed by those who belonged to the Rachna Doab. Elsewhere, only a few local leaders occupied any territory. It has been possible to identify fortyone out of fiftythree Sikh chiefs mentioned in the previous pages. All these fortyone came from the countryside. Only one of them was a carpenter, that is, Jassa Singh Ramgarhia; and only one was a Kalāl, that is, Jassa Singh Ahluwalia. We know at least two instances of Khatri chiefs: Tahil Singh Chhachhi and Dharm Singh. All the remaining chiefs were Jat. With the exception of two Jat Sikh chiefs, we know their clan names. They were Sandhus, Sidhus, Mans, Randhawas, Virks, Khairas, Gills, Kahlons, Kangs, a Dhillon, a Dhaliwal, a Ghumman, a Bhangu and a Waraich. However, there is no such information for about twelve chiefs. There is a possibility that the number of non-Jats among them was perhaps more considerable. It may also be added that though the majority of the Jat Sikh chiefs sprang from ordinary families of cultivators, more than half a dozen of them belonged to the families of *chaudharīs*. Presumably, some intermediary *zamīndārs* joined the political movement after its initial success. Significantly, among the most important Jat Sikh chiefs, there was none with the background of an intermediary.

During the late eighteenth century, the most powerful of the chiefs made use of their relatively large resources and extended their territories. This resulted in the subversion of a number of principalities even before the end of the eighteenth century. It may be noted here that all the principalities obliterated during the period belonged to Muslim chiefs. This is understandable. Since the area of the upper Doabs of the Punjab was the stronghold of the most important Sikh chiefs, it was natural for them to subjugate others either by annexing their territories or obliging them to pay tribute as vassal chiefs. Of the seven principalities obliterated during the period, two were in the Jalandhar Doab, namely Kapurthala and Nakodar. The former was taken over by Jassa Singh Ahluwalia and the latter by Tara Singh Dallewalia. Qadian, in the Bari Doab, was taken over by Jassa Singh Ramgarhia. The Chatthas in the Rachna Doab went down before Charhat Singh Sukarchakia who took over two chiefships in the Sindh Sagar Doab as well, that is, Pind Dadan Khan and Ahmadabad. The Gakkhar stronghold of Rawalpindi was taken over by Milkha Singh. We find that most of these principalities were taken over either by the strongest among the Sikh chiefs or by a combination of the Sikh leaders.

By the last decade of the eighteenth century, there was no inclination or incentive among the Sikh chiefs to combine their resources for further aggrandizement. For defence, however, they were left with little choice when Zaman Shah invaded the Punjab. In the process of forming a combined force against him, Ranjit Singh emerged as an important leader. With the consistent support of Fateh Singh Ahluwalia and Sada Kaur, he was able to subjugate the smaller chiefs rather easily. Even the important chiefs were no match for the combined resources of the Sukarchakia, Ahluwalia and the Kanhiya chiefs. In any case, before he signed the treaty of Amritsar with the British in 1809, Ranjit Singh had subjugated more than three dozen chiefs. Nearly half a dozen more, including Sahib Singh Bhangi, were subjugated before the end of 1810. The supporters or the allies of Ranjit Singh were able to retain their territories longer. But after the elimination of Sada Kaur's principality in 1821, only Fateh Singh Ahluwalia was left. He too lost his territories in the Bari Doab in 1825 and came to serve Ranjit Singh as a subordinate chief. Thus, the fall of the Sikh principalities was more rapid than their rise. But the fall of their principalities did not mean the end of Sikh rule. They were all united into a larger and stronger state.

3

CHIEFS OF THE LOWER DOABS

In the lower Doabs of the Punjab, there were fifteen principalities in all: seven in the Bari Doab, three each in the Rachna and Sindh Sagar Doabs and two in the Chaj Doab. The number of Muslim chiefs was much larger than that of the Sikh chiefs: twelve against three. Five of the chiefs were Jat, three each were Afghan and Rajput, two were Baloch and one each was a Shaikh and a Sayyad. Moreover, there were three outside chiefs who held large territory in the lower Doabs: the chiefs of Bahawalpur, Dera Ghazi Khan and Dera Ismail Khan. They were also Muslim. The chiefs of Bahawalpur were Afghan and those of the Deras, Baloch.

I

The most important principality of the lower Doabs was that of Multan. The Mughal province of Multan had been taken over by Ahmad Shah Abdali in 1752. However, he chose Shakar Khan, son of the Mughal governor Zahid Khan, a Saddozai Afghan, for the governorship of the province. Shakar Khan was succeeded by his brother Shuja Khan in the governorship in 1766. Ahmad Shah Abdali's successor Timur Shah appointed Haji Sharif Khan as the governor of Multan and Shuja Khan had to retire to Shujabad which he had founded earlier. Soon, however, Multan was invaded and occupied by Jhanda Singh Bhangi. When Timur Shah recovered Multan in 1780, he appointed Muzaffar Khan, the son of Shuja Khan, as its governor. Muzaffar Khan was thus the fourth governor of Multan from the same Saddozai family.[1]

---

[1] Zahid Khan was a Saddozai Afghan whose ancestors had migrated to Multan in the reign of Shah Jahan and served the Mughal empire for two or three generations before Zahid Khan was appointed as the governor of Multan. In 1752, he was replaced by Ali Muhammad Khan. But in 1762,

It is stated in a document of 1788 that Timur Shah sent his *sazawals* to Muzaffar Khan for the collection of grain and cloth.[2] It is not clear whether or not Muzaffar Khan was sending revenues of the province to the Afghan ruler at Kabul.[3] In a report of the late 1790s, Muzaffar Khan is not well disposed towards Zaman Shah just as he had not been well disposed towards Timur Shah.[4] However, the fact that Muzaffar Khan was not dislodged from Multan by the rulers of Kabul, even when they were inclined to do so, suggests that he went on paying tribute to them from time to time.

In the early years of the nineteenth century, Ranjit Singh obliged Muzaffar Khan to pay tribute to him and, thus, to transfer his allegiance from Kabul to Lahore.[5] In 1803, the amount of *nazrāna* extorted from Muzaffar Khan was rather nominal but subsequently it was fixed at 50,000 rupees a year. By 1810, Ranjit Singh was demanding two lacs of rupees on the assumption that this was the amount which Muzaffar Khan used to pay to the rulers of Kabul.[6] Finally in 1818, the Maharaja took over Multan. Nawab Muzaffar Khan died fighting along with six of his sons. Two of his sons, Sarafraz Khan and Zulfiqar Khan, were taken to Lahore and subsequently given a *jāgīr*. After the annexation of

---

Ahmad Shah Abdali appointed Shuja Khan, the second son of Zahid Khan, as the governor of Multan: Shahamat Ali, *History of Bahawalpur*, London, 1848, 63-64. *SR Muzaffargarh* (1882), 49. *DG Multan* (1883-84), 26-27. Lepel Griffin, *The Panjab Chiefs*, 479-80.

[2] Extract of a letter dated 19 December 1788, *Calender of Persian Correspondence, 1788-89*, VIII, 365.

[3] Extract of a letter dated 19 December 1789, *Poona Residency Correspondence, 1785-94*, I, 360. Already in 1785, George Forster had noticed that the 'chief of Multan has assured a great degree of independence and shows only such observance to the orders sent from Kabul as may be correspondent with his own conveniency': 'Observations on the Sikhs', *Early European Accounts of the Sikhs* (ed. Ganda Singh), 85.

[4] Foreign/Political Consultation, 7 July 1797, No. 3; 25 January 1797, No. 9.

[5] Ahmad Shah, *Tārīkh-i-Panjab* (Pbi. tr.), 72. H.L.O. Garrett & G.L. Chopra (tr.), *Events at the Court of Ranjit Singh (1810-1817)*, 9-11.

[6] Sohan Lal, *Umdat-ut-Tawārīkh* (Pbi. tr.), II, 106, 131 & 220. Foreign/Secret Consultation, 3 April 1810, No. 19. Foreign/ Political Proceedings, 15 August 1836, No. 17. *SR Muzaffargarh* (1882), 93.

the kingdom of Lahore in 1849, they received pension from the British rulers.[7]

Adjoining the territories of Multan between the Ravi and the old bed of the Beas was the principality of Gogera, founded by Kamr Singh Nakkai, the son of a local *chaudharī*. Kamr Singh proved to be the most important chief of the principality. Before his death in 1780, he had conquered Kabirwala and Kamalia in the Rachna Doab. However, he lost Sayyadwala to the chief of Bharwal and it was during his attempt to recover it that he died in 1780.[8] He was succeeded by his brother Wazir Singh who lost Kamalia to the Kharals but recovered Sayyadwala from the Bharwal chief. On his death in 1790, he was succeeded by his son Mihr Singh who lost his territories to Ranjit Singh in 1804 and got a *jāgīr* in Gogera worth 4,000 rupees a year.[9]

Between the old bed of the Beas and the river Satlej, there were six principalities. However, much of this area belonged to the chiefs of Bahawalpur. Mubarak Khan Daudputra, the younger brother of Bahawal Khan I, had occupied places like Lodhran, Kahror, Mailsi, Dunyapur and Jalalpur between the river Satlej and the old bed of the Beas. His ancestor Daud Khan was a Mughal *mansabdār* in the lower Sindh Sagar Doab. Bahadur Khan Daudputra, a descendant of Daud Khan, had moved to Shikarpur during the reign of Aurangzeb because of a dispute with his collaterals, the Kalhoras.[10] In the early eighteenth century, the Daudputra chief Sadiq Khan was obliged to leave Shikarpur and to settle down as a *zamīndār* to the south of the Satlej, between the territories of Multan and Jaisalmer. He submitted to Nadir Shah and obtained a large territory.[11] His son and successor, Bahawal Khan, known as Bahawal Khan the first, could extend his territory to the south of the Satlej in

---

[7] Hugel, *Travels in Kashmir and the Panjab*, 378. Prinsep, *Origin of the Sikh Power*, 91-93. *DG Multan* (1883-84), 29. Lepel Griffin, *The Panjab Chiefs*, 488-89.

[8] Aliuddin, *Ibratnāma* (Pbi. tr.), 315. Lepel Griffin, *The Panjab Chiefs*, 511. *SR Montgomery* (1878), 32-33. *DG Montgomery* (1883-84), 31.

[9] Ram Sukh Rao, *Sri Fateh Singh Partap Prabhakar*,411. Lepel Griffin, *The Panjab Chiefs*, 511. *SR Montgomery* (1878), 32.

[10] George W. Forrest, 'Masson's Journals', *Selections From the Travels and Journals Preserved in the Bombay Secretariat*, Bombay, 1906, 182 (cited hereafter as *Selections*). Shahamat Ali, *History of Bahawalpur*, 14 & 182-84. *DG Bahawalpur* (1904), 47-49.

[11] Shahamat Ali, *History of Bahawalpur*, 21, 24-25 & 184. *SR Muzaffargarh* (1882), 47.

return for the support he extended to Diwan Kaura Mal who had been sent by Ahmad Shah Abdali against Shah Nawaz Khan at Multan.[12] With this background, Mubarak Khan had found it easy to cross the river Satlej during Ahmad Shah Abdali's invasions of the Punjab in search of new conquests.

The death of Mubarak Khan synchronized with the death of Ahmad Shah Abdali and the conquest of Multan by Jhanda Singh Bhangi. Mubarak Khan had been paying tribute to the rulers of Kabul through the Afghan governor of Multan. His successor, Bahawal Khan II, refused to pay tribute to Timur Shah.[13] There are references to Timur Shah's expeditions against Bahawal Khan II for the collection of tribute, indicating that the Daudputra chief was reluctant to send regular tribute to Kabul. After the death of Timur Shah, Bahawal Khan II came to assert his independence more clearly and became a sovereign ruler at the beginning of the nineteenth century.[14]

During his long reign Bahawal Khan II was able to extend his dominions.[15] He refused to pay revenues to the governor of Multan and the chief of Dera Ghazi Khan for territories which had been taken on *ijara* by his predecessors.[16] In the 1790s, when the river Indus changed its course, Bahawal Khan II occupied the territory which was formerly on the east of the river but now on its west.[17] On the whole, thus, he came to possess a large belt of territory on both sides of the river Satlej below Mailsi. There is no indication that either Bahawal Khan II, who died in 1806, or his successor Sadiq Khan II, paid any tribute to Maharaja Ranjit Singh before 1809.

Since the treaty of Amritsar signed by the East India Company with Ranjit Singh in 1809 recognized him as the sole sovereign ruler on the west of the river Satlej, Ranjit Singh tended to presume that he was the overlord of the chief of Bahawalpur for his territories on the right of the river Satlej. Indeed, the tribute paid by the chief of Bahawalpur to the Maharaja amounted in due course to two lacs of ru-

---

[12] Shahamat Ali, *History of Bahawalpur*, 34, 36-37. *DG Bahawalpur* (1904), 53-54.

[13] Shahamat Ali, *History of Bahawalpur*, 189 & 200. *SR Montgomery* (1878), 34.

[14] Extract of a letter dated 18 March 1789, *Calender of Persian Correspondence, 1788-89*, VII, 457. *Poona Residency Correspondence, 1785-94*, I, 339-40. Forrest, 'Masson's Journals', *Selections*, 12.

[15] *SR Muzaffargarh* (1882), 48.

[16] Shahamat Ali, *History of Bahawalpur*, 199.

[17] Ibid., 149. *SR Muzaffargarh* (1882), 5 & 48.

pees a year. It was in this context that, when Ranjit Singh conquered Dera Ghazi Khan in 1821, he entrusted the territory to Sadiq Khan II for three lacs of rupees.[18] Sadiq Khan II and his successor Bahawal Khan III continued to pay tribute to the Maharaja. The arrears of tribute and *ijara* gave Ranjit Singh the pretext to annex the territories of Bahawal Khan III on the west of the river Satlej in 1831, when the British were thinking of a commercial treaty with the Maharaja.[19]

Adjoining the territory of Bahawalpur, between the old bed of the Beas and the river Satlej, was the principality of Pakpatan established by Shaikh Muhammad Abdus Subhan, a descendant of Shaikh Farid whose *khanqah* at Pakpatan was the recipient of revenue-free grants from a number of Mughal rulers. Shaikh Subhan had seized a number of villages around Pakpatan, joined hands with the chief of Bahawalpur and come into possession of a considerable territory on both sides of the river Satlej.[20] He defended himself against the Hans and Nakkai chiefs till his death in 1767. His successor, Shaikh Ghulam Rasul, was able to retain control of his territories against his neighbours.[21] Shaikh Muhammad Yar, who succeeded Ghulam Rasul, was made tributary by Ranjit Singh before his territory was taken over in the 1820s. Shaikh Muhammad Yar was given a subsistence *jāgīr*.[22]

In the north of Pakpatan was the principality of Malka Hans. During the reign of Aurangzeb, Shaikh Qutb Hans was given a grant worth 10,000 rupees a year in the *pargana* of Qabula. One of his descendants, Muhammad Azim, established himself as the chief of Qabula and Malka Hans. However, he had to defend himself against Jhanda Singh Bhangi. He had to fight against Pakpatan too. In 1767, Muhammad Azim was defeated and imprisoned by Kamr Singh Nakkai when the Hans chief had marched upon Kamalia and the chief of

---

[18] H.L.O. Garrett & G.L. Chopra (tr.), *Events at the Court of Ranjit Singh (1810-17)*, 194. R.B. Whitehead, *Catalogue of Coins in the Punjab Museum*, xxxix. Foreign/Secret Consultation, 30 January 1832, No. 12. Prinsep, *Origin of the Sikh Power*, 115.

[19] Shahamat Ali, *History of Bahawalpur*, 199-200 & 206-07. *SR Montgomery* (1878), 34.

[20] *Ā'īn-i-Akbarī* (Eng. tr.), III, 404. *Akbarnāmā* (Eng. tr.), 404. Foreign/Political Proceedings, 23 June 1854, No. 205. *SR Montgomery* (1878), 35.

[21] *SR Montgomery* (1878), 33-35.

[22] Sohan Lal, *Umdat-ut-Tawārīkh* (Pbi. tr.), II, 185. Shahamat Ali *History of Bahawalpur*, XXIX. Foreign/Political Proceedings, 23 June 1854, No. 205.

Kamalia had sought Kamr Singh's help. Muhammad Azim's brother Muhammad Hayat succeeded him at Malka Hans. He too had to fight against the Shaikhs of Pakpatan and the Nakkais of Bharwal. He was overpowered by Bhagwan Singh Nakkai in 1790 and his territories were taken over.[23]

Adjoining Pakpatan and the river Satlej was the principality of the Wattus. They had settled in these parts during the seventeenth century and acquired *zamīndārī* rights on both sides of the river Satlej. Around 1750, Lakha Wattu established himself as a chief with his headquarters at Haveli Lakha Wattu, generally referred to simply as Haveli. In the 1760s, he was succeeded by his grandson Ahmad Yar Khan who established good relations with the chief of Pakpatan by supporting him against the Nakkais. Around 1767, Ahmad Yar Khan was ousted from the Bari Doab by Lehna Singh of Lahore. His son Jahan Khan ruled over the Wattu possessions on the other side of the Satlej till 1807, when Ranjit Singh took over his territory.[24]

The principality of Dipalpur in the north-west of Haveli was established by Daud Khan. He founded Jalalabad, after the name of his son Jalaluddin Khan, to serve as his headquarters for the territory around. In 1761, he occupied Dipalpur and the surrounding area. On his death in 1772, he was succeeded by Jalaluddin Khan. In 1780, Ran Singh Nakkai obliged Jalaluddin Khan to pay tribute. Ghiyasuddin Khan succeeded Jalaluddin Khan on his death in 1804. Three years later, the territory of Dipalpur was taken over by Ranjit Singh, and Ghiyasuddin Khan accepted service with the Maharaja.[25]

The seventh principality in the lower Bari Doab was that of the Sayyads of Hujra Shah Muqim. Like the descendants of Shaikh Farid, the ancestors of Sayyad Sadruddin, the chief of Hujra, had received revenue-free lands from the Mughal emperors at several places in the area. In order to consolidate his position, he cultivated friendly relations with his neighbours. A similar attitude was adopted by his successor Qutb Ali who was able to rule from Hujra till 1807 when his territories were

---

[23] Giani Gian Singh, *Raj Khalsa*, 567. *SR Montgomery* (1878), 30, 33-34 & 36. H.A. Rose, *A Glossary of Tribes and Castes*, III, 261. *DG Montgomery* (1933), 37.

[24] *SR Googaira* (1860), 28-29. H.A. Rose, *A Glossary of Tribes and Castes*, III, 491. *SR Montgomery* (1878), 35-36. *DG Montgomery* (1883-84), 34.

[25] Ahmad Shah, *Tārīkh-i-Panjab* (Pbi. tr.), 75. Aliuddin, *Ibratnāma* (Pbi. tr.), 318. *SR Montgomery* (1878), 36-37. *DG Montgomery* (1883-84), 69.

taken over by Ranjit Singh. Sayyad Qutb Ali was subsequently killed in a quarrel with Sahib Singh Bedi of Una who had been given a *jāgīr* in the Hujra territories.[26]

II

In the lower Rachna Doab, there were three principalities. Along the river Chenab were the principalities of Jhang and Chiniot. The lower portion of the Doab was covered by the territories of the Kharals along the river Ravi. Before the incursion of the Sikhs into this region, it was dominated by the Kharals of Kamalia and the Sials of Jhang and Chiniot.

The Sials had settled near Pakpatan in the thirteenth century but shifted to Jhang during the fifteenth. They consisted of several important clans with *zamīndārī* rights over Maghiana, Khiwa, Shorkot, Mirak, Masson, Pipalwala, Karianwala and Jalalpur in the Rachna Doab. During the early eighteenth century, Walidad Khan was recognized by the Mughal authorities as the *zamīndār* of all the Sial territories. The other clan chiefs were given service *jāgīrs*. Walidad Khan got Chiniot and the adjoining territory in reward for his services, and his supremacy came to be acknowledged over the entire territory from Chiniot to the confluence of the rivers Chenab and Ravi. He was able to wrest Kamalia from the Kharals before his death in 1747, but the latter recovered it from his successor Inayat Ullah Khan.[27]

In 1760, Hari Singh Bhangi occupied Chiniot and invaded Jhang. Inayat Ullah Khan managed to retain the territories of Jhang by paying tribute. His successor Sultan Khan was killed by his half brother Sahib Khan in a bid to rule over the principality. Sahib Khan himself was killed by his cousin Kabir Khan. On his death in 1801, Kabir Khan was succeeded by his son Ahmad Khan who was obliged two years later to pay 60,000 rupees a year as tribute to Ranjit Singh.[28] Four years later,

---

[26] *SR Montgomery* (1878), 35-37. *DG Montgomery* (1883-84). 69.

[27] *SR Jhang* (1860), 3-4 & 35-36. Denzil Ibbeston, *Panjab Castes*, 147-48. *DG Chenab Colony* (1904), 15-16. *SR Jhang* (1882), 35. H.A. Rose, *A Glossary of Tribes and Castes*, III, 417. *SR Montgomery* (1878), 31. Lepel Griffin, *The Panjab Chiefs*, 504 & 511.

[28] Qazi Nur Muhammad, *Jangnāmā*, 59-60. *DG Jhang* (1883-84), 32. *SR Jhang* (1882), 37-38. Lepel Griffin, *The Panjab Chiefs*, 504-05. Ahmad Shah, *Tārīkh-i-Panjab* (Pbi. tr.), 72 & 74. Prinsep, *Origin of the Sikh Power*, 45.

he tried unsuccessfully to resist the Maharaja's forces. For several years then, he served Ranjit Singh as a vassal till 1816 when he was asked to pay a lac of rupees as tribute; he was reluctant to pay and consequently he lost his territories. Imprisoned for some time, he was given a service *jāgīr* worth 12,000 rupees a year in 1817.[29]

In the *Ā'īn-i-Akbarī*, the Kharals are mentioned as zamīndārs of seven *mahals*. Only two of these were in the Bari Doab. They were holding 1,50,000 *bighas* of land yielding over 2,70,000 rupees as revenue and were commanding 900 cavalry and 8,500 infantry.[30] They were divided into five major clans, including the Lakheras who emerged as the most powerful of them all before the end of the seventeenth century. Kamal Khan Lakhera had founded Kot Kamalia in the early seventeenth century, and his grandson Sa'adat Yar Khan, the first, came to hold a high *mansab* under Aurangzeb, with a *jāgīr* worth a lac of rupees. In the early eighteenth century, however, Sa'adat Yar Khan was subjugated by the Sials.[31] After his death in 1747, his son Muhammad Yar Khan recovered Kamalia from the Sials. It appears, however, that Muhammad Yar Khan lost large territories on both sides of the river Ravi to the Nakkai chiefs. In 1767, Kamalia itself was taken over by Kamr Singh Nakkai who had actually come to Muhammad Yar Khan's support against the chief of Malka Hans. On Kamr Singh's death in the 1780s, Ran Singh Nakkai of the Bharwal family occupied Kamalia. In the 1790s, the Kharal chief Sa'adat Yar Khan II was able to recover it. He lost it to Muzaffar Khan of Multan for a short time during the invasion of Zaman Shah. In 1804, Ranjit Singh took over all his territories and enlisted him in service.[32]

As we noticed earlier, Chiniot was occupied by Hari Singh Bhangi in 1760. It was given to Karam Singh, known as Dulu because

---

[29] H.L.O. Garrett & G.L. Chopra (tr.), *Events at the Court of Ranjit Singh (1810-17)*, 177, 222 &239. *SR Jhang* (1860), 5. H.A. Rose, *A Glossary of Tribes and Castes*, III, 417. Sohan Lal, *Umdat-ut-Tawārīkh* (Pbi. tr.), II, 212. Debi Parsad, *Gulshan-i-Panjab* (Pbi. tr.), 27. Foreign/Political Consultation, 12 March 1852, No. 98. Lepel Griffin, *The Panjab Chiefs*, 505.

[30] *Ā'īn-i- Akbarī* (Eng. tr.), II, 332-35.

[31] *SR Montgomery* (1878), 44. Denzil Ibbetson, *Panjab Castes*, 174. H.A. Rose, *A Glossary of Tribes and Castes*, I, 498. *SR Googaira* (1860), 25. *SR Jhang* (1860), 4.

[32] *SR Montgomery* (1878), 30-31, 32 & 33. *DG Montgomery* (1873), 36. H.A. Rose, *A Glossary of Tribes and Castes*, II, 19. Sohan Lal, *Umdat-ut-Tawārīkh* (Pbi. tr.), II, 25. Lepel Griffin, *The Panjab Chiefs*, 511.

of his gallantry and generosity, who had joined Hari Singh in the campaign. In 1778, however, he was ousted from Chiniot by the Sial chief Inayat Ullah Khan. He was able to recover Chiniot only in 1787. He went to the support of Sahib Singh of Gujrat against Mahan Singh Sukarchakia in 1790 but he was defeated by the young Ranjit Singh. On Karam Singh's death in 1800, he was succeeded by his son Jassa Singh who sided with Sahib Singh against Ranjit Singh. Chiniot was besieged by Ranjit Singh in 1802 and Jassa Singh failed to defend himself. His territories were occupied and he was given a subsistence *jāgīr* worth 50,000 rupees a year.[33]

III

In the lower Chaj Doab, there were two principalities: Sahiwal and Bhera. Sahiwal was ruled over by the Baloch chief Mubarak Khan in the 1750s. His ancestor Bajjar Khan had been recognized by Babur as *zamīndār* of the Shahpur area and he settled near Khushab. Sahiwal was added to the *zamīndārī* of his son in the time of Humayun. In the early decades of the eighteenth century, Langar Khan was the chief at Sahiwal. After his death in 1735, a dispute about succession arose among his sons. In the beginning, Mubarak Khan was obliged by his brother Lal Khan to leave Sahiwal. In 1749, however, Mubarak Khan succeeded in killing his brother, but he was again ousted from Sahiwal by Lal Khan's son Fateh Khan. Eventually, Mubarak Khan succeeded in occupying Sahiwal, while Fateh Khan's brother Jafar Khan founded a separate principality at Khushab.[34]

The decline of the principality began in the time of Mubarak Khan's son and successor Muhammad Khan. In 1771, he lost Bhera and the territory around to Jhanda Singh Bhangi. In 1804, his son Fateh Khan submitted to Ranjit Singh and agreed to send twentyfive horses and twentyfive camels as the annual tribute. This tribute was commuted in 1809 into 12,000 rupees a year.[35] In the year following, the tribute was increased to 85,000 rupees and on his failure to pay, the principality of Sahiwal was taken over by the Maharaja. Fateh Khan

---

[33] Aliuddin, *Ibratnāma* (Pbī. tr.), 388. Foreign/Political Proceedings, 29 December 1849, No. 47A. *SR Jhang* (1882), 33, 37 & 38.

[34] *Bābur-Nāmā* (Eng. tr.), 383. *SR Shahpur* (1866), 48. Lepel Griffin, *The Panjab Chiefs*, 546-47.

[35] *DG Shahpur* (1883-84), 17. *SR Shahpur* (1866), 38. Prinsep, *Origin of the Sikh Power*, 45. Lepel Griffin, *The Panjab Chiefs*, 548.

was given a service *jāgīr* worth 14,400 rupees for fifty horsemen. Some years later, he left Ranjit Singh's service and went to Bahawalpur where he died in 1820, but his son agreed to serve the Maharaja as a *jāgīrdār*.[36]

The Bhera territory lost by the Sahiwal chief developed into a separate principality. Jhanda Singh Bhangi gave Bhera to his associate Dhanna Singh Bajwa who belonged to Kalalwala in the Rachna Doab. He was already in possession of some villages and he now strengthened his position by a matrimonial alliance: his son Jodh Singh was married to the daughter of Sahib Singh of Gujrat. On his death in 1793, he was succeeded by Jodh Singh who allied with Sahib Singh against Ranjit Singh in 1800. Three years later, he was attacked by Ranjit Singh and obliged to evacuate Bhera. His territories were taken over by the Maharaja. For a few years, he was able to hold on to his possessions in the Rachna Doab but in 1806-07, he was compelled to accept a service *jāgīr*, while his territories worth about 60,000 rupees in the Sialkot region were annexed to the kingdom of Lahore.[37]

IV

Besides the territories of Multan and Bahawalpur and the territories of the chiefs of Dera Ghazi Khan and Dera Ismail Khan in the lower Sindh Sagar Doab, there were three other principalities. As we have already noticed, one of these was Khushab, founded by Jafar Khan in the 1750s. Another was Nurpur, founded by the Rajput chief Sher Khan. The third was Mankera: it acquired the status of a principality only in the 1790s.

Jafar Khan, the founder of Khushab, survived into the nineteenth century without much activity to his credit during the eighteenth. In 1803, he supported Khan Beg Khan against his brother Khan Muhammad Khan Tiwana, the chief of Nurpur. In the year following, Jafar Khan was obliged to pay tribute to Ranjit Singh, an obligation which went on increasing with the passage of years till his territories

---

36 Sohan Lal, *Umdat-ut-Tawārīkh* (Pbi. tr.), II, 111. Prinsep, *Origin of the Sikh Power*, 63. Ganesh Das, *Chār-Bāgh-i-Panjab* (Pbi. tr.), 152. Ahmad Shah, *Tārīkh-i-Panjab* (Pbi. tr.), 81. H.L.O. Garrett & G.L. Chopra (tr.), *Events at the Court of Ranjit Singh (1810-17)*, 18-27. Foreign/Political Proceedings, 16 December 1859, No. 46. *SR Shahpur* (1866), 44. *DG Shahpur* (1897), 39.

37 Munshi Amin Chand, *A History of the Sialkot District*, 11 & 150. *SR Shahpur* (1866), 37 & 39. Lepel Griffin, *The Panjab Chiefs*, 368-69.

were taken over by the Maharaja in 1810 and he was given *jāgīr* for subsistence.[38]

The Tiwana Rajputs had settled in the Nurpur region in the late seventeenth century. In 1745, Sher Khan founded a new principality with his headquarters at Nurpur Tiwana. For more than twenty years, he contended with his neighbours, particularly the Awans and the Baloches, and succeeded in increasing his territories. On his death in 1767, he was succeeded by his elder son Khan Muhammad Khan. Against his wishes, his younger brother, Khan Beg Khan, occupied Miththa Tiwana, a town in the south-west of Khushab. Khan Muhammad Khan overpowered him but forgave the offence. In the early years of the nineteenth century, Khan Beg Khan sought help from the Sials and the neighbouring Baloch chiefs against his brother. Khan Muhammad Khan felt obliged to seek help from Ranjit Singh. Payment of tribute to the Maharaja was the price he paid for the defeat and death of his rebel brother. Khan Muhammad Khan was succeeded by his son Ahmad Yar Khan who was obliged by Ranjit Singh to become a *jāgīrdār*. During Ranjit Singh's campaign against Mankera in 1821, the Tiwanas fought gallantly on the side of the Maharaja and this became the basis of their long service with him.[39]

For the emergence of Mankera as a principality, we have to consider the background of Baloch politics in the region. The Hot and Mirrani Baloches had come to the region from Kech Mekran in the fifteenth century and held lands on the west of the Indus. Later on they took possession of the territory on the east as well. By the end of the century, the Hots were well established at Dera Ismail Khan and in the territory between Mianwali and Bhakkar in the Sindh Sagar Doab. The Mirranis were well established at Dera Ghazi Khan and in the territory between Bhakkar and Leia in the Sindh Sagar Doab. They ruled as independent chiefs till the time of Akbar who obliged them to pay regular tribute. The Hots held their possessions throughout the Mughal rule. The Mirranis, however, were ousted from their territory in 1620 by Baloch Khan, a Baloch of the Jaskani tribe.[40]

Baloch Khan was recognized as the chief of the territory between Leia and Bhakkar by several other chiefs and was succeeded by Baloch

---

[38] *DG Shahpur* (1883-84), 18-19. *SR Shahpur* (1866), 37-38. Prinsep, *Origin of the Sikh Power*, 45.

[39] *DG Shahpur* (1883-84), 17. *SR Shahpur* (1866), 28 & 37 & 40-41. Lepel Griffin, *The Panjab Chiefs*, 521-24.

[40] *DG Dera Ismail Khan* (1883-84), 30-34.

Khan II who died in 1746. His son and successor Fateh Khan ruled over his territory for nearly a quarter of a century. Around 1770, however, Fateh Khan was defeated by the chief of Dera Ismail Khan. Fateh Khan and his son committed suicide. Hayat Khan, the grandson of Fateh Khan, was a minor at this time and the *wazīr* of Fateh Khan started ruling in his name. Upon attaining majority, Hayat Khan took over the reins of government. In 1787, he was killed by a collateral chief of the Sarghani tribe. Hayat Khan's brother Muhammad Khan defeated the aggressor. However, Muhammad Khan was not left in peace. Only a year later, he was defeated by Abdul Nabi, the chief of the Kalhoras. Timur Shah recognized Abdul Nabi as the chief but only for a few years before Muhammad Khan Saddozai, a cousin of Muzaffar Khan of Multan, was authorized to occupy the territory of the Kalhoras in the lower Sindh Sagar Doab. Muhammad Khan did so in 1792 and became the chief, acknowledging Timur Shah as his overlord.[41]

On Timur Shah's death in 1793, Zaman Shah succeeded to the throne at Kabul. His brother, Prince Humayun, opposed his succession but he was defeated and fled to Leia. He was captured by Muhammad Khan and sent to Zaman Shah. As a reward, Dera Ismail Khan was also given to Muhammad Khan by the Kabul ruler. Muhammad Khan ousted Nusrat Khan, the Hot chief from his entire territory, including the area in the Sindh Sagar Doab in 1794, gave him a subsistence *jāgīr* and appointed his own deputy at Dera Ismail Khan.[42]

Thus, Muhammad Khan came to possess the entire territory from Mianwali to Leia together with Dera Ismail Khan. He adopted Mankera as his headquarters. Subsequently, he extended his influence towards the north and the north-west. The chiefs of Kalabagh and Isa Khel were obliged to pay tribute and some territory was added to the principality of Mankera. A few other chiefs are also said to have become tributary to him. Before his death in 1816, Muhammad Khan came into control of a territory yielding ten lacs of rupees and containing a large number of forts.[43]

Muhammad Khan was succeeded by Sher Muhammad Khan, the son of his daughter. Ranjit Singh demanded tribute from the chief of Mankera soon after his succession. The forts of Khangarh and Mahmud

---

[41] Ibid., 35 & 199. Forrest, 'Masson's Journal', *Selections*, 20.

[42] Forrest, 'Masson's Journals', *Selections*, 147 & 150. *DG Dera Ismail Khan* (1883-84), 31-32, 36-37 & 70-74.

[43] Charles Masson, *Narrative of Various Journeys*, I, 64. Sita Ram Kohli, *Maharaja Ranjit Singh*, 162.

Kot were occupied by the Maharaja and Sher Muhammad Khan felt compelled to pay over a lac of rupees as yearly tribute. Sher Muhammad Khan paid an increasing tribute for four or five years before Ranjit Singh occupied all his forts and territory in 1821. Sher Muhammad Khan was allowed to retain Dera Ismail Khan as a vassal of the Maharaja. Fifteen years later, in 1836, Dera Ismail Khan was taken over and Sher Muhammad Khan was given a subsistence *jāgīr*.[44]

V

As in the case of the chiefs of the upper Doabs of the Punjab so in the case of the chiefs of the lower Doabs, the resources of the new principalities ranged rather widely. Three of the chiefs commanded resources worth over eight lacs of rupees: those of Multan, Mankera and Jhang. Four of the chiefs could collect more than a lac of rupees as the annual revenue: those of Sahiwal, Kamalia, Khushab and Gogera. Three of them held territories yielding less than one lac but more than 50,000 rupees. It has been possible to identify a few chiefs whose resources were less than 50,000 rupees a year.

In contrast with the chiefs of the upper Doabs of the Punjab, the majority of the chiefs of the lower Doabs were *zamīndārs* and *jāgīrdārs* of the Mughals or the Afghans : like the chiefs of Bahawalpur, Haveli and Dipalpur in the Bari Doab; the chiefs of Kamalia and Jhang in the Rachna Doab; the chief of Sahiwal in the Chaj Doab; and the chiefs of Khushab, Nurpur, Leia and Mankera in the Sindh Sagar Doab. Two of the most important principalities were founded by the Afghan governors appointed by the rulers of Kabul, namely Multan and Mankera. Two of the chiefs were descendants of very eminent grantees: the chiefs of Pakpatan and Hujra Shah Muqim. Of the three Sikh chiefs, the chief of Gogera belonged to a family of *chaudharīs*. The Sikh chiefs of Chiniot and Bhera had sprung from ordinary peasant families. Once again we notice that, whereas nearly all the non-Sikh chiefs made use of the politico-administrative framework of the Mughal empire or the state of

---

[44] Sohan Lal, *Umdat-ut-Tawārīkh* (Pbi. tr.), II, 226., 241, 248-49, 308, 341, 344, 353, 356 & 360. H.L.O. Garrett & G.L. Chopra (tr.), *Events at the Court of Ranjit Singh (1810-17)*, 245. Prinsep, *Origin of the Sikh Power*, 88. Foreign/Political Consultation, 8 August 1836, No. 6; 29 August 1836, No. 32; 24 October 1836, No. 20. *SR Muzaffargarh* (1882), 50. *DG Dera Ismail Khan* (1883-84), 199-200.

Kabul, the majority of the Sikh chiefs were of plebian origins working against the holders of power at all levels.

It is a significant reflection on the polity of the times that most of the chiefs survived into the nineteenth century in the lower Doabs of the Punjab as well as in the upper Doabs, despite a wide range in their resources and power. Only two principalities, namely Malka Hans and Haveli, established in the lower Doabs during the eighteenth century, were obliterated before the end of the century. It is interesting to note that both of these were subverted by Sikh chiefs, the former by Bhagwan Singh Nakkai and the latter by Lehna Singh of Lahore. The principalities of Sahiwal, Jhang and Kamalia lost parts of their territories during the late eighteenth century. When Ranjit Singh appeared on the scene with a much greater striking power, all the principalities of the lower Doabs were subverted by him; those which were closest to his dominions were subverted first and the others later. The chiefs of Jhang, Nurpur, Multan, Mankera and Bahawalpur were subjugated by Ranjit Singh only when he had consolidated his power in the rest of the Punjab. In almost all cases, the chiefs were made tributary before their territories were annexed.

4

ADMINISTRATIVE ARRANGEMENTS

We have already noticed that the government and administration of the principalities in the hills had always remained under the control of their chiefs. Therefore, for our present purpose, it is not the change that we are seeking to understand so much as the administrative arrangements. The majority of the chiefs in the lower Doabs made use of the politico-administrative framework of the Mughal empire and any possible change can be appreciated only with reference to the arrangements of the Mughal times. The maximum change may be expected in the areas subjugated by the Sikh chiefs who rose into power not with the help of but in spite of the politico-administrative arrangements of the Mughals. In their case too, the change can be appreciated with reference to what was there earlier.

I

According to Hutchison and Vogel, the hereditary aristocracy in the hills had practically no administrative duties and little power or responsibility. The administration was carried on by the chief through high officers, bearing the title of *wazīr*, each of whom either lived in the area under his jurisdiction, known as *wazārat*, or visited the area from time to time. They worked through lower officials, and exercised both judicial and executive powers. For revenue purposes, the lower officials of the principality worked under a revenue officer called *thare-dā-mahta*. The military accounts were in the charge of an officer called *bakhshi* who was responsible also for the administration of the camp. The administrative sub-division of *wazārat* was called *pargana*, and its official dealt with petty cases by fine and imprisonment. Because of a lock-up, called *kothi*, in the headquarters of the *pargana*, it was also referred to as *kothi*. There was another officer at the *pargana* headquarters known as the *kotwāl* whose duties were military, judicial and fiscal. He was assisted by an official called *jinsali* who had charge of the military stores of the *pargana*. An officer called *thare-da-kotwāl* performed the duties of a chief constable in the capital. The official in charge of the *pargana* itself was known as *chata* or *char* who combined in his office the executive, judicial and revenue powers. He was assisted by an official called *likhnehāra* in collecting the revenue and in keeping accounts. Below him were some other functionaries who carried out the orders of the superior officers in dealing with the village headmen or *lambardārs*.[1]

This description of the administrative arrangements in the hills suggests that the chief at the headquarters was assisted by a revenue officer for the entire principality, by a *bakhshi* for the forces and by a chief constable for the capital. The principality was divided into *wazārats* though a *wazīr* did not necessarily live outside the capital. The *wazārat* was divided into *parganas*, and *parganas* were sub-divided into circuits of hamlets. At the *pargana* level, there was a general administrator assisted by a number of officials for collecting revenues through the village headmen, and for keeping accounts. There was another officer at the *pargana* headquarters whose duty was primarily of a military character. He too was assisted by a subordinate official. From the references of Hutchison and Vogel to the *wazīr* in the late eighteenth and the early nineteenth century, it appears that he acted as a minister as well as an administrator.[2]

When we turn to other contemporary or near contemporary evidence, much of the description of administrative arrangements given by Hutchison and Vogel gets confirmed. There are references, for instance, to *parganas, kārdārs, qānūngos, kotwāls* and *muqaddams*, which appear to refer basically to the officials and functions mentioned by Hutchison and Vogel. In the *Settlement Report of Kangra*, there is a reference to *chaudharīs* exercising jurisdiction over a number of villages for the collection of revenue. They were expected to encourage cultivation and to arrest criminals. They appear to be the 'circuit officials' of Hutchison and Vogel. In a contemporary document, it is stated that Raja Sansar Chand's order was inscribed by his *wazīr* Khushala. This too indicates that *wazīr* Khushala was not the counterpart of the 'provincial governor'.[3]

---

[1] Hutchison & Vogel, *Hill States*, I, 69-71, 187, 206, 322-23, 324-25, 361; II, 391, 393, 467 & 505.

[2] Loc. cit.

[3] Foreign/Political Proceedings, 16 April 1852, No. 60. *SR Sialkot* (1865), 57. *SR Kangra* (1889), 16-17. Ahmad Shah, *Tārīkh-i-Panjab* (Pbi. tr.), 57.

On the whole, administrative arrangements in the hill principalities during the late eighteenth century do not appear to have undergone any appreciable change. This is understandable. In the general circumstances of the late eighteenth century there was hardly any need for change. The removal of the suzerain's political control by itself did not affect the administrative arrangements. If in some ways they appeared to be similar to what was prevalent in the plains under the Mughal rule, it could be due to a certain degree of assimilation during the period of Mughal rule itself.

II

As we suggested at the beginning, it is necessary to refer to the arrangements prevalent under the Mughals for a proper appreciation of administrative arrangements of the principalities of the plains during the late eighteenth century. It is difficult to assume that the administrative arrangements in the province of Lahore or Multan remained the same throughout the Mughal rule. It is also likely that there was a certain degree of overlapping in the functions of the provincial officials. Nevertheless, it is possible to see that during the seventeenth and the early eighteenth century in the Punjab, the administration of the province was carried on by three major functionaries with the help of officials at lower rungs in different parts of the province.

The most important functionary in the province was its governor, generally called *sūbadār*. His functions were primarily military and executive. The safety of the province against any outsiders and the maintenance of peace and order within the province were his main concern. He was supported by a number of *faujdārs* posted in different parts of the province. Some of the *faujdārs* in turn were assisted by *thānadārs* in charge of small garrisons. In the Punjab, as in some other provinces, a few of the *faujdārs* were entrusted with the duties of dealing with the vassal chiefs. They generally enjoyed higher rank and were given the privilege of directly communicating with the emperor. The *faujdārs* of Jammu and Kangra, for instance, belonged to this category. The *'āmil* in the *pargana* was also expected to perform *faujdāri* duties, but he was placed under the *dīwān* rather than the *sūbadār*.[4]

---

[4] P. Saran, *The Provincial Government of the Mughals*, 157-74 & 210-13. M. Athar Ali, 'Provincial Governors under Aurangzeb - An Analysis', *Medieval India: A Miscellany*, I, 96-133. Jadunath Sarkar, *Mughal Administration*, 43-44. Hutchison & Vogel, *Hill States*, I, 235.

The second important functionary in the province was the *dīwān*. His primary duty was the assessment and collection of revenues. For this purpose, he had to keep all revenue accounts. He was not placed under the *sūbadār*. He was responsible to the *dīwān* at the centre and through him to the emperor who actually appointed all provincial *dīwāns* in consultation with the *dīwān* at the centre. The provincial *dīwān* was assisted by *'āmils* in the *parganas*.[5]

The third important functionary in the province was the *sadr* who was responsible to the *sadr-us-sudūr* at the centre and not to the *sūbadār*. He looked after the administration of justice and charitable grants. In the performance of his duties, he was assisted by *qāzīs* and *muftīs*, not only in the cities of the province but also in some of the small towns. The court of the *qāzī* was accessible to all for matters relating to property. In these matters it was accessible to Muslims and non-Muslims alike.[6]

The most important unit of administration was the *pargana*. In the province of Lahore under Akbar, there were nearly 234 *parganas*. This number increased to about 300 by the end of the seventeenth century. The number of *parganas* within the rivers Indus and Satlej in the province of Multan was 53 towards the end of the sixteenth century.[7] This number presumably also increased during the seventeenth century though we have no definite information on the point. Assuming the increase to be nearly the same as in the Province of Lahore, the total number of *parganas* in the lower Doabs would come to about fiftyfive. The total area of this region was more than 30,000 square miles. Therefore, the average area of the *pargana* was over 500 square miles. In the upper Doabs, however, the total area was about 60,000 square miles and the average area of the *pargana* was therefore less than 200 square

---

[5] Ishtiaq Hussain Qureshi, *The Administration of the Mughal Empire*, 232.

[6] P. Saran, *The Provincial Government of the Mughals*, 158, 163, 182 & 320-21. Noman Ahmad Siddiqi, *Land Revenue Administration*, 19 & 89-90. J.S. Grewal, *In the By-Lanes of History*, 7-8; 'The Qazi in the Pargana', *Historian's Punjab: Miscellaneous Articles*, 38-73. Zaheeruddin Siddiqi, 'The Institution of the Qazi under the Mughals', *Medieval India: A Miscellany*, I, 247-59.

[7] *Ā'īn-Akbarī* (Eng. tr.), II, 319, 329-36. Sujan Rai Bhandari, *Khulāsat-ut-Tawārīkh* (Pbi. tr.), 91.

miles.[8] This would enable us to draw the inference that the size of the *pargana* in the lower Doabs was much larger than the size of the *pargana* in the upper Doabs. This did not imply, however, that the *pargana* of the Mughal Province of Multan yielded higher revenues. The upper Doabs on the whole were much more productive.

The administrator *par excellence* of the Mughal *pargana* was the *'āmil* who was assisted by accountants and assessment officers, measurers of land, watch and ward officers, and treasurers. The assessment and collection of land revenue as well as the maintenance of peace and order and extension of cultivation were the primary duties of the *'āmil*. In the countryside, he was assisted by a *chaudharī* or *chaudharīs* in the *pargana*, each of whom had jurisdiction over a number of villages. In each village, there was a *muqaddam* or a few *muqaddams* who were responsible for the collection of revenue. All revenue records at the *pargana* level were kept by a *qānūngo*, and at the village level by a *patwārī*.[9]

When we turn to the principalities of the plains during the late eighteenth century, we find that there is no mention of the *sadr*. However, the *qāzī* does find mention in the near contemporary records. For example, Nawab Bahawal Khan I gave a grant of revenue-free land to Sayyad Muhammad Saleh for performing the duties of a *qāzī*. Similarly, Sohan Lal refers to Qazi Gul Mohammad of Mankera as the *vakil* sent to the court of Ranjit Singh. Shahamat Ali mentions that if a person was dissatisfied with the decision of a *qāzī* in the principality of Bahawalpur, he could go to the chief himself for justice. He refers also to the *qāzī* at the court of the chief.[10] This reference suggests the possibility that the duties of the *qāzī* at the court were similar to those of the *sadr*. It is certain that the *qāzī* at the court was appointed by the chief himself.

There are references also to the *dīwān* in Jhang, Leia and Mankera. One Bhawani Das was the *dīwān* of the Sial chief Inayat Ullah Khan.

---

[8] This has been calculated from the figures given in James Douie, *The Panjab, North-West Frontier Province and Kashmir*, 234-41, 245-68, 278, 280, 283-85, 286, 288 & 299.

[9] P. Saran, *The Provincial Government of the Mughals*, 157, 163, 175, 177-81, 267-71. Irfan Habib, *Agrarian System of Mughal India*, 131-32, 280-81 & 291-92. Noman Ahmad Siddiqi, *Land Revenue Administration under the Mughals (1700-1750)*, 81-82 & 90-91.

[10] Foreign/Political Proceedings, 12 December 1856, No. 255. Sohan Lal, *Umdat-ut-Tawārīkh* (Pbi. tr.), II, 162. Shahamat Ali, *History of Bahawalpur*, xii-xiii.

Laddha Ram is referred to as the *dīwān* under Muhammad Khan Jaskani. Manak Rai is similarly referred to as the *dīwān* at Mankera. He was later appointed as the administrator of Dera Ismail Khan.[11] We may be sure that the *dīwāns* were appointed by the chiefs themselves, and were directly responsible to them. Thus, in place of the virtually independent *sadrs* and *dīwāns*, we have in these principalities *dīwāns* and *qāzīs* appointed by the chief who had taken the place of the Mughal *sūbadār* with the difference that he was not subordinate to any emperor. The existence of *wazīrs* in many of the non-Sikh principalities of the plains indicates that they regarded themselves as independent potentates. Hasan Khan Laskrani, for instance, was the *wazīr* of Fateh Khan Jaskani, the chief of Leia and Bhakkar. There is a similar reference to a *wazīr* under Nawab Sher Muhammad Khan of Mankera.[12]

In contemporary and near contemporary records, a large number of terms refer to the functionaries of the Sikh principalities: *sūbadār*, *nāzim*, *dīwān*, *kārmukhtār*, *kārdār*, *'āmil*, *tehsīldār*, *thānadār*, *faujdār*, *qānūngo*, *tappadār*, *chaudharī*, *muqaddam*, *toshakhānia*, *munshī*, *qāzī*, *muftī*, *chobdār*, *nāib*, *deodidār*, *lāngarī*, *muqarrab*, *naqīb* and *khidmatgār*. However, all of these terms do not appear to have any essential bearing on the administrative arrangements of the Sikh principalities. The terms *deodidār*, *lāngarī*, *naqīb*, *khidmatgār* and *chobdār*, for instance, refer to persons at the court of the ruler. The term *toshakhānia* is used for the treasurer. The terms *sūbadār* and *nāzim* are used only in connection with Multan when it was temporarily conquered by Jhanda Singh Bhangi. Similarly, the use of the term *faujdār* is rather rare. The term *munshī* is frequently used for a writer.[13] Thus, the terms which appear to have a bearing on the administrative arrangements are *kārmukhtār*, *nāib*, *dīwān*, *kārdār*, *'āmil*, *tehsildār*, *thānadār*, *tappadār*, *qānūngo*, *chaudharī*, *muqaddam*, *qāzī* and *muftī*.

---

[11] *SR Jhang* (1882), 37. *DG Dera Ismail Khan* (1883-84), 33-34, 36-37, 70 & 74. *Punjab Government Records, Ludhiana Agency, 1808-15*, II, 192. Ram Sukh Rao, *Jassa Singh Binod* (ms), ff 206 a, 225 ab. Prinsep, *Origin of the Sikh Power*, 102.

[12] Charles Masson, *Narrative of Various Journeys*, I, 42-43. *DG Dera Ismail Khan* (1883-84), 37.

[13] Ram Sukh Rao, *Sri Fateh Singh Pratap Prabhakar*, 306-07. Sohan Lal, *Umdat-ut-Tawārīkh* (Pbi. tr.), II, 56-57. Foreign/ Political Proceedings, 5 September 1846, No. 114; 7 January 1853, No. 231. Lepel Griffin, *The Panjab Chiefs*, 596. Ganesh Das, *Chār-Bāgh-i-Panjab* (Pbi. tr.), 132. Kirpa Ram, *Gulabnāma* (Eng. tr.), XI.

The references to *kārmukhtārs* or *nāibs* in the Sikh principalities are few.[14] The context clearly suggests that the persons so designated were acting as deputies of the chiefs, particularly in their absence. Thus, the position of the *nāib* or *kārmukhtār* was rather rare and it was clearly distinct from the position of the *wazīr* in the hill principalities or the non-Sikh principalities in the plains.

The person next in importance to the chief in the Sikh principalities is frequently referred to as the *dīwān*. There are references to the *dīwāns* under Gujjar Singh and Sahib Singh at Gujrat, under Charhat Singh and Mahan Singh at Gujranwala, under Jassa Singh and Bhag Singh at Kapurthala, under Milkha Singh at Rawalpindi, under Hari Singh and Jhanda Singh at Amritsar, under Haqiqat Singh and Jaimal Singh at Fatehgarh Churian, and under Jai Singh at Batala. Nearly all of these were rather important principalities. However, considering that the primary function of the *dīwān* was related to finances, particularly land revenue, it is safe to assume that the office of the *dīwān*, or its counterpart, did exist in nearly all the Sikh principalities. In some cases, there is a reference to more than one *dīwān* at one and the same time.[15] It is possible, therefore, that in matters of the state finance the services of more than one person were utilized. It is interesting to note, incidentally, that this was the position under Ranjit Singh in the early years of the nineteenth century.

References to *kārdārs* are more frequent than to the *'āmil*, the *tehsīldār* or the *thānadār*. In some contemporary documents, the term *'āmil* is used for the office for which the term *kārdār* is also used.[16] The literal meaning of these two terms and the functions performed by those who were so designated clearly show that the two terms were used for the same office. It has been argued recently that the term *pargana* and *ta'alluqa* were used synonymously during the late eighteenth and early nineteenth centuries in the Punjab.[17] It is clear, therefore, that the *kārdār* was the general administrator of the *ta'alluqa* who combined in

---

[14] Sohan Lal, *Umdat-ut-Tawārīkh* (Pbi. tr.), II, 41, 65, 105 & 123-24.

[15] Ram Sukh Rao, *Jassa Singh Binod* (ms), ff 159a, 192b, 206a & 225b; *Fateh Singh Partap Prabhakar*, 143 & 152. Aliuddin, *Ibratnāma* (Pbi. tr.), 305 & 309. Ganesh Das, *Early Nineteenth Century Panjab* (Eng. tr.), 98. Lepel Griffin, *The Panjab Chiefs*, 295. Sohan Lal, *Umdat-ut-Tawārīkh* (Pbi. tr.), II, 31.

[16] B.N. Goswamy and J.S. Grewal, *The Pindori Documents*, XVIII-XXI, XXV, XXIX & XXXIV. Foreign/Political Proceedings, 27 May 1853, Nos. 193 & 208; 4 July 1856, No. 153; 1 Nov. 1857, No. 419.

[17] Indu Banga, *Agrarian System of the Sikhs*, 66-67.

his office the fiscal, executive and some judicial powers. It appears that when his function as a revenue collector was underlined, the term *tehsīldār* was used for his office. To underline his concern for peace and order, the term *thānadār* was occasionally used.[18] It is possible, however, that in some principalities *thānadārs* were appointed specifically for maintaining small garrisons at strategic points. By far the most important administrator outside the headquarters of the chief was the *kārdār*. There is only one reference to the administrator of a *tappa* as the sub-division of a *pargana*.[19] This is understandable because only a few *parganas* in the Mughal Punjab were divided into *tappas*.

The *qānūngos*, the *chaudharīs* and the *muqaddams* are mentioned in connection with a large number of principalities. Karori Mal, for instance, was the *qānūngo* of Eminabad under Charhat Singh Sukarchakia; Jai Singh was the *qānūngo* of Wazirabad under Jodh Singh Wazirabadia; Kishan Chand was the *qānūngo* of Batala under Jassa Singh Ramgarhia; Jawala Sahai was at Gogera under Kamr Singh Nakkai; and Pahar Mal at Sujanpur under Amar Singh Bagga. Among the *chaudharīs* in the Sikh principalities can be mentioned Roop Chand under Fateh Singh Ahluwalia, Usman Khan and Jhanda Singh under Jai Singh Kanhiya, Ahmad Khan under Kapur Singh Saurianwala, Ghulam Qadir under Jodh Singh Wazirabadia and Suba Khan under Bagh Singh Hallowalia. A few of the *muqaddams* specifically mentioned were Bahadur Singh under Jai Singh Kanhiya, Naurang Singh under Jassa Singh Ramgarhia, Yar Singh under Gurbakhsh Singh Wazirabadia, Sahib Khan under Nar Singh Chamiariwala, and Nur Burhan under Ran Singh Nakkai.[20] It appears in fact that the holders of all these positions occupied them on a hereditary basis. At any rate, even when the persons were changed, the functions of the holders of these positions remained the same now as in the Mughal times.

---

[18] Ganesh Das, *Chār Bāgh-i-Panjab* (Pbi. tr.), 131-32. Ram Sukh Rao, *Jassa Singh Binod* (ms), f. 211; *Sri Fateh Singh Partap Prabhakar*, 63, 214 & 385.

[19] Ganesh Das, *Chār Bāgh-i-Panjab* (Pbi. tr.), 131-32.

[20] Ganesh Das, *Early Nineteenth Century Panjab* (Eng. tr.), 45, 57, 58, 93-94 & 110. *SR Googaira* (1860), 19. Lepel Griffin, *The Panjab Chiefs*, 300. Foreign/Political Consultation, 18 June 1852, No. 183. Foreign/Political Proceedings, 16 April 1852, No. 55; 9 January 1857, Nos., 230, 234 & 274; 27 May 1853, No. 208; 3 June 1853, No. 119; 11 July 1856, No. 211; 8 August 1856, No. 207; 5 September 1856, Nos. 111, 113 & 114; 27 March 1857, Nos. 243 & 247; 17 April 1857, No. 603; 29 May 1857, No. 197; 31 December 1858, No. 318.

By contrast, references to *qāzīs* and *muftīs* are not many. Qazi Kamaluddin is mentioned as performing his duties at Wazirabad, Qazi Haji at Gujrat and Qazi Abdul Rahman at Gujranwala. Only in the case of Batala, do we come across the names of five *qāzīs*. The available evidence does suggest that wherever they remained in existence, they continued to perform the same functions as they used to perform under the provincial *sadr* during the Mughal times. We have detailed references to *bai'nāmas*, *girvīnāmas*, *tazkaras* and *iqrarnāmas* executed in the court of the *qāzī* of Batala. It is interesting to note that these transactions took place between Muslims and Muslims, between Muslims and non-Muslims, and between non-Muslims and non-Muslims. The non-Muslims chose to go to the *qāzī's* court because of the uniform application of the law.[21]

III

For further clarification of the position regarding administrative arrangements in the Sikh principalities, we may turn specifically to the chiefs traditionally called Bhangi. To assist the Bhangi chiefs in the administration was a *dīwān* at the headquarters, who used to look after the revenue affairs of the principality. He was assisted by *kārdārs* at the *pargana* level. The primary duty of the *kārdār* was to supervise the collection of revenues and to maintain peace and order within his jurisdiction. He was assisted by a *qānūngo* who prepared revenue assessment records. The services of a local hereditary official called the *chaudharī* were utilized to collect the revenues from the *muqaddams*.

There is a reference to the appointment of Diwan Singh as the *nāzim* of Multan after its occupation by Jhanda Singh in 1772. But this arrangement was exceptional and also temporary as Diwan Singh remained in office only till the recovery of Multan by Timur Shah in 1780.[22] There is no reference to a *nāzim* under any other Bhangi chief, or any of the Sikh chiefs of the late eighteenth century.

There are references to *dīwāns* under Hari Singh, Jhanda Singh, Gujjar Singh and Sahib Singh. Gujjar Singh ruled over Gujrat for

---

[21] J.S. Grewal, *In the By-Lanes of History*, Documents, II, III, X, XIII, XV, XVIII & XXXII; 'The Qazi in the Pargana', *Historian's Punjab: Miscellaneous Articles*, 38-73. Sohan Lal, *Umdat-ut-Tawārīkh* (Pbi. tr.), II, 94 & 108.

[22] Ganesh Das, *Chār Bāgh-i-Panjab* (Pbi. tr.), 132. Indu Banga, 'Sikh Revenue Administration: The Framework', *Studies in Local and Regional History* (ed. J.S. Grewal), 55.

nearly twentythree years. To serve him as *dīwāns* were Sobha Ram Handa for eight years, Dilbagh Singh for ten years and Sharda Ram for five years. During Sahib Singh's rule, the *dīwāns* were Ratan Chand, a Brahman who served for eight years; Chait Singh, a Kalal who served for nine years; and Mohkam Chand, a Khatri who served for two years. There are references also to Diwan Guttu Mal who served Gujjar Singh and Sahib Singh throughout his life. His son served Sahib Singh as a *dīwān* till 1810 when Ranjit Singh took possession of the chief's territories.[23] Thus, the context clearly suggests that the services of more than one *dīwān* were required by Gujjar Singh and Sahib Singh for regulating the civil affairs of the large tract over which they ruled.

There are references to the *kārdār* at *ta'alluqa* Manawar under Gujjar Singh, at Nuruddin under Gulab Singh, at Talwandi under Lehna Singh, and at Zafarwal under Bagh Singh Hallowalia.[24] The *kārdārs* were primarily fiscal officers and their most important duty was to collect revenue. They were also required to execute the orders of their chiefs relating to alienation of revenues in favour of individuals and institutions.

There are references to the *qānūngos* at Gujrat and Rawalpindi. Shiv Dayal Handa, for instance, is referred to as the hereditary *qānūngo* of Gujrat under Gujjar Singh. Ismatullah has also been referred to as a *qānūngo* of Gujrat under Gujjar Singh, suggesting that there was more than one *qānūngo* of Gujrat under Gujjar Singh for the preparation of revenue-assessment records.[25]

There are several references to *chaudharīs* under the Bhangi chiefs, as to Rahmat Khan Waraich, the *chaudharī* of Jalalpur under Gujjar Singh, to Dasaunda Khan, the Rajput *chaudharī* of Chamiari under Nar Singh Chamiariwala, and to Teeka Khan, the *chaudharī* of Talwandi under Bagh Singh Hallowalia. Khudadad Khan and Yadgar Khan are mentioned as the *chaudharīs* at Firozke under Suddh Singh Chhina. For the administration of the towns, services of the *chaudharīs* of different *muhallas* were also utilized by the Bhangi chiefs. These *chaudharīs* used to be the headmen of different professional classes. Their opinion was taken on all important matters connected with the town or its

---

[23] Ganesh Das, *Early Nineteenth Century Panjab* (Eng. tr.), 65. A.C. Elliot, *The Chronicles of Gujrat*, 79. Ram Sukh Rao, *Jassa Singh Binod* (ms), f. 192b. Lepel Griffin, *The Panjab Chiefs*, 464.

[24] Foreign/Political Proceedings, 27 May 1853, Nos. 193 & 208; 4 July 1856, No. 153; 1 May 1857, No. 419.

[25] Foreign/Political Proceedings, 9 January 1857, No. 274. Ganesh Das, *Chār Bāgh-i-Panjab* (Pbi. tr.), 131.

neighbourhood. Among the *chaudharīs* of Lahore were Mian Muhammad Āshiq, Mian Mohkam Din, Mir Shadi Khan and Mir Badaruddin. There are references also to *chaudharīs* in Gujrat under Gujjar Singh.[26]

To assist the *chaudharī* and the *kārdār* in the collection of revenues, there was at least one headman or *muqaddam* in every village. We may refer to a few instances which find mention in contemporary records. Gulab Singh Gill was a *muqaddam* of *mauza*' Kot Budha under Gulab Singh; Muhammad Din was a *muqaddam* of *mauza*' Saggian under Lehna Singh; and Sahib Khan was a *muqaddam* of Musapur under Nar Singh Chamiariwala. There are references also to more than one *muqaddam* in a village under the Bhangi chiefs: to Budhu and Puran in *mauza*' Ghat and to Maggu and Raj Kaur in *mauza*' Sutra under Nar Singh Chamiariwala, for instance.[27]

References to a *tehsīldār* and a *tappadār* suggest that the persons in charge were performing duties similar to those of a *kārdār* and a *chaudharī* respectively.[28] A *qāzī* at Gujrat under Gujjar Singh finds mention in a near contemporary source.[29]

IV

As in the Mughal times so during the late eighteenth century, the most important unit of administration was the *pargana*. It became in fact the primary unit of administration in a principality instead of being a secondary unit in the Mughal empire. Significantly, it survived in the entire area under our present consideration. In the orders of Ranjit Dev of Jammu, there are references to the *parganas* of Sialkot and Shakargarh. The *pargana* of Kangra is referred to in an order of Sansar Chand. In the contemporary documents transcribed or summarized in the

---

[26] Foreign/Political Proceedings, 27 May 1853, No. 208; 3 June 1853, No. 119. Aliuddin, *Ibratnāma* (Pbi. tr.), 281. Sohan Lal, *Umdat-ut-Tawārīkh* (Pbi. tr.), II, 49-50. Ganesh Das, *Early Nineteenth Century Punjab* (Eng. tr.), 58.

[27] Foreign/Political Proceedings, 5 December 1856, No. 212; 9 January 1857, No. 230; 29 May 1857, No. 197.

[28] Ganesh Das refers to the appointments made by Gujjar Singh Bhangi in his conquered territory in the Sindh Sagar Doab. Jodh Singh Atariwala was appointed *tehsīldār* of Pothohar and Ran Singh Pidda as a *tappadār* of Sarai Kala: *Chār Bāgh-i-Panjab* (Pbi. tr.), 131-32.

[29] Ganesh Das, *Early Nineteenth Century Panjab* (Eng. tr.), 58.

Catalogue of Bhuri Singh Museum, nearly a dozen *parganas* in the hills are mentioned.[30] Similarly, in the territories of non-Sikh chiefs, the term *pargana* remained current. This is evident from the orders of Ghulam Muhammad Chattha, Nawab Bahawal Khan I, Nawab Sadiq Muhammad Khan, Nawab Shuja Khan, Qutbuddin Khan, Walidad Khan and Ahmad Khan Sial, Jalal Khan Bhatti, and the Khokhar chief of Pind Dadan Khan. In the territory of Mankera, there are references to about a dozen *parganas*.[31]

In the territories of the Sikh chiefs, however, the term *ta'alluqa* as well as *pargana* was current. In the first decade of the nineteenth century, Talwan, Rahon, Nakodar, Sham Chaurasi, Shergarh, Hariana, Malot, Garhdiwala, Nur Mahal, and more than a score of other *parganas* are named in the Jalandhar Doab. This could not be a new development. Indeed, most of these names are the same as in the *Ā'īn- i-Akbarī*. In the Bari Doab too, there are a few references to *parganas* in the late eighteenth century.[32] In a few contemporary documents, the terms *pargana* and *ta'alluqa* are used for one and the same area. Lahore, for instance, has been referred to as *pargana* and *ta'alluqa* Lahore in an order of Gujjar Singh. Pathankot, Adinanagar, Batala, Qasur, Qila Sobha Singh, Shakargarh, and Ghaniwala have been similarly mentioned.[33] In fact, a comparison of the list of *ta'alluqas* in the territories of the Sikh chiefs compiled from contemporary and near contemporary sources and compared with the list of *parganas* in the *Ā'īn-i-Akbarī* shows that at least fifty to sixty names were common.[34] This evidence supports the

---

[30] Foreign/Political Proceedings, 19 December 1856, No. 172; 9 January 1857, No. 221; 31 December 1858, No. 318. Vogel, *Catalogue of Bhuri Singh Museum*, 11-12, 70-71.

[31] Foreign/Secret Consultation, 7 July 1797, No. 3. Foreign/ Political Proceedings, 27 May 1853, No. 202; 25 June 1854, No. 205; 22 March 1856, No. 132; 28 November 1856, No. 139; 5 December 1856, No. 210; 12 December 1856, No. 255; 25 June 1858, No. 275.

[32] *Ā'in-i-Akbarī* (Eng. tr.), II, 320-21. Foreign/Secret Proceedings, 24 June 1809, No. 7. Foreign/Political Proceedings, 4 July 1856, No. 152; 5 December 1856, No. 210; 1 May 1857, No. 418.

[33] Foreign/Political Proceedings, 14 January 1853, Nos. 213 & 235. 4 July 1856, No. 152; 29 August 1856, No. 249; 28 November 1856, No. 131; 5 December 1856, No. 211; 9 January 1857, No. 262; 29 May 1857, No. 197; 31 December 1858, No. 3315; 5 September 1859, No. 110. B.N. Goswamy & J.S. Grewal, *The Pindori Documents*, Documents XXXII & XXXIV.

[34] *Ā'īn-i-Akbarī* (Eng. tr.), II, 320-26. Sita Ram Kohli, *Catalogue of the Khalsa Darbar Records*, Vol. II. Foreign/Political Proceedings, 21

view put forth by Indu Banga that the terms *pargana* and *ta'alluqa* were used synonymously in the territories of the Sikh chiefs.[35]

Even in the Mughal times, the size of the *pargana* was not uniform. The disparity in the revenue figures of the various *parganas* of the Bari Doab in the Mughal province of Lahore is so large that it suggests a certain degree of difference in size.[36] During the late eighteenth century, a *pargana* or a *ta'alluqa* of the same name as in the *Ā'īn-i-Akbarī* did not necessarily have the same boundaries. The *pargana* of Talwan, for instance, figures in the territories of Fateh Singh Ahluwalia. But villages worth about 10,000 rupees a year from the Mughal *pargana* of Talwan were under Baghel Singh and this unit of villages was also referred to as the *pargana* of Talwan.[37] If we compare the revenue figures of *parganas* in the *Ā'īn-i-Akbarī* with the revenue figures of *parganas* of the Sikh territories, the difference in every case cannot be explained in terms of the difference in the rate of assessment, area under cultivation, or the difference in prices, or even all these put together. The difference can be explained only in terms of the difference in size. The *pargana* of Nakodar, for instance, during the Sikh times yielded a little over 31,000 rupees whereas the corresponding figure in the *Ā'īn-i-Akbarī* is nearly 93,000 rupees.[38] The *pargana* of Shaikhpur, by contrast, yielded a little over 1,18,000 rupees in the time of Akbar, but about 2,65,000 rupees under Fateh Singh Ahluwalia.[39] Similarly, the revenue of Jalandhar under Buddh Singh Faizullapuria exceeded 4,75,000 rupees whereas in the *Ā'īn-i-Akbarī*, the revenue was slightly less than 3,69,000 rupees.[40]

February 1851, No. 218; 7 January 1853, No. 234; 14 January 1853, Nos. 219, 238 & 241; 10 June 1853, Nos. 218-19; 12 December 1856, No. 253.

[35] *Agrarian System of the Sikhs*, 67-69. Cf. Bhagat Singh, *Sikh Polity in the Eighteenth & Nineteenth Centuries*, 247.

[36] For illustration, the *pargana* of Patti Haibatpur has been shown as yielding 28, 395, 380 *dāms* (7,09,885 rupees) as revenues; by contrast, the *pargana* of Sherpur in the same Doab was yielding only 4,80,000 *dāms* (12,000 rupees). This is not the only example; we can find similar instances in the Jalandhar, Rachna, Chaj and the Sindh Sagar Doabs too: *Ā'īn-i-Akbarī* (Eng. tr.), II, 320-28.

[37] Foreign/Secret Proceedings, 24 June 1809, No. 7.

[38] *Ā'īn-i-Akbarī* (Eng. tr.), II, 321. Foreign/Secret Proceedings, 24 June 1809, No. 7.

[39] *Ā'īn-i-Akbarī* (Eng. tr.), II, 321. Foreign/Secret Proceedings, 24 June 1809, No. 7.

[40] Foreign/Secret Proceedings, 24 June 1809, No. 7. *Ā'īn-i-Akbarī* (Eng. tr.), II, 320.

It is interesting to note that in several cases the difference in the revenue figures is rather small. The *pargana* of Garhdiwala, for instance, yielded 66,752 rupees in the time of Akbar, and about 61,525 rupees under Mohar Singh, a *jāgīrdār* of the Ramgarhias during the late eighteenth century.[41] The size of the *pargana* or the *ta'alluqa* during the late eighteenth century appears to be related to the nature of the political process and the mode of territorial occupation. While some of the *parganas* were partitioned among more than one chief, some others were taken over entirely by a single chief. Consequently, there were *ta'alluqas* with the same size as that of the Mughal *parganas* and also *ta'alluqas* larger than the former Mughal *parganas* when a single chief took over a *pargana* and added villages to it taken from another, or when parts of several *parganas* were made into a single *ta'alluqa*.

There are only a few references to the *'āmil* in the *pargana* or *ta'alluqa* in the late eighteenth century. But this is only because he came to be called *kārdār*. Indeed, there are several references to *kārdārs* even in the lower Doabs, as to Hamid under Muhammad Khan of Mankera and to Suleman Khan under Bahawal Khan II. These references occur in a *Settlement Report* written in the early 1880s.[42] It is likely, therefore, that the term *kārdār* came to be used for the former *'āmils* after the conquest of these territories by Ranjit Singh. There are references to *qānūngos*, *chaudharīs* and *muqaddams* which suggest that hardly any change was introduced in the administrative arrangements at the *pargana* level.[43] In the case of the Sikh principalities, we have already seen that the *kārdār* was indeed the administrator *par excellence* of the *ta'alluqa* or *pargana*. He looked after the law and order in the area under his jurisdiction and also performed some judicial functions, but his primary concern was with the collection of revenues. He was assisted by *qānūngos*, *chaudharīs* and *muqaddams*. Every village was covered by a *patwari*, though every village did not have a *patwari* exclusively for itself.

---

[41] Similarly, the *pargana* of Naya Nangal yielded about 57,850 rupees under Akbar and about 51,000 rupees under Jodh Singh Ramgarhia: *A'īn-i-Akbarī* (Eng. tr.), II, 321 Foreign/Secret Proceedings, 24 June 1809, No. 7.

[42] *SR Muzaffargarh* (1882), 16-17 & 21. *SR Jhang* (1882), 35. *DG Muzaffargarh* (1917), 60.

[43] Foreign/Political Proceedings, 9 January 1854, No. 221; 31 March 1854, No. 232; 29 August 1856, Nos. 240-41; 27 March 1857, Nos. 243 & 247. *SR Googaira* (1860), 10.

V

The army during the late eighteenth century can be placed in two categories: the troops of the chief, that is, his *khās fauj*, and the troops of his *jāgīrdārs*. Revenue from land was assigned to the *jāgīrdār* in lieu of the salary for his service and that of his men. The *khās fauj* was divided into *deras*, with a *sardār* as its leader. The *deras* were further divided and placed under *sarkardas* and *jama'dārs*. The soldiers were paid every six months, partly in kind and partly in cash. They were also given a share in the booty.[44]

Cavalry was the major part of the army. Almost everyone preferred to fight as a horseman (*ghurcharha*). The high figures of cavalry under the Punjab chiefs reflect their interest in the horsemen. The chiefs used to procure horses from their vassals as tribute. The horses and arms were the personal property of *ghurcharhas*. Each one of them was furnished with two blankets, which were placed beneath the saddle with a gram bag and heel ropes; this in fact was the baggage of a horseman. The *ghurcharhas* sometimes were paid large sums through *jāgīrs* in recognition of their meritorious services: Dyal Singh, Pahar Singh Man, Diwan Singh Batalia, Kapur Singh, Amir Singh, Gajja Singh, Bakhshish Singh, Prem Singh and Sarja Singh, for instance.[45]

The infantry soldiers were considered altogether inferior to the cavalry and were left behind to garrison forts in the times of war. They were also employed for night watch. They consisted of *khidmatgārs*, *pahlwans*, *beldārs* and the like.[46]

---

[44] Foreign/Secret Consultation, 7 July 1797, No. 3. C.Grey, *European Adventurers of Northern India, 1785- 1849*, 60-64. Ram Sukh Rao, *Sri Fateh Singh Partap Prabhakar*, 311. Hugh David Sandeman, *Selections form Calcutta Gazettes of the years 1806 to 1815 inclusive*, IV, Government Printing, Calcutta, 1868, 206. William Franklin, *Military Memoirs of Mr. George Thomas*, London, 1805, 113. Ganda Singh, *Sardar Jassa Singh Ahluwalia*, 73. Fauja Singh, *Military System of the Sikhs*, 72.

[45] Ganesh Das, *Chār Bāgh-i-Panjab* (Pbi. tr.), 144. Lepel Griffin, *The Panjab Chiefs*, 192, 249, 461 & 463. Ram Sukh Rao, *Jassa Singh Binod*, (ms), ff 76, 95b, 96a, 119a, 159a & 195b. William Franklin, *Military Memoirs of Mr. George Thomas*, 109. Foreign/Political Proceedings, 29 December 1849, No. 49A; 7 January 1853, No. 228; 14 January 1853, Nos. 219 & 235; 27 May 1853, No. 219.

[46] Mahan Singh had four prominesnt *pahlwāns*: Nadir Singh Dalpatia, Tara Singh Chhina, Khushal Singh and Fateh Khan Awan: Sohan Lal, *Umdat-ut-Tawārīkh* (Pbi. tr.), II, 22.

The main weapon was the sword with which the *ghurcharhas* were very skilful. Bows and arrows were used by the infantry. Matchlocks and muskets were also used. Small cannons, swivels, spears, wall pieces, *zambūraks* and seige guns were also used.[47] Sansar Chand of Kangra established a factory of small arms.[48] William O'Brien under Sansar Chand of Kangra, Sultan Ali under Muzaffar Khan of Multan, Ghosi Khan and Mian Khushal Topchi under Mahan Singh Sukarchakia and Imam Shah Hussain under Jodh Singh Wazirabadia were some of the artillery officers of the chiefs of the Punjab during the late eighteenth century.[49] The chiefs were usually armed with steel caps, breast-plates, arm-guards, gauntlets and shields.[50] It is a significant reflection on the state of artillery in the Punjab during the late eighteenth century that the big Zamzama gun called *Bhangian-wali-Top*, which changed hands several times from the Sukarchakias to the Chatthas and from the latter to the Bhangis, was not used at all in any campaign.

The forts were the main basis of defence. They were also the repositories of treasure and war-material. There are references to a number of forts in the jurisdiction of each chief. Muzaffar Khan of Multan had nineteen forts; Sahib Singh of Gujrat had twelve; and Nizamuddin Khan of Qasur had ten. Construction of many new forts is also referred to. Nawab Muhammad Khan got constructed twentythree forts in Leia and Bhakkar; Fateh Singh Ahluwalia built eight; and Kamr Singh Nakkai built five. In the *pargana* of Amritsar alone, seven forts were constructed by the Sikh chiefs.[51]

---

[47] Raja Prithi Singh of Nurpur had 200 swivels and ten cannons. Sahib Singh Bhangi had a gun called Shah Basant. Gulab Singh Bhangi and Sahib Singh Sialkotia had four pieces of cannons and six wall pieces each. Karam Singh Dulu had ten pieces of cannons, eight wall pieces and fifty *zambūraks* or camel guns: Foreign/Secret Consultation, 23 January 1797, No. 5; 20 February 1797, No. 16; 7 July 1797, No. 3. W.S. Setton Karr, *Selections from Calcutta Gazettes*, II, 467.

[48] C. Grey, *European Adventurers of Northern India*, 18. Hutchison & Vogel, *Hill States*, I, 193.

[49] *Punjab Government Records, Ludhiana Agency*, 1808-15, II, 188-89. Lepel Griffin, *The Panjab Chiefs*, 468.

[50] C. Grey, *European Adventurers of Northern India*, 18.

[51] Foreign/Secret Consultation, 7 July 1797, No. 3; 29 December, 1849, No. 46. Ram Sukh Rao, *Sri Fateh Singh Pratap Prabhakar*, 151, 230, 408-09. *DG Muzaffargarh & Leiah Tehsil* (1919), 50-51. Ahmad Shah, *Tārīkh-i-Panjab* (Pbi. tr.), 26. Kirpa Ram, *Gulabnāma* (Eng. tr.), 46 n79.

A great degree of reliance was placed on these forts. After a reverse in the open, the fort was the last resort of a fugitive. He could hope to be safe as long as he had sufficient supplies. The siege craft formed a vital part of the warfare.[52] The strong forts were usually reduced by strict investment, starving out the garrison and sometimes cutting out the supply of water to the fort. The chiefs did not have heavy guns. Therefore, they usually resorted to bribing the inmates for treachery. In 1765, Gujjar Singh and Lehna Singh bribed one Dyal Singh and guided by him, they entered the fort of Lahore through a drain and succeeded in occupying it. Similarly, the fort of Multan could be occupied by Jhanda Singh only when Sharif Beg, the frustrated governor of Multan, opened the gates for the Sikh force.[53]

There are references to the military strength of the chiefs of the Punjab. Sansar Chand of Kangra had a force of 16,000 men; Muzaffar Khan of Multan, 11,000; Ranjit Dev of Jammu, 10,000; Mahan Singh Sukarchakia and Jassa Singh Ramgarhia, 5,000 each; Milkha Singh of Rawalpindi, Baghel Singh Karora Singhia and Amanat Khan Jodrah of Pindi Gheb, 4,000 each; Haqiqat Singh Kanhiya and Tara Singh Pathankotia, 2,000 each; Dal Singh Akalgarhia, 1,000; and Bandu Khan Chib of Khari Khariali had only 600 men.[54] We have some more detail about a few of the chiefs. Sahib Singh of Gujrat had a regular army of 2,000 men but in an emergency he was able to collect 8,000 horsemen and 4,000 foot; Sahib Singh Sialkotia had a permanent force of 1,500 men but he could also muster a force of 3,000 horsemen and 1,000 foot. Similarly, Karam Singh Dulu had about 2,000 men in his regular army but on occasions he was able to raise a force of 7,000 horsemen and 4,000 foot.[55]

VI

In contemporary and near contemporary sources, information having bearing on administrative arrangements is not available for all the principalities. This is understandable. Both in the hills and the plains,

---

[52] Fauja Singh, *Military System of the Sikhs*, 26-27.

[53] Veena Sachdeva, 'The Rule of the Bhangis (1765-1810)', M. Phil Dissertation, 13-14, 19-23.

[54] Foreign/Secret Consultation, 7 July 1797, No. 3. Foreign/Secret Proceedings, 24 June 1809, No. 7. Foreign/Political Consultation, 2 January 1797, No. 24. G.T. Vigne, *Travels in Kashmir*, I, 107.

[55] Foreign/Secret Consultation, 7 July 1797, No. 3.

only a few principalities were large enough to be taken notice of. If the total area of the Punjab under consideration was about 90,000 square miles and there were nearly 125 principalities in this area, then on the average a principality covered only about 720 square miles, which was less than four average *parganas*. Actually, however, some of the principalities were rather large and some others were very small, covering even less than a *pargana*. That is why we find references to the administrative arrangements in the principalities like Kangra, Jammu, Chamba, Mandi, Suket and Nurpur in the hills, the non-Sikh principalities like Multan, Mankera, Jhang and Qasur, and the Sikh principalities like Amritsar, Kapurthala, Gujrat, Lahore, Gujranwala, Batala and Sri Hargobindpur. What we have said about the administrative arrangements in the Punjab during the late eighteenth century applies mainly to the larger principalities.

From our discussion of administrative arrangements in the Punjab during the late eighteenth century, it is also evident that virtually no change took place at the village level and no appreciable change took place even at the *pargana* or the *ta'alluqa* level. The size of *parganas* and the designation of functionaries changed but not the basic framework and functions. At levels higher than the *pargana*, the changes introduced were not uniform for the entire area. In the principalities of the non-Sikh chiefs, the *sadr* was either absent or his jurisdiction was curtailed; the *dīwān* became subordinate to the chief and the office of the *wazīr* was created. In the Sikh principalities, the *dīwān* was clearly subordinate to the chief and there was no *sadr* or his counterpart and no *wazīr* or his counterpart.

5

POLITICAL ORGANIZATION

I

Suzerain-vassal relationship was an essential feature of Indian polity even before the Turks conquered northern India, and this feature of Indian polity was effectively used by the Mughal rulers to give a certain degree of political unity to nearly the whole of the Indian subcontinent. When Ahmad Shah Abdali took over the Mughal provinces of Kabul, Kashmir, Lahore and Multan, he assumed the former position of the Mughal rulers in their capacity as the suzerains of vassal principalities in the hills as well as the plains.

During the late eighteenth century, the successors of Ahmad Shah Abdali tried to assert their suzerain claims not only over the old vassal principalities but also over new chiefs. Their attempt met an increasing failure but they did not give up their claims even after the end of the eighteenth century. In the case of the hills chiefs, for instance, we find Timur Shah and Zaman Shah claiming suzerainty over Raja Sampuran Dev of Jammu, Raja Raj Singh and Raja Jit Singh of Chamba, and some of the other hill chiefs.[1] Timur Shah and Zaman Shah demanded and received tribute also from Muzaffar Khan of Multan, Muhammad Khan of Mankera, Bahawal Khan of Bahawalpur, and Nizamuddin Khan of Qasur.[2] In the last decade of the eighteenth century, Zaman Shah was making offers severally to Sikh chiefs to accept his superior political claim as the condition of holding their territories.[3] It was in this context

---

[1] Foreign/Secret Consultation, 25 January 1797, No.9. Vogel, *Catalogue of Bhuri Singh Museum*, 61-65, cc. 17, 45, 46 & 47.

[2] *Poona Residency Correspondence, 1785-94*, I, 339-40. *Calender of Persian Correspondence, 1788-89*, VIII, 365. Foreign/Secret Consultation, 25 January 1797, No. 9. Foreign/Political Proceedings, 30 December 1800, No. 90. Shahamat Ali, *History of Bahawalpur*, 191.

[3] Foreign/Political Consultation, 28 October 1796, No. 22. Extract of a letter of 23 December 1798, *Poona Residency Correspondence*, VIII,

that he offered the *sūbadārī* of Lahore to Lehna Singh.[4] According to contemporary reports, he succeeded in collecting cash from some of the Sikh chiefs during his invasions in 1797 and 1799.[5]

By far the large majority, however, of the rulers of the Punjab during the late eighteenth century did not pay tribute to the successors of Ahmad Shah Abdali, or to Ahmad Shah Abdali himself. This does not mean that every chief of the Punjab during this period remained independent all the time. We have already noticed how some of the hill chiefs tried to assert their superior political claims over others. Raja Ranjit Dev of Jammu is said to have successfully asserted such claims over a large number of hill principalities: Mankot, Basohli, Chenini, Kirmchi, Bandralta, Bhadarwah, Bhadu, Bhau, Dalpatpur, Samba, Tirikot, Jasrota, Riasi, Akhnur, Bhimber and Khari Khariali.[6] Frederic Drew makes the statement that the chiefs of Akhnur, Dalpatpur and Kirmchi paid tribute and rendered military service to Raja Ranjit Dev. 'During a portion of the year they would be present at Jammu itself, attending the court of the ruler and having separate ones themselves'.[7] According to Ganesh Das, the vassal chieftains used to sit on the left in the court of Ranjit Dev in order of their importance.[8]

Ranjit Dev was not the only hill chief to assert suzerain claims over others. Sansar Chand of Kangra acted as the overlord of several principalities: Guler, Kotla, Mandi, Suket, Siba, Datarpur, Kulu, Nurpur, Jaswan, and Kahlur.[9] Raj Singh of Chamba acted as the overlord of Bhadarwah and Kashtwar and his successor Jit Singh obliged the chiefs of Bhadu, Basohli, and Bandralta to pay tribute.[10] The chiefs

102 & 112. Mountstuart Elphinstone, *An Account of the Kingdom of Caubul*, II, 315.

[4] Foreign/Secret Consultation, 23 January 1797, No. 5.

[5] Ibid., 23 January 1797, No. 7. Foreign/Political Proceedings, 25 January 1799, No. 28. Mountstuart Elphinstone, *An Account of the Kingdom of Caubul*, II, 317. Ganesh Das, *Chār Bāgh-i- Panjab* (Pbi. tr.), 140.

[6] George Forster, *A Journey From Bengal to England*, I, 272-73 & 344.

[7] *The Jummoo and Kashmir Territories*, 9.

[8] *Rajdarshīnī* (Eng. tr.), 12-13.

[9] *SR Kangra* (1874), 113.

[10] Vogel, *Catalogue of Bhuri Singh Museum*, cc. 22, 32-37, 38, 40, 42, 48 & 50. Hutchison & Vogel, *Hill States*, I, 318.

of Kahlur used to get tribute from the petty chiefships known as Bara Thakurian till 1793.[11]

The non-Sikh chiefs of the plains did not have any strong regional tradition of suzerain-vassal relationship because nearly all the vassal chiefs attached to the province of Multan were outside the area under our present consideration.[12] However, there are indications that the Gakkhars and the Janjuas were treated by the Mughal emperors as vassal chiefs though the contemporary chronicles refer to them as *zamīndārs*.[13] It is interesting to note in this context that Muhammad Khan of Mankera started collecting tribute from the chiefs of Kalabagh, Isa Khel, Kulachi, Marwat, and Mangal by the early nineteenth century.[14]

Among the Sikh chiefs, there is no reference to assertion of suzerain rights over one another during the late eighteenth century. But there are numerous references to Sikh chiefs collecting tribute or asserting suzerain rights in some other way over non-Sikh chiefs, both in the hills and the plains. Jassa Singh Ahluwalia, for instance, collected tribute from Rai Ibrahim Bhatti of Kapurthala, Churh Mal of Phagwara, Rai Ahmad Khan Manj of Talwan, Dharm Das Topi of Jodhanagri, and Dayal Das and Saran Das of Jandiala.[15] Similarly, Charhat Singh Sukarchakia collected tribute from the Chatthas of Rasulnagar, Amanat Khan Jodrah of Pindi Gheb, Rai Jalal Gheba of Kot, and the Awans of Shamsabad. Among the chiefs who paid tribute to Mahan Singh were Shabt Khan Janjua of Kusak, and the chiefs of Jammu and Akhnur.[16] Hari Singh Bhangi is said to have collected tribute from the Sial chief of Jhang and the Khokhar chief of Pind Dadan Khan, and his successor Jhanda Singh, from Raja Ranjit Dev of Jammu.[17] The hill principalities of Kangra, Guler, Jaswan, Siba,

---

[11] Hutchison & Vogel, *Hill States*, II, 497.

[12] Ahsan Raza Khan, *Chieftains in the Mughal Empire*, 61-73.

[13] *Babur Nāmā* (Eng. tr.), I, 379-80 & 387. *Akbarnāma* (Eng. tr.), I, 599. *DG Dera Ismail Khan* (1883-84), 17, 30-31.

[14] Charles Masson, *Narrative of Various Journeys*, I, 71-72. *DG Dera Ismail Khan* (1883-84), 36-37, 70-74.

[15] Ram Sukh Rao, *Jassa Singh Binod* (ms), ff 76a, 93a, 95b, 96a,b, 119a, 125b, 135b, 140b, 152b, 159a, 177b, 187b, 195b, 206a, 225a,b & 230b. Lepel Griffin, *The Rajas of the Punjab*, 503-04, 511-12.

[16] Sohan Lal, *Umdat-ut-Tawārīkh* (Pbi. tr.), II, 30. Lepel Griffin, *The Panjab Chiefs*, 536, 539 & 605.

[17] George Forster, *A Journey From Bengal to England*, I, 286-87. Sohan Lal, *Umdat-ut-Tawārīkh* (Pbi. tr.), II, 11. *DG Jhang* (1883-84), 32.

Datarpur, Mandi, Nurpur, Suket, Basohli, Chamba, and Bhadarwah were obliged to accept the overlordship of Jassa Singh Ramgarhia for five years,, from 1770 to 1775, and of Jai Singh Kanhiya from 1775 to 1786. The hill chiefs of Bhimber, Khari Khariali and Akhnur accepted the suzerainty of Gujjar Singh and his successor Sahib Singh.[18] Baghel Singh Karora Singhia collected tribute from Muhammad Khan Manj of Talwan; Ran Singh Nakkai, from Jalaluddin Khan of Dipalpur; and Milkha Singh Thepuria, from the Gakkhars of Khanpur and the Afghans of Sarai Niamat Khan.[19]

Thus, we find that suzerain-vassal relationship remained an essential feature of polity in the Punjab during the late eighteenth century. The tradition being strong in the hills, it is not surprising that every powerful hill chief tried to invoke this age old institution to increase his political influence and to some extent his resources. The strength of the tradition is underlined by the fact that many of the Sikh chiefs were tempted to make use of this institution for political aggrandizement on a considerable scale. One very significant feature of the suzerain-vassal relationship was that the two rulers concerned entered into this relationship in their capacity as individuals. When a chief accepted the overlordship of another, he retained control over the government and administration of his territories.

II

Notwithstanding the common feature of suzerain-vassal relationship in the polity of the late eighteenth century Punjab, many historians have depicted Sikh polity as peculiar to themselves. Joseph Davey Cunningham, for example, characterized the late eighteenth century Sikh polity as 'theocratic confederate feudalism'. The peculiar features of this polity in his view were the meetings of the Sarbat Khalsa at Amritsar, the assembly of the chiefs termed 'Gurumatta', the 'Dal of the Khalsa' or the 'army of the theocracy of Singhs', and 'confederacies called Misals'.[20] Cunningham also refers to the system of *rākhī* or protection money collected from territories which were subdued but not

---

[18] Indu Banga, *Agrarian System of the Sikhs*, 41-42. Ganesh Das, *Chār Bāgh-i-Panjab* (Pbi. tr.), 133.

[19] *DG Rawalpindi* (1895), 52-53. *DG Jullundur* (1904), 34-35 & 77.

[20] *A History of the Sikhs*, 85, 94 & 96.

occupied by the Sikhs.[21] However, Cunningham was not the first historian to refer to these features of the late eighteenth century Sikh polity. They had figured in the works of A.L.H. Polier, George Forster, James Browne, John Malcolm, and Henry T. Prinsep. N.K. Sinha, in the twentieth century, accepts the general formulation of the late eighteenth century Sikh polity as theocratic confederate feudalism and refers to the 'Sarbat Khalsa', the 'Dal Khalsaji', the '*gurmata*', the '*misl*' and the 'Rakhi' as the features of that polity.[22] Although the historians of the Sikhs do not have the same conception or understanding of these features, it is generally assumed that the late eighteenth century Sikh polity was markedly different from the Sikh polity of the early nineteenth. That is why, whereas the reign of Ranjit Singh and his successors is treated as a monarchy, the late eighteenth century in Sikh history is referred to as the *misl* period. Nevertheless, the use of the term *misldārī* for the late eighteenth century Sikh polity does not exclude the features of polity which have been mentioned above. For a proper understanding of that polity, therefore, we have to clarify our conception of the *sarbat khālsa*, the *gurmata*, the *dal khālsa*, the *rākhī* and the *misl*.

III

That Cunningham equated *sarbat khālsa* with the entire body of the Khalsa is evident from the following statement: 'Year by year the "Sarbat Khalsa" or whole Sikh people, met once at least at Amritsar, on the occasion of the festival of the mythological Rama, when the cessation of the periodical rains rendered military operations practicable'.[23] Prinsep, however, had used the term *sarbat khālsa* for an assembly of the chiefs: 'There was generally an assembly of the chiefs called the Sarbat Khalsa, held twice a year at Amritsar during the Baisakhi and Diwali festivals which occur in April and October'.[24] N.K. Sinha looks upon the *sarbat khālsa* as a diet which acted as the central government of the Sikhs: 'The Central Government of the Sikhs during the misl period consisted of a tumultuous diet, the "Sarbat Khalsa", which met twice a year at Amritsar during the Baisakhee and the

---

21 Ibid., 95 n 1.

22 *Rise of the Sikh Power*, 57, 108-11 & 115.

23 *A History of the Sikhs*, 94.

24 *Origin of the Sikh Power*, 26.

Dewali'.[25] Thus, we find that these three historians do not have the same conception of the *sarbat khālsa.*

In its literal meaning, the term refers to the entire Khalsa, generally in a situation in which every member in theory has the right to participate in deliberations having bearing on the general interests of the Khalsa. During the 1750s and 1760s, the Khalsa used to come to Amritsar almost every year at the time of the Baisakhi and the Diwali in very large numbers. These gatherings could be referred to as the *sarbat khālsa*. It is doubtful, however, that all the members of the Khalsa participated in the deliberations at Amritsar. Nevertheless, because of the doctrine that Guruship was vested in the Khalsa Panth, as the collective body of the Khalsa, the gathering of the Khalsa at Amritsar and their deliberations did possess a mystic connotation for all the members. Though all the Sikhs were never present in Amritsar on any occasion, and all the Sikhs present did not necessarily participate in meetings, those who deliberated in the name of the *sarbat khālsa* were regarded as doing so on behalf of the entire body of the Khalsa. It is clear that the *sarbat khālsa* cannot be regarded as the central government of the Sikhs; nor can it be equated merely with the assembly of the chiefs. The *sarbat khālsa* was an ideal norm and not a formal political institution.

A similar confusion has existed with reference to the term *gurmata*. Polier regarded *gurmata* as the 'greatest council' of the Sikhs.[26] James Browne used the phrase 'Grand Diet' and Forster refers to *gurmata* as the 'grand convention' of the Sikhs.[27] Malcolm and Prinsep also use the terms 'national council' or 'special council'.[28] The Sikh historian, Ratan Singh Bhangu, writing in the early 1840s clearly refers to *mata* or *gurmata* as the decision or resolution adopted by a body of the Khalsa present at one time at a given place.[29] According to Ganda Singh, 'Mata literally means opinion or resolution, and it is called Gur-matā, opinion or resolution endorsed by the Guru because the Guru is believed to be always presiding over the deliberations of the Khalsa held in presence of the Holy Book the *Guru Granth Sahib*'.[30] It

---

[25] *Rise of the Sikh Power*, 108.

[26] Ganda Singh (ed.), *Early European Accounts of the Sikhs*, 61.

[27] Ibid., 17. George Forster, *A Journey From Bengal to England*, I, 330.

[28] John Malcolm, *Sketch of the Sikhs*, 95- 96. Prinsep, *Origin of the Sikh Power*, 71.

[29] *Prāchīn Panth Parkāsh*, 221-22, 331, 405, 407-08 & 416.

[30] Ganda Singh (ed.), *Early European Accounts of the Sikhs*, 16 n 9.

is clear that *gurmata* was not a council or a government of the Sikhs. It was a decision taken by a body of the Khalsa in a given situation in the presence of the Holy Granth. However, the term *gurmata*, that is, the decision of the Guru, was used for such resolutions not merely because of their adoption in the presence of the Holy Granth but primarily because the Guru was assumed to be present among the Khalsa. In fact, since the Khalsa during the eighteenth century subscribed to the doctrine of Guru-Panth, in certain situations even five members of the Khalsa brotherhood could act on behalf of the Khalsa. Obviously, all *gurmatas* of historical importance were not adopted at Amritsar. Also, a *gurmata* was supposed to be morally binding on those who may not even be present in the actual deliberations.

We come upon different views on the scope as well as the mode of *gurmata*. According to Malcolm, the 'gur-mata' was 'convened by the Akalis'.[31] Here again we can see that Malcolm is not thinking of *gurmata* as a resolution but as a council. Therefore, this reference to the Akalis as conveners does not make any sense. We have already noticed that all *gurmatas* were not adopted in Amritsar where the Akalis were generally assumed to be present. The context in which Ratan Singh Bhangu refers to *gurmatas* clearly suggests that whatever the place, the leaders of the Khalsa decided to meet and resolve on behalf of their followers.[32] It does not follow, however, that most of the important *gurmatas* were not adopted in Amritsar, or at the Akal Takht in Amritsar. During the eighteenth century, Amritsar had become the most important centre for the collective activities of the Khalsa. When the leaders as well as their followers, together with other Sikhs, came to visit the Golden Temple at the time of Baisakhi or Diwali, matters of importance concerning the Sikh Panth could be discussed and resolved upon. Ratan Singh Bhangu refers to four specific *gurmatas* adopted at the Akal Takht in such situations.[33]

According to N.K. Sinha, the grand diet of the Khalsa made decisions about the important expeditions to be undertaken and about matters of general concern.[34] According to Ratan Singh Bhangu, a resolution was adopted by the Khalsa at one time to get Bhai Taru Singh released from the clutches of the Mughal *faujdārs*.[35] Resolutions

---

[31] *Sketch of the Sikhs*, 95-96.

[32] *Prāchīn Panth Parkāsh*, 221-22, 331, 405, 408 & 416.

[33] Ibid., 221-22, 280, 331 & 416.

[34] *Rise of the Sikh Power*, 108.

[35] *Prāchīn Panth Parkāsh*, 280.

were passed to oust Zain Khan from Sarhind, to sack the city and to build Gurdwaras at places associated with Guru Gobind Singh's mother and his two younger sons.[36] Another *gurmata* related to a pitched battle with Ahmad Shah Abdali.[37] From these instances, it is clear that *gurmatas* related generally to political activity, to matters of defence and offence, and to the gratification of religious sentiments. Such resolutions covered temporary alliances, battles to be fought and expeditions to be undertaken. However, all the *gurmatas* did not necessarily have only an immediate effect. There is an indication in Ratan Singh Bhangu's work that *gurmatas* related also to territorial occupation.[38] This would account not only for a very large number of very small Sikh chiefs but also for the freedom of movement through the territories belonging to others.

It has been observed recently that 'the decisions which the Sikh leaders took from time to time at Amritsar were ad hoc deliberations of voluntary gathering and their scope was confined to matters concerning the preservation or augmentation of striking power; they stopped short of territorial occupation and rule'.[39] We have seen, however, that *gurmatas* were not always confined to matters concerning 'striking power'. They embraced territorial occupation sometimes.

It is true, however, that *gurmatas* stopped short of administrative arrangements. The *gurmatas* remained important only as long as the Sikhs were faced with a common enemy. After the final departure of Ahmad Shah Abdali from the Punjab, when the Sikhs became territorial chiefs, there was hardly any occasion for a united front. We do not hear of any *gurmatas* at Amritsar during the last quarter of the eighteenth century. When Zaman Shah invaded the Punjab in the last decade, the Sikh chiefs who were otherwise opposed to him found it difficult to adopt a common resolution at Amritsar or elsewhere. George Forster was already saying it in the early 1780s that the grand assembly was 'rarely summoned'.[40] The common notion that the last *gurmata* was held in 1805 does not take into account the political realities of the time and it is meaningless to blame Ranjit Singh for abolishing the institution of *gurmata*. The great days of this institution belonged to

---

36 Ibid., 405, 407 & 408.

37 Ibid., 430.

38 Ibid., 400: It was because of a *gurmata* that those who occupied a village or two were not to be ousted by a more powerful leader of the Khalsa.

39 J.S. Grewal, 'Eighteenth Century Sikh Polity', *Essays in Sikh History: From Guru Nanak to Maharaja Ranjit Singh*, 98-99.

40 *A Journey from Bengal to England*, I, 331.

the phase of territorial occupation during the 1750s and 1760s. In no case was the scope of the *gurmata* extended to arrangements for government and administration.

About the *dal khālsa*, there has been a similar lack of unanimity or clarity among the historians. According to James Browne, the *dal khālsa* was formed by Jassa Singh Ahluwalia, Charhat Singh Sukarchakia and Karora Singh during the governorship of Mir Mannu in 1748. Browne equates the *dal khālsa* with the 'Army of the State'.[41] Prinsep looks upon the *dal khālsa* as 'the joint forces of several Misals' for 'expeditions of importance or any matters of more than ordinary moment'.[42] Cunningham refers to the 'Dal of the Khalsa' as the army of the theocracy of 'Singhs' and he attributes to Jassa Singh Ahluwalia the creation of this new power.[43] N.K. Sinha refers to *dal khālsa* as the 'grand army' of the confederacy.[44] H.R. Gupta thinks of the *dal khālsa* as the 'standing national army' consisting of the 'whole body of fighting units'.[45]

If we turn to Ratan Singh Bhangu, we find that the *dal khālsa* is supposed to be constituted by two wings: the *buddha dal* and the *taruna dal*. Each of these *dals* was formed by a combination of several *misls*.[46] If we examine the actual activity of the *dal khālsa*, we get the impression that the *dal khālsa* was essentially a combination of the forces of several leaders for a specific purpose. The *dal khālsa*, therefore, was not a standing army or a single unit but a temporary combination of several units acting in concert.[47] During the 1750s and 1760s, there were many important occasions on which the leaders of the Khalsa combined to act as a collective body and therefore the actions of the *dal khālsa* during these two decades proved to be of vital importance in the history of the Sikhs. In fact, not only for defence but also for the occupation of territories, the combined action of the *dal khālsa* proved to be of great importance. However, the *dal khālsa* never became a standing army or a single unit. Our discussion in the previous chapter of the armies of the chiefs during the late eighteenth century, including the Sikh chiefs, clearly demonstrates that there was no *dal khālsa* in the

---

41 Ganda Singh (ed.), *Early European Accounts of the Sikhs*, 33.

42 *Origin of the Sikh Power*, 26.

43 *A History of the Sikhs*, 85.

44 *Rise of the Sikh Power*, 108.

45 *History of the Sikhs*, II, 90.

46 *Prāchīn Panth Parkāsh*, 400-02.

47 J.S. Grewal, 'Eighteenth Century Sikh Polity', *From Guru Nanak to Maharaja Ranjit Singh*, 98. Indu Banga, *Agrarian System of the Sikhs*, 31.

sense of a standing army or a single unit. These terms were appropriate for the army of every single chief.

Consequently, the days of the *dal khālsa* were over when no need was felt for a combined or a joint action. When Timur Shah invaded Multan to recover it from Desa Singh Bhangi, no Sikh chief went to the latter's assistance.[48] In fact, after the occupation of territories each Sikh chief used his discretion as to whether or not he should combine his forces with another chief for any purpose.[49] In the last decade of the eighteenth century, when Zaman Shah invaded the Punjab, the Sikh chiefs did not form the *dal khālsa* to give him battle, though some of them did join their forces in self-interest.[50] The *dal khālsa* played an important role precisely during the phase in which the *gurmatas* remained operative. Indeed, the *gurmata* and the *dal khālsa* were the reverse and the obverse of the same political coin. Just as the former refers to a resolution of the Khalsa present at a given time and place upon a matter of common concern, the latter refers to the joint action of the Khalsa to put the resolution into effect.

IV

Writing in the 1770s, Polier noticed that the Sikhs had come into possession of 'the whole *soubah* of Lahore, the greatest part of that of Multan and part of that of Delhi, including all the country called Punjab'. At this time, the Sikh chiefs used to collect a certain yearly tribute from some areas of the Delhi and Agra provinces which were not in their possession. This tribute, according to Polier, was called *răcky* that is, *rākhī*. Polier goes on to say that 'in general a trifle will satisfy them, from two to five per cent on the revenues, particularly if at a distance; and provided this is regularly paid, it is said no further hindrance or molestation will be received from them. On the contrary the chief, to whom the tribute or *răcky* is paid, takes the district under

---

48 *Calender of Persian Correspondence*, V, No. 1843.

49 Ganda Singh (ed.), *Early European Accounts of the Sikhs*, 61, 99, 102-03.

50 Foreign/Political Consultation, 2 January 1797, No. 24; 20 February 1797, No. 52; 25 January 1799, Nos. 26-27. Foreign/Secret Consultation, 23 January 1797, No. 7. Foreign/Political Proceedings, 11 January 1799, No. 30. Ganda Singh (ed.), *Early European Accounts of the Sikhs*, 103.

his protection and is ready to fight against any of the brethren who might think of disturbing it'.[51]

James Browne reinforces this idea of *rākhī*, adding at the same time a significant dimension to the situation. 'In the districts not reduced to their absolute subjection, but into which they make occasional incursions, they levy a tribute which they call Raukey, and which is about one fifth (as the Marhatta Chout is one fourth) of the annual rent; whenever a Zamindar has agreed to pay this tribute to any Sick chief, that chief not only himself refrains from plundering him, but will protect him from all others; and this protection is by general consent held so far sacred that even if the grand army passes through a Zamindary where the safe guards of the lowest Sick chief are stationed, it will not violate them'.[52] There is a suggestion in this description that there was a consensus among the Sikh chiefs regarding the imposition of *rākhī*. Prinsep refers to the collection of *rākhī* on the basis of *gurmatas*.[53] Cunningham also states that *rākhī* was collected from tracts which were subdued but not occupied by the Sikhs.[54] Both Prinsep and Cunningham refer to it as 'Black Mail', but Cunningham was aware that the literal meaning of *rākhī* is protection and therefore, the amount levied was 'in a higher sense tribute'.[55]

N.K. Sinha simply repeats the ideas expressed by the early European writers. H.R. Gupta, however, takes a more serious view of the system of *rākhī*: 'The Sikhs offered a plan to the villages individually. The villagers were to place themselves under the protection of the Dal Khalsa on a promise to pay one-fifth of their income twice a year in May and October, at the end of each harvest, Asarhi and Saoni, known also as Rabi and Kharif. The Sikhs in return were to afford them full protection against plunder, theft or molestation of any other kind either by themselves or by their neighbours and Government troops'.[56] Elsewhere H.R. Gupta appears to think of this system of *rākhī* as a definite phase in the political career of the Sikhs, a

---

[51] Ganda Singh (ed.), *Early European Accounts of the Sikhs*, 62.

[52] Ibid., 16 & 100.

[53] *Origin of the Sikh Power*, 26.

[54] *A History of the Sikhs*, 95 n 1.

[55] Prinsep, *Origin of the Sikh Power*, 26. Cunningham, *A History of the Sikhs*, 95 n 1.

[56] *History of the Sikhs*, II, 127. N.K. Sinha, *Rise of the Sikh Power*, 115.

step that 'supplied them with the idea of raising themselves into territorial chieftains'.[57]

It has been observed recently that the system of *rākhī* did serve as a prelude to annexation but *rākhī* as a system was not a definite phase in the political history of the Sikhs. 'Territorial occupation and *rākhī* could be established by one and the same chief at one and the same time in two different areas. Rakhi was thus a transitional arrangement existing side by side with territorial occupation. The areas once brought under *rākhī* were often, but not always, actually occupied and directly administered sooner or later'.[58] However, we may agree with H.R. Gupta that *rākhī* signified the Sikh chief's claim to a part of the produce from land in return for protection against all other claimants.

We have already seen that some of the contemporary European observers saw the system of *rākhī* in operation in the Ganga-Jamuna Doab in the 1770s. There is documentary evidence to suggest that territorial occupation by the Sikhs in the province of Lahore had started in the early 1750s.[59] It is obvious, therefore, that the system of *rākhī* was not a phase prior to territorial occupation. Nevertheless, it can be emphasised that the system of *rākhī*, like the *gurmata* and the *dal khālsa*, played its most important role during the 1750s and 1760s. With the increasing striking power of the Sikhs, and the institutions of the *gurmata* and the *dal khālsa*, it became increasingly possible for the Sikh leaders to provide effective protection to those who agreed to pay a part of the revenues to them. The system of *rākhī* became popular not only because the cultivators had to pay a much smaller part of their produce as revenue or *rākhī* but also because they felt increasingly reassured that they were safe against others who might demand the revenues from them. The system of *rākhī*, thus, became an important instrument of establishing political control over a large part of the Punjab. However, in the areas which were not eventually occupied, collection of *rākhī* could appear to be merely 'plundering raids'.

---

[57] *History of the Sikhs*, II, 128. Bhagat Singh, *Sikh Polity in the Eighteenth and Nineteenth Centuries*, 82. Sita Ram Kohli, *Sunset of the Sikh Empire*, 5.

[58] Indu Banga, *Agrarian System of the Sikhs*, 27-28.

[59] Jai Singh Kanhiya started using his seal for formal orders in A.D. 1750: B.N. Goswamy and J.S. Grewal, *The Mughals and the Jogis of Jakhbar*, Documents XXV & XVIII-XXIX.

V

The most important unit of Sikh polity during the late eighteenth century is generally believed to be the *misl*. It is interesting to note, however, that Polier, George Forster, James Browne and John Malcolm do not use the term *misl*. This was noted by Cunningham when he pointed out that Prinsep was 'the first who perceived and pointed out the Sikh system of "Misals" '. Cunningham also commented on 'the uncertainty and irregularity natural to the system of "Misals" and indeed to all powers in process of change or development'.[60] According to Cunningham, there was no justification for 'making the Nishanias and Shahids regular Misals'.[61] Thus, Cunningham was a little sceptical about the system called the 'Misal system'. Nevertheless, he accepted the notion that the entire Punjab in the 1760s was divided among the twelve *misls* enumerated by Prinsep.[62]

Prinsep's description of the *misls* is as follows: 'The Sardars or chiefs of the Sikh nation had been followed into the field by relations, friends and volunteers and not ordinarily by hired retainers. Most of these looked upon themselves as partners and associates in each enterprize, and regarded the lands now acquired as a common property in which each was to have his share, according to the degree in which he might have contributed to the acquisition. The associations were called Misals, implying that they were confederacies of equals, under chiefs of their own selection. The chief was to lead in war, and act as arbiter in peace: he was respected and treated with deference by the inferior Sardars, but these owned no obligation to obey, beyond what they might consider to be for their own reciprocal benefit or for the well being of the Misal'.[63] The twentieth century historians like N.K. Sinha and H.R. Gupta have merely assumed the correctness of Prinsep's understanding of the *misl*.[64]

However, if we turn to near contemporary evidence, the concept of the *misl* and *misldār* is not very clear. Ahmad Shah of Batala writing in the 1820s uses the term *misl* but without defining it. According to him, there were more than four or five hundred *sardārs* but pre-eminent for their armies, followers and territories were only a few groups. He

---

60 *A History of the Sikhs*, 97 n 1.

61 Ibid., 97 n 2.

62 Ibid., 96.

63 *Origin of the Sikh Power*, 23.

64 N.K. Sinha, *Rise of the Sikh Power*, 57-61. H.R. Gupta, *History of the Sikhs*, II, 91-92.

refers to *sardār* and *misldār* in terms which make the latter clearly subordinate to the former. In other words, a number of *misldārs* were subordinate to a single *sardār*.[65] The evidence of Ahmad Shah of Batala suggests that the *sardār* and his associate *misldārs* made joint conquests and partitioned among themselves the territories they conquered. Each *misldār* made his own administrative arrangements without reference to another *misldār*, or even to the *sardār*. For administrative purposes, therefore, there was no difference between the *sardār* and the *misldār*.[66] From this it appears, as suggested by Prinsep, that for the purpose of territorial occupation, a number of the leaders of the Khalsa could combine their forces voluntarily, accepting the leadership of one in a given situation.[67]

For further clarification, we may examine the position of a few so- called *misls*. The label of 'Bhangi', for instance, is used for Hari Singh, Jhanda Singh, Ganda Singh, Charhat Singh, Desa Singh, Gulab Singh and Gurdit Singh. They all belonged to the family of Hari Singh and succeeded to chiefship one after the other until Gurdit Singh was ousted from Amritsar by Ranjit Singh in the first decade of the nineteenth century. Obviously, they formed a dynasty of chiefs. There were eight other chiefs who are believed to have been associated with the 'Bhangis', namely Lehna Singh of Lahore, Gujjar Singh of Lahore and Gujrat, Karam Singh Dulu of Chiniot, Milkha Singh of Rawalpindi, Karam Singh Man of Mananwala, Gurbakhsh Singh of Doda, Sanwal Singh Randhawa of Chamiari and Dhanna Singh Kalalwala of Bhera. None of these chiefs was related to Hari Singh 'Bhangi' and they were not related to one another either. Each respectively was succeeded by Chait Singh, Sahib Singh, Jassa Singh, Jiwan Singh, Ram Singh, Suddh Singh, Nar Singh, and Jodh Singh, forming altogether eight dynasties of rulers. Indeed, the principle of hereditary succession was well recognized by all the Sikh chiefs during the late eighteenth century. It may be interesting to add here that the label 'Bhangi' is also used for some other chiefs who actually had no formal connection with the chiefs mentioned above. These chiefs were Bagh Singh of Hallowal, Karam Singh Chhina of Firozke and Sahib Singh, Jiwan Singh, Natha Singh and Mohar Singh, all of Sialkot. The

---

[65] Ahmad Shah, *Tārīkh-i-Panjab* (Pbi. tr.), 38.

[66] J.S. Grewal, 'Ahmad Shah of Batala on Sikh Polity', *From Guru Nanak to Maharaja Ranjit Singh*, 89-90. Indu Banga, *Agrarian System of the Sikhs*, 32-33.

[67] *Origin of the Sikh Power*, 23.

only possibility that remains is that some of these chiefs collaborated for territorial occupation.[68] Taken together, their territorial possessions in the Bari, Rachna, Chaj and the Sindh Sagar Doabs were almost contiguous, a pattern which suggests that there was perhaps some kind of an association between them for the purpose of conquest. There are some references to close co-operation between two or more of the chiefs called 'Bhangi'.[69]

At the same time, there are several references to the association of 'Bhangi' chiefs with some other Sikh chiefs.[70] Before the end of the eighteenth century, some of the 'Bhangi' chiefs entered into alliance even with non-Sikh chiefs.[71] The chiefs of the second generation at any rate were entirely independent in their relations with other chiefs, whether Sikh or non-Sikh. Furthermore, at no time was any 'Bhangi' chief subordinate to Hari Singh Bhangi or any of his successors. We have already seen that every chief made administrative arrangements within his territories independently of others. This would also be evident from their alienation of land revenue in *jāgīr* and *dharmarth*.[72] Thus, each of the 'Bhangi' chiefs was as much autonomous in his internal administration as in his political relations with others.

This was true as much of the chiefs called 'Kanhiya', 'Dallewalia', and 'Nakkai' as of the 'Bhangis'. The case of the 'Nakkais', in fact, is rather interesting. The family of Gogera and the family of Bharwal had no relationship with one another. They did not associate with each other at any stage. In fact, they fought against each other on several occasions. The apparent justification for using the term Nakkai lies in the fact that the original villages of the founders of these principalities were in the region called Nakka in the south of Lahore.

---

68 Veena Sachdeva, 'The Rule of the Bhangis (1765- 1810)', 7-58.

69 The invasion on the territory of the Sial chief was made jointly by Hari Singh Bhangi and Karam Singh Dulu. Whereas Hari Singh imposed tribute on Inayat Ullah Khan, Karam Singh took Chiniot as his share. Similarly, Sialkot was invaded by four 'Bhangi' chiefs who later divided it. Lahore too was conquered jointly by Gujjar Singh and Lehna Singh.

70 It has already been noticed that the Chaj and the Sindh Sagar Doabs were jointly invaded by Gujjar Singh and Charhat Singh Sukarchakia who later partitioned the conquered territory.

71 Jhanda Singh Bhangi, for instance, went to assist Raja Ranjit Dev of Jammu against the combination of Charhat Singh Sukarchakia, Jai Singh Kanhiya, Haqiqat Singh and Brij Raj Dev. Veena Sachdeva, 'The Rule of the Bhangis (1765-1810)', 24-25.

72 Ibid., 69-81.

But this fact has no bearing on polity. In the case of the 'Ahluwalias' and the 'Ramgarhias', no associates of the founders are mentioned at any stage in their history.[73] Furthermore, there are several chiefs who are not known to have associated with any of the '*misls*' enumerated by the historians. Among these chiefs were Sobha Singh Sandhu of Lahore, Jodh Singh Saurianwala, Nidhan Singh Daskewala, Sahib Singh Virk of Shaikhupura, Arbel Singh Sidhu, Nahar Singh Man, Sahaj Singh Bhangu of Makhowal, Karam Singh of Povind and Lal Singh of Kanganpur. They occupied territories on their own and they were totally independent chiefs.

Thus, we find that the term '*misl*' in its application to the Sikh polity of the late eighteenth century does not possess the kind of significance which is attributed to it. Every Sikh chief in theory, and the majority in practice, was entirely independent of others in the internal administration of territories and political relations. Many of the chiefs occupied territories without associating themselves with others. Those who joined forces for conquest did not extend their association to the realm of politics, government and administration after territorial occupation. Just as the *gurmata*, the *dal khālsa* and the *rākhī* proved to be important instruments of territorial occupation, so did the combination of two or more leaders. But to refer to such combinations, or '*misls*', in terms suggestive of political units is without justification. The term *misldārī* system carries little meaning for the polity of the Sikh chiefs during the late eighteenth century.

VI

The coins struck by the Sikh chiefs during the late eighteenth century are generally believed to have a peculiar bearing on their polity. Cunningham, for instance, says that the Sikh chiefs assembled at Amritsar in 1765 and 'proclaimed their own sway and the prevalence of their faith, by striking a coin with an inscription to the effect that Guru Gobind Singh had received from Nanak "Deg, Tegh and Fath", or Grace, Power and Rapid Victory'.[74] Cunningham was basing himself on the

---

[73] It is interesting to note in this connection that Jassa Singh Ahluwalia and Khushal Singh were at one stage associated with Nawab Kapur Singh but subsequently each of them came to be treated as the leader of a separate *misl*, namely the Ahluwalia and the Faizullapuria or Singhpuria.

[74] *A History of the Sikhs*, 93-94.

earlier European writers. According to James Browne, after the expulsion of the functionaries of Ahmad Shah Abdali from the Punjab, the Sikhs held a 'general Diet' at Amritsar, 'in which they determined to call in the rupees which were struck in the name of Jessa Kalal, and to strike them for the future in the name of their Gooroos, with an inscription to this effect, "Gooroo Gobind Singh received from Nanuck the Daig, the sword and rapid victory", which coin is current throughout their dominions to this day'.[75] N.K. Sinha refers to the coins of 1765 as struck by 'the Sikh Commonwealth'.[76] He argues at length that no coin could have been struck by Jassa Singh Ahluwalia. Indeed, for a Sikh chief to strike a coin in his own name, according to N.K. Sinha, was to be 'selfish and undemocratic'.[77] Thus the coin struck by the Sikh chiefs at Lahore in 1765 is regarded as the declaration of the collective sovereignty of the Khalsa.

The absence of the name of any chief in the inscriptions of the Sikh coins is the strongest presumption in support of the view that the Sikh coins symbolized collective sovereignty. Indeed, every Mughal ruler of India had struck a coin in his own name. In fact, some of their vassal chiefs also struck coins in the name of their suzerain. It was in this context that Ranjit Dev of Jammu minted a coin in the name of Shah Alam.[78] At a later stage, Ranjit Dev struck coins in his own name, which may be taken as a declaration of his sovereign status.[79] When Ahmad Shah Abdali invaded the Punjab in 1748, he struck his own coin at Lahore.[80] Subsequently, he struck coins from the mints in Multan, Lahore, Sindh, Kashmir and Sarhind. He issued coins from Lahore for several years before 1765, and also after 1765.[81] We can see, therefore, that Ahmad Shah Abdali was trying to declare from time to time that his writ ran in the Punjab. In this context, the Sikh coin of 1765 may certainly be treated as a declaration that political power had passed into the hands of the Sikhs.

This impression is reinforced by the fact that all the new rulers of the Punjab during the late eighteenth century did not strike their own

---

[75] Ganda Singh (ed.), *Early European Accounts of the Sikhs*, 40-41.

[76] *Rise of the Sikh Power*, 55.

[77] Ibid., 54-56 n 3.

[78] C.J. Rodgers, 'Some Coins of Ranjit Deo, King of Jammu a Hundred Years Ago', *Journal of the Asiatic Society of Bengal*, LIV (1885), Part I, 64.

[79] Ibid., 65-66.

[80] C.J. Rodgers, 'The Coins of Ahmad Shah Abdali', *Ibid.*, 69.

[81] Ibid., 69-71.

coins. We do not come upon any coins of the non-Sikh chiefs of the Punjab. In all probability, they went on using the coins issued in the name of the Afghan rulers of Kabul after the death of Ahmad Shah Abdali. Even the Sikh chiefs of Patiala, Nabha and Jind struck coins in the name of Ahmad Shah Abdali.[82] The coin struck at Lahore,which bears the names of Guru Nanak and Guru Gobind Singh in the inscription rather than that of any potentate, does underline its peculiar significance.[83]

However, to draw the inference that coins struck at Lahore in 1765 symbolized the declaration of the collective sovereignty of the Khalsa is not so obvious. It is true that this Gobind Shāhī coin became current in the Punjab, covering the dominions of many Sikh chiefs. However, all the coins were not minted at Lahore. In fact, in 1778, a new mint was established at Amritsar to strike coins which bore a totally different inscription and which came to be known as Nanak Shāhī coins and which eventually replaced the Gobind Shāhī.[84] It is

---

[82] Ibid., 75. Lepel Griffin, *The Rajas of the Punjab*, 313-14, 316.

[83] The inscription was:

دیگ و تیغ و فتح و نصرت بیدرنگ
یافت از نانک گورو گوبند سنگھ

On the reverse were the words:

ضرب دار السلطنت لاہور
سمت ۱۸۲۲ میمنت مانوس

The Sikh chiefs struck similar coins at Lahore in the years 1766, 1767, 1768, 1769, 1770, 1771, 1773, 1774, 1775, 1776 & 1777. C.J. Rodgers, 'On the Coins of the Sikhs', *Journal of the Asiatic Society of Bengal* (1881), 79; 'The Coins of Ahmad Shah Abdali', *Journal of the Asiatic Society of Bengal* (1885), 75.

[84] It has the following verse inscribed on it:

سکہ زد بر ہر دو عالم تیغ نانک واہب است
فتح گوبند سنگھ شاہ شاہان فضل سچا صاحب است

On the reverse were the words:

ضرب سری امرت سر
جلوس تخت اکال بخت سمت ۱۸۳۵

C.J. Rodgers, 'On the Coins of the Sikhs', *Journal of the Asiatic Society of Bengal* (1881), 80. For similar coins struck at Amritsar in the years, 1779, 1780, 1781, 1784 and 1797, ibid., 80-82.

interesting to note that the inscription of neither the Gobind Shāhī nor the Nanak Shāhī coin was an original composition. The former had been used by Banda Bahadur on his seal and the latter on his coin.[85] This would explain the acceptability of these coins in the dominions of the Sikh chiefs. We have already seen that the individual chief acted independently of others in his relations with outside powers and in the internal administration of his territories. Even if the inscriptions on the coins were meant to indicate that sovereignty was derived from the Gurus and God, the coin enabled each individual chief to assert his independence of any temporal lord. He was, 'a sovereign ruler not in spite of the coin but because of it'.[86]

Indeed, the contention that the inscriptions on the Sikh coins symbolized collective sovereignty has the status of an assumption that remains unsupported by evidence. If we turn to the available seals of the late eighteenth century Sikh chiefs, we find that in the seals too the help of God is invoked but the name of the chief is mentioned.[87] In other words, the Sikh chief did not mind issuing orders in his own name. We also notice that the epithet Khalsaji was used for the individual chief, as for Charhat Singh Sukarchakia, Gulab Singh Bhangi, Sada Kaur, Milkha Singh of Rawalpindi, Gulab Singh Khaira, Bagh Singh Hallowalia, Nar Singh Chamiariwala and Sahib Singh Randhawa.[88] The chief was also referred to as Singh Sahib, like Gujjar Singh and Sahib Singh Bhangi, Mahan Singh Sukarchakia and Jai Singh Kanhiya.[89] The term Sarkar too was used for several of the Sikh chiefs: Gujjar Singh Bhangi, Jai Singh Kanhiya, Haqiqat Singh and Jaimal Singh, Jodh Singh Saurianwala and Nar Singh Chamiariwala as

---

[85] Ganda Singh, *Baba Banda Singh Bahadur*, 9.

[86] Indu Banga, *Agrarian System of the Sikhs*, 36.

[87] In the orders of Hakumat Singh, Jai Singh, Gurbakhsh Singh (Sada Kaur), Amar Singh, Bhag Singh and Sahib Singh, we can see their seals with Akāl Sahāi and the name of the concerned chief on it: B.N. Goswamy & J.S. Grewal, *The Pindori Documents*, XVIII- XXXII. For the seal of Bhag Singh, *The Jogis of Jakhbar*, XVII.

[88] B.N. Goswamy & J.S. Grewal, *The Pindori Documents*, XXIX-XXXI. Foreign/Political Proceedings, 22 March 1856, No. 130; 1 May 1856, No. 419; 11 July 1856, No. 208; 5 September 1856, No. 111; 5 December 1856, No. 217; 1 May 1857, Nos. 416 & 419.

[89] B.N. Goswamy & J.S. Grewal, *The Pindori Documents*, XXXII. Ganesh Das, *Early Nineteenth Century Panjab* (Eng. tr.), 17. Foreign/ Political Proceedings, 11 July 1856, No. 219.

well as for Qutbuddin Khan of Qasur.[90] In combination, the two terms produced the phrase Sarkar Khalsaji and was used for Jodh Singh Ramgarhia.[91] This was the legacy that Ranjit Singh kept alive.

VII

In retrospect we can see that an important feature of the late eighteenth century polity of the Punjab was the survival of the idea of suzerain-vassal relationship. Whereas the suzerainty of the Mughal emperors was nominally recognized in many parts of the country, the new rulers of the Punjab did not recognize the Mughals as their suzerains. For sometime suzerainty was claimed by Ahmad Shah Abdali. His successors too did not relinquish their claims over the Punjab, and in the absence of a direct control they tried to assert suzerain claims over the indigenous rulers of the Punjab, though with decreasing success. What was more significant, however, the new rulers themselves started asserting superior political authority over one another. In the plains as well as the hills, among the Sikh and the non-Sikh chiefs, the more powerful rulers were successful in obliging some others to pay annual tribute to them as the hall mark of their subordination. Crucial to the suzerain-vassal relationship was the autonomy of thc individual chief. Whether sovereign or subordinate, he remained in full control of the administration of his territory.

The administrative arrangements made by all the chiefs of the Punjab during the late eighteenth century clearly reinforce the view that political power was vested in the individual chief. It is in this context that a reappraisal of the institution of the *gurmata*, the *dal khālsa*, the *rākhī* and the *misl* become obligatory for the historian of the Punjab. All these institutions played a vital role in the political history of the Sikhs, particularly in the 1750s and the 1760s. It is difficult to imagine that ordinary people could have risen into political power without these institutions. But these institutions did not have any

---

90 B.N. Goswamy & J.S. Grewal, *The Pindori Documents*, XXV. Foreign/Political Proceedings, 7 January 1853, No. 234; 3 June 1853, No.119; 4 July 1856, No. 152; 11 July 1856, No. 208; 29 August 1853, No. 250.

91 Foreign/Political Proceedings, 13 August 1852, No. 49. Ganesh Das is not off the mark when he uses the term Badshah for Hari Singh, Jhanda Singh, and Ganda Singh and for Jassa Singh Ahluwalia: Ganesh Das, *Early Nineteenth Century Panjab* (Eng. tr.), 16.

significant bearing on the polity of the Sikh chiefs after they had occupied territories and started ruling over them. The coins struck by the Sikhs have to be seen in this light. The invocation of the grace of the Gurus enabled each individual chief to be sovereign in his own place. This was in conformity with the general belief of the Khalsa during the eighteenth century that Guru Gobind Singh had prophesied a kingdom for every horseman.

6

LAND REVENUE, JĀGĪRS AND DHARMARTH

In the work of the contemporary European writers on the Sikhs, there is rather meagre and cursory information on agrarian production or agrarian relations. Writing in the 1770s, Polier observed that the possessions of the Sikh chiefs were 'exceedingly well cultivated, populous and rich'. He also observed that the revenues were generally collected in kind and not in money, an arrangement favourable to the cultivators. Six or seven years later, George Forster referred to the large revenues of the extensive and fertile territories of the Sikhs. Without precise information on the revenues of the Sikh times, Forster thought that there was 'no great decrease in the revenues collected during the reign of Aurangzeb'. James Browne referred to 'a state of high cultivation' in the Sikh territories and added that the 'rent' was moderate and the cultivator was never molested. In the 1790s, John Griffiths referred to grains, cotton, indigo, jaggery, and a variety of fruits produced in the Punjab. Towards the end of the eighteenth century, William Francklin stated that grain in the Punjab was cheaper than in any other part of India. He also referred to the abundance of sugarcane, wheat, barley, rice, pulses of all sorts, tobacco, and various fruits produced in the Punjab which was also well supplied with cattle. Writing in the early nineteenth century, Malcolm referred to one half of the produce taken by the chiefs as revenue but added that the chief never levies the whole of his share; and 'in no country, perhaps, is the Rayat, or cultivator, treated with more indulgence'.[1]

Henry Prinsep does not talk about agricultural production but he does talk about tenures which involved agrarian relations. According to him, there were four kinds of tenures in the territories of the Sikhs:

---

[1] George Foster, *A Journey from Bengal to England*, I, 336-37. Ganda Singh (ed.), *Early European Accounts of the Sikhs*, 17, 93, 101-02 & 336-37. John Malcolm, *Sketch of the Sikhs*, 125-26.

pattidārī, *misldārī*, *tābadārī* and *jāgīrdārī*. The first two related actually to arrangements between the larger and the smaller chiefs. The two latter referred to the system of *jāgīrs*. Prinsep also added that, as in the rest of the country, in the territories of the Sikh chiefs one could find 'religious and charitable appropriations and grants, those made to Sikh Gurus, Sodhis and Bedis or to endowments for temples and for charitable distribution of alms, and sometimes even to Musalman Pirzadas'.[2]

Among the twentieth century historians, N.K. Sinha merely repeats less than what we find in the early European writers and H.R. Gupta adds small bits of information without adding anything to our understanding of agricultural production and agrarian relations during the late eighteenth century in the territories of the Sikh chiefs.[3] In the light of the recent study of the agrarian history of medieval India, we can see that the early European writers provide meagre but significant information on the subject. Besides general agrarian prosperity and adequate revenues, they refer to the low rates of assessment, the collection in kind, the major produce from land, the *jāgīrdārī* system and the alienation of revenues for charitable purpose.

Indeed, in a recent study of the agrarian system of the Sikhs, it has been shown that *batāī* and *kankūt* were the most prevalent methods of assessment in the Sikh dominions. Cash rates were charged on wells and ploughs and certain crops were assessed in cash in some areas. Cash rates per unit area were limited to a few crops. The rates of assessment varied from place to place and from time to time but they were generally lower than what they had been in the Mughal times. The cultivators were encouraged to extend cultivation. The *jāgīrdārī* system under the Sikh rulers closely resembled the one prevalent earlier and *dharmarth* grants formed even a more important feature of the state patronage now than earlier. There were proprietary and tenant cultivators in the Sikh dominions as in the Mughal provinces of Lahore and Multan.[4] Thus, we find that in spite of the political change, there was a large degree of continuity in the system of agricultural production, agrarian relations and land tenures. We have already noticed that the degree of politico-administrative change in the non-Sikh principalities was smaller than in the Sikh principalities. Therefore, we may expect

---

2 *Origin of the Sikh Power*, 27-29.

3 N.K. Sinha, *Rise of the Sikh Power*, 112-13, 114-15. H.R. Gupta, *History of the Sikhs*, IV, 363-72.

4 Indu Banga, *Agrarian System of the Sikhs*, 88 & 187.

greater continuity in the system of agrarian production, agrarian relations and land tenures in the territories of the non-Sikh chiefs. With these observations, we may now turn to available information on the subject.

I

During the Mughal period, three major methods of assessment were used, namely *kankūt*, *batāī* and *zabt*. The first involved the assessment of the share of the government on the basis of standing crop before it was harvested; the second involved the division of crop after harvesting; and the third involved cash assessment per unit area. In the Punjab as a whole, the system of *zabt* was the most prevalent during the early eighteenth century, followed by *batāī* and *kankūt*. The collection of revenue in the case of *kankūt* was generally made in cash and even in the case of *batāī*, the share of the government could be sold at the spot. The rate of assessment for *kankūt* and *batāī* was generally one-half and the rate in the case of *zabt* was generally about 40 per cent of the estimated yield.[5]

Turning to the late eighteenth century, we find that all the three systems of *kankūt*, *batāī* and *zabt* prevailed in the hill principalities. Batāī, for instance, was prevalent in the territories of Jammu and Guler; *kankūt* was prevalent in Jaswan and Nurpur; and *zabt* as well as *kankūt* was prevalent in Kangra and Chamba. The revenue in the hill principalities was collected both in cash and kind.[6] Similarly, in some of the non-Sikh principalities for which evidence is available, all the three methods of assessment were current: *batāī* in Mankera, Shahpur, Pakpatan and Multan, *kankūt* in Pindi Gheb, Kot, Rawalpindi and Jhang, and *zabt* in Muzaffargarh. It may be pointed out, however, that the *zabt* system was applied in the hills as well as in the plains of the Punjab only to crops like sugarcane, cotton, tobacco, and perishable crops. It must be added here that in some of the non-Sikh principalities like Multan and Pakpatan, revenues on cash crops like indigo and

[5] Irfan Habib, *Agrarian System of Mughal India*, 193, 219-20, 222-23 & 237. Noman Ahmad Siddiqi, *Land Revenue Administration*, 47-48, 56 & 58.

[6] *SR Kangra* (1889), 50. *SR Sialkot* (1865), 51. Ranjit Dev of Jammu, for instance, always collected revenues in kind. But in the Kangra hills, revenue was collected in cash as well as in kind: *SR Sialkot* (1865), 51. *DG Kangra* (1883-84), 212. Hutchison & Vogel, *Hill States*, I, 68.

cotton too were collected in kind. Therefore, almost everywhere the revenue was collected in both cash and kind.[7] This was also the position in the Sikh territories. In Lahore and Sialkot, for instance, *batāī* was the prevalent method and in Kapurthala *kankūt* and *zabt* as well as *batāī*.[8] About the rate of assessment, only in a few places it is mentioned as one-half; generally it was less, going down to even one-fifth or one-sixth of the produce.[9] This variation in the rates of assessment from region to region was due to differences in the condition of the soil, mode of irrigation and the expense of cultivation.

If we turn to the early nineteenth century, we find that *batāī* and *kankūt* were more important than *zabt*. In fact, the system of *zabt* was limited to a few crops. The government share in *batāī* and *kankūt* could be commuted into cash only if the cultivator agreed. The rate of assessment on the average was two-fifth.[10] Thus, there was a clear shift towards *batāī* and *kankūt* and a lower rate of assessment. The evidence which we have on the late eighteenth century suggests that this shift had largely taken place.

Before the division of the crop between the state and the cultivator, deductions were made for the expenses of cultivation and on account of *pachotra* or the five per cent share of the *chaudharī* or the *muqaddam*. On the other hand weighman's fees and carriage were charged from the cultivator, besides some other cesses. The share of the government in the case of indigo was assessed in cash per maund. This share was called *moghla* and was prevalent under the Bahawalpur chiefs. It was generally fixed at five rupees per maund. The rate varied

---

[7] *SR Googaira* (1860), 33 & 41-42. *SR Rawalpindi* (1865), 67, 75 & 154. *SR Shahpur* (1866), 78. *DG Multan* (1883-84), 24 & 165. *SR Muzaffargarh* (1882), 83.

[8] *SR Sialkot* (1865), 52. *DG Lahore* (1883-84), 129. *DG Jullundur and Kapurthala State* (1904), 27. *SR of the Narowal Pargana of Amritsar District* (1860), 156.

[9] Sansar Chand of Kangra, Gujjar Singh of Gujrat, Jassa Singh Ahluwalia and the rulers of Sialkot collected one-half as revenues. Ranjit Dev of Jammu collected one-third, and the Sial chiefs of Jhang and the rulers of Lahore collected one-fourth as their share. In the lower Sindh Sagar Doab, one-fifth or one-sixth of the produce was collected by the chiefs of Mankera and Bahawalpur: *SR Gujrat* (1861), 46. *SR Sialkot* (1865), 51-52. *SR Jhang* (1882), 6 & 113. *SR Muzaffargarh* (1882), 83. *DG Kangra* (1883-84), 212. *DG Lahore* (1884), 129.

[10] Indu Banga, *Agrarian System of the Sikhs*, 88-117.

according to the market price.[11] A grazing tax called *tirnī* was collected from pastoral tribes. The *tirnī* tax was common in the lower parts of the Doabs where irrigation facilities were scarce and a large proportion of land was lying waste. Even the cultivators who kept large number of camels and herds of cattle paid *tirnī*. This tax was not inconsiderable, for the Nakkai chief of Gogera is said to have collected nearly 60,000 rupees a year from the Sayyadwala area.[12]

Some other cesses in addition to land revenue were also collected in certain areas. These were *hak-buha*, *tik* and *ghiana*. A house tax called *hak-buha* or *ghardwaru* used to be collected from the *kamins* and non-proprietary residents of villages. In Mankera, Lodhran and Multan, a tax called *tik* was taken by the non-Sikh chiefs at a rate of two to four rupees per thirtytwo maunds of grain. In the hills, the owners of cows and buffaloes who did not pay *tirnī* tax used to pay a cess called *ghiana* which was always paid in clarified butter (*ghee*).[13] Relevant information on all the principalities is not available but there is no reason to doubt the general prevalence of cesses and taxes in addition to the land revenue. Perhaps, the practices of the Mughal times were either not discarded or they were revived.

The important *rabi* crops were wheat, barley, gram, tobacco, fodder, and vegetables. The important *kharīf* crops were maize, rice, sugarcane, pulses, cotton, and turmeric. Several additional crops were grown in some areas in both the harvests, like indigo in Multan and Muzaffargarh, and fruits in the hills as well as the plains. Multan was known for its date trees.[14]

---

[11] *SR Muzaffargarh* (1882-83), 83. *DG Gujrat* (1883-84), 58. *SR Rawalpindi* (1865), 67.

[12] *SR Jhang* (1882), 161. G.W. Hamilton, 'On the Tirnī Tax of Jhung', *Selections from Public Correspondence*, October 1851, 104. In Chiniot, *tirnī* tax was imposed by Jassa Singh Dulu and at first the collections amounted to 5,000 rupees only: *DG Jhang* (1883-84), 155-56. *SR Shahpur* (1866), 73, 79 & 111. *SR Muzaffargarh* (1882), 83. *DG Kangra* (1883-84), 217. *DG Montgomery* (1883-84), 174. *DG Chenab Colony* (1904), 20.

[13] *SR Sialkot* (1865), 51. *DG Kangra* (1883-84), 217. *SR Rawalpindi* (1865), 67. *SR Muzaffargarh* (1882), 83. *SR Siba* (1882), 3 & 19.

[14] Moorcraft & Trebeck, *Travels in the Himalayan Provinces of Hindustan and the Punjab*, II, 303. *SR Sialkot* (1865), 19. *SR Gujrat* (1861), 94. *SR Jullundar* (1852), 15. *SR Hoshiarpur* (1860), 44-45. Mountstuart Elphinstone, *An Account of the Kingdom of Cabul*, 28.

Artificial means of irrigation, which are known to have been there during the Mughal period, were used during the late eighteenth century. In the lower portions of the Doabs, where rainfall was inadequate, the new chiefs took several steps to cater to the needs of the cultivators. The non-Sikh chiefs of Mankera, Multan and Bahawalpur are said to have constructed about seventeen inundation canals in the territories under their jurisdiction. That the Shah Nahr, also called Hasli, remained in use during the late eighteenth century is evident from the orders of Jai Singh Kanhiya and Sada Kaur in which they exempt the grantees from the tax on water from the Shah Nahr for the irrigation of their revenue-free lands. Jai Singh Kanhiya, for instance, directed the authorities of the Shah Nahr in 1775 to give water free of charge to Mahant Prem Nath for his *khudkāsht* land in *pargana* Gurdaspur.[15] It is clear that the cultivators used to pay *nahrāna* or water tax for the canal water used for irrigation.

Besides constructing new inundation canals, the chiefs of the Punjab took several steps to revive agrarian prosperity during the late eighteenth century. To quote a settlement officer of Gujrat: 'the names of Gujjar Singh and Sahib Singh Bhangi are often in the mouths of people of this district who look back to their rule without the smallest bitterness. They seem indeed to have followed an enlightened and liberal policy, sparing no effort to induce the people to settle down to peaceful occupations. Agriculture was encouraged, the system of *in'āms* and *chahāramis* introduced, and every effort made to induce the people to settle down to their previous pursuits'.[16]

The Bhangi chiefs were not an exception. We have references to waste land being given by some other chiefs of the Punjab to several individuals for bringing it under cultivation. The grantees in these cases were not to pay any revenue to the state. Jalal Khan Bhatti, for instance, granted over 63 *ghumāons* of land in *mauza*' Kot Jahan of Pargana Hafizabad to Jahan Khan, a Rajput, for cultivation. Muzaffar Khan of Multan, Sada Kaur of Batala, and Jassa Singh Ahluwalia gave similar grants.[17] The motive behind the grants of waste land to religious institutions and individuals was the same. It was in this

[15] Foreign/Political Proceedings, 16 December 1853, No. 189; 7 January 1853, No. 219. *SR Muzaffargarh* (1882), 14-21.

[16] *SR Gujrat* (1861), 4-5. *DG Gujrat* (1883-84), 17. A.C. Elliot, *The Chronicles of Gujrat*, 31.

[17] Foreign/Political Proceedings, 14 January, 1856, Nos. 213, 219-20 & 241; 5 September 1856, Nos. 111 & 114; 26 September 1856, No. 244; 7 May 1858, No. 222.

context that the contemporary European travellers noted in their works the 'exceedingly well cultivated, populous and rich possessions of the Sikhs' and their 'attachment and application in the midst of warfare to the occupations of agriculture'; they also observed that 'the country is in a state of high cultivation', and 'the cultivation of their lands is attended with much assiduity'.[18]

II

Prinsep was the first historian to refer to *jāgīrdārī* in the late eighteenth century Punjab. According to him, *jāgīrs* were given to 'needy relations, dependents and the soldiers who deserved well, and the holders were liable to be called upon for their personal services at all times with their quotas or contingents, equipped and mounted at their own charge, according to the extent of the grant'. Prinsep goes on to add that *jāgīrs* were 'hereditary' only according to the chiefs' pleasure. Furthermore, it is implied in his statement that all *jāgīrs* were military *jāgīrs*. Prinsep's cryptic remarks have been repeated by some of the twentieth century historians of the Punjab.[19] H.R. Gupta, however, has tried to say something on his own. The additional information given by him relates to the fixed number of horsemen and foot-soldiers to be maintained by the *jāgīrdār*.[20] This information makes only a marginal advance upon Prinsep.

The publication of Indu Banga's *Agrarian System of the Sikhs* has placed the study of the subject on a different footing altogether. Though there is larger concentration on the early nineteenth century, the author takes the late eighteenth century also into account. Three types of *jāgīrs* are identified: service, *in'ām* and subsistence. These categories have been clearly defined for the purpose of analysis. Service *jāgīr* was primarily either military or civil: 'When a *jāgīrdār* was required to serve with a certain number of horsemen he was assigned *jāgīrs* not only for his personal services but also for the maintenance of those horsemen'. The civil *jāgīrdār* was paid only for his personal services. This is illustrated with reference to a number of cases. Charhat Singh

---

[18] Ganda Singh (ed.), *Early European Accounts of the Sikhs*, 17, 62, 100, 336-37.

[19] *Origin of the Sikh Power*, 29. Cf. N.K. Sinha, *Rise of the Sikh Power*, 116. Bhagat Singh, *Sikh Polity in the Eighteenth and Nineteenth Centuries*, 91.

[20] *History of the Sikhs*, IV, 369-70.

Sukarchakia, for instance, gave a *jāgīr* worth 65,000 rupees to Sahib Singh Kāliānwala for maintaining 80 horsemen. Jassa Singh Ahluwalia granted four villages worth 4,000 rupees in *jāgīr* to Jagat Singh, Prem Singh, and Des Raj on condition of service of four horsemen. The administrators performing civil duties too were paid in *jāgīr*, like Diwan Shiv Dyal under Charhat Singh Sukarchakia, Diwan Guttu Mal under Gujjar Singh Bhangi, Diwan Sulakhan Mal and his sons under Milkha Singh of Rawalpindi, and Qazi Abdul Rahman under Mahan Singh Sukarchakia.[21]

The *in'ām jāgīr* is defined as land held on 'the same basis as the service *jāgīr* but not against any office, or with any obligation to the state'. Such *jāgīrs* were generally given by the Sikh rulers 'by way of reward'. The recipient of these grants were largely *chaudharīs* and *muqaddams*. But *in'ām jāgīrs* were also given to those who brought wasteland under cultivation. Subsistence *jāgīrs* were given 'without involving the idea of either reward or service'. Gujjar Singh of Gujrat, for instance, gave such a *jāgīr* to his father-in-law. The subsistence and *in'ām jāgīrs* were hereditary. The system of *jāgīrs* implied a distinction between the *khālisa* and *jāgīr* lands, and it could not work without the maintenance of revenue records.[22]

Given the background of the Mughal times and the process of political change during the eighteenth century, we could expect *a priori* that the non-Sikh chiefs would alienate land-revenue in favour of their *jāgīrdārs*. Indeed, there are several references in contemporary records to *jāgīrs* of all kinds given by the non-Sikh chiefs. Ghafur Khan Afghan, for instance, was commanding 100 horsemen under Ahmad Khan Sial as a military *jāgīrdār*. Similarly, Khiwa Khan Bhatti was holding a *jāgīr* worth 10,000 rupees under Qutbuddin Khan of Qasur. Nur Muhammad Khan and his descendants served Bahawal Khan as *jāgīrdārs* in Bahawalpur. Ali Muhammad Khan held a *jāgīr* worth 5,000 rupees in Multan under Muzaffar Khan. Shah Muhammad Khan was another *jāgīrdār* of Muzaffar Khan with a *jāgīr* worth 10,000 rupees in Dera Dinpanah. That *jāgīrdārī* was prevalent in Multan on a large scale is evident from the fact that Muzaffar Khan of Multan alienated land-revenue worth four lacs of rupees in favour of his *jāgīrdārs* who supplied a total force of 2,000 horse and 4,000 foot. Similarly, Muhammad Khan of Mankera gave *jāgīrs* worth 1,64,000 rupees to his

---

21 Indu Banga, *Agrarian System of the Sikhs*, 118, 124-25n 29, 138-39.

22 Ibid., 84-85, 130-31 & 143.

jāgīrdārs in Dera Ismail Khan alone. It is interesting to note that the land revenue alienated in *jāgīr* was more than what was retained as *khālisa*. In Multan, the *khālisa* was worth three lacs of rupees against a total land-revenue of about seven lacs. In the case of Dera Ismail Khan, however, the lands held in *khālisa* were worth 1,36,000 rupees against a total revenue of three lacs of rupees.[23] Like the non-Sikh chiefs of the Punjab plains, the chiefs of the hills also gave *jāgīrs* to those who rendered service to the state. Sansar Chand of Kangra, for example, gave a whole *pargana* in *jāgīr* to the European Commander Willam O'Brien who used to serve him with 2,000 horsemen. Dulcha Singh entered the service of Ranjit Dev of Jammu and he was given a *jāgīr* for guarding the frontier with a fixed number of horsemen.[24]

There are known instances of revenues alienated by the non-Sikh chiefs in favour of persons who were not performing military service. Walidad Khan Sial, for example, granted 60 *bighas* of land worth 25 rupees a year to Roshan Ram, a *qānūngo*. Nawab Bahawal Khan granted 85 *bighas* of land worth 100 rupees to Muhammad Saleh for performing the duties of a *qāzī*. Similarly, Sultan Muqarrab Khan Gakkhar of Rawalpindi granted land worth 95 rupees to Muhammad Wali, a boatman (*mallāh*), for his services at the Dangli ferry.[25] The non-Sikh chiefs granted *jāgīrs* also as *in'ām* and subsistence. Nizamuddin Khan of Qasur granted land worth two hundred rupees to a *lambardār*, Sujan Khan. Murad Bakhsh Bhatti of Hafizabad granted *jāgīrs* in *in'ām* to Pir Bakhsh and Muazzam Khan for bringing waste-land under cultivation. Subsistence *jāgīr* was granted by Kabir Khan Sial to one Ahmad Khan Sial.[26] From the known examples of *jāgīrs* for civil and military service, for subsistence and as *in'ām*, it may be safely inferred that the *jāgīrdārī* system in general remained prevalent in the territories of the non-Sikh chiefs in the Punjab during the late eighteenth century.

There is enough information on the Sikh chiefs of the late eighteenth century to suggest that they adopted the *jāgīrdārī* system not

---

[23] Foreign/Secret Consultation, 7 July 1797, Nos. 3-4. Lepel Griffin, *The Panjab Chiefs*, 258-59 & 497. *DG Multan* (1883-84), 60.

[24] C. Grey, *European Adventurers of Northern India, 1785 to 1849*, 64. Lepel Griffin, *The Panjab Chiefs*, 414.

[25] Foreign/Political Proceedings, 31 March 1854, No. 232; 12 December 1856, No. 255; 9 January 1857, No. 274. Vogel, *Catalogue of Bhuri Singh Museum*, 12.

[26] Foreign/Political Proceedings, 31 March 1854, No. 232; 5 December 1856, No. 212; 7 May 1858, No. 222. *DG Dera Ismail Khan* (1883-84), 32.

long after the occupation of territories. As elsewhere, in their territories too the military *jāgīrdārs* were assigned *jāgīrs* not only for their own services but also for the maintenance of horsemen. There is no separate information on the amount paid on account of the latter but there is hardly any doubt that the lump sum payment made to them, for which information is available in contemporary and near contemporary records, included the payment made on account of horsemen. In many cases, the number of horsemen to be maintained is not mentioned, but there are other instances in which the number is clearly stipulated.

There are numerous references to *jāgīrdārs* with merely the amount payable to them. To cite a few examples, Dasaunda Singh Randhawa was a *jāgīrdār* under Hari Singh of Amritsar receiving 20,000 rupees a year; Mian Khan under Sada Kaur was receiving 15,000 rupees; Katha Singh Chahal under Lehna Singh, 5,000 rupees; Gajjan Singh Chashmawala under Jai Singh Kanhiya, 4,000 rupees; and Nodh Singh Majithia under Amar Singh Bagga, 2,000 rupees. Sahib Singh was granted Tung with some adjacent villages by Jassa Singh Ahluwalia. Ram Singh Kahlon of Bhagowal was similarly granted two villages by Bhag Singh Bagga.[27]

There are a few cases in which the number of troops required is also mentioned. Gaura Singh Atariwala, for example, took service under Gujjar Singh of Gujrat on a *jāgīr* of 18,000 rupees a year when he was required to serve the chief with twentyfive horsemen. Similarly, Charhat Singh was granted Nur Mahal worth 50,000 rupees by Jassa Singh Ahluwalia on the condition of maintaining 150 horsemen. Jagat Singh was granted four villages worth 4,000 rupees in *jāgīr* on the condition of furnishing four horsemen for Jassa Singh Ahluwalia. Mahan Singh Sukarchakia granted a few villages to Khudadad Khan, son of the *chaudharī* of Jalalpur, on the condition of serving with twenty horsemen.[28]

Some of the *jāgīrs* were rather large. For instance, Sahib Singh Kāliānwala, a *jāgīrdār* of Charhat Singh Sukarchakia, held a *jāgīr* worth 65,750 rupees. Desa Singh Kontal enjoyed a *jāgīr* worth 45,000 rupees under Jai Singh Kanhiya. Godh Singh Kamla held a *jāgīr* worth 40,000 rupees under Hari Singh of Amritsar. His nephew Jai Singh Kamla

---

[27] Foreign/Political Proceedings, 14 January 1854, No. 232. *SR Amritsar* (1860), 148. Lepel Griffin, *The Panjab Chiefs*, 84, 303, 437 & 459.

[28] Foreign/Secret Proceedings, 24 June 1809, No. 7. Foreign/Political Proceedings, 29 December 1849, No. 47A. Foreign/Political Consultation, 12 March 1852, No. 95.

received a *jāgīr* worth 50,000 rupees under Gulab Singh. To cite a few more examples, Bhag Singh Chhichhawalia held a *jāgīr* worth 40,000 rupees under Gujjar Singh of Gujrat. Sobha Singh Bhakka was granted a *jāgīr* worth 40,000 rupees by Haqiqat Singh Kanhiya. Another *jāgīrdār* of Charhat Singh Sukarchakia was Dyal Singh Chhachhi who received *jāgīr* worth 37,000 rupees in Mian Daud Khel and elsewhere on the left bānk of the Indus.[29]

Sometimes a single *ghurcharha* was granted a considerable *jāgīr*. Dyal Singh of Dadubajra in Sialkot district entered the service of Tara Singh Pathankotia as a trooper, served his master in many expeditions and received from him a *jāgīr* worth 5,000 rupees in Pathankot. Similarly, Pahar Singh Man entered Charhat Singh Sukarchakia's service as a trooper, and soon distinguished himself to obtain a grant of four villages worth 3,277 rupees. Diwan Singh was given the villages of Butala and Pahladpur by Charhat Singh Sukarchakia. Sahaj Singh, who had served Jassa Singh Ahluwalia in his *khās fauj* was granted Bhakna and Bhulana in *jāgīr* by Bhag Singh Ahluwalia. Some other cases of individual horsemen getting handsome *jāgīrs* are also known: Kapur Singh under Jaimal Singh Kanhiya; Amir Singh, Gajja Singh and Bakhshish Singh under Nar Singh Chamiariwala; and Prem Singh under Jassa Singh Ramgarhia.[30]

Some of the descendants of *chaudharīs*, *muqaddams* and *jāgīrdārs* of the Mughal times also joined the service of the new rulers and received *jāgīrs*. For example, one Ladda was authorized to collect revenues of twentytwo villages by one of the Mughal emperors. The office remained with the family for many generations. On the decline of the Mughal empire, the family accepted the Sikh faith. Sarja Singh offered his services to Charhat Singh Sukarchakia and he was granted a *jāgīr*. His sons were also given separate *jāgīrs*. Lakha Singh, son of Chaudharī Churh Mal, joined Charhat Singh Sukarchakia and obtained Ranjitgarh with four other villages in Gujranwala district in *jāgīr*. The families of *chaudahrīs* whose members accepted service with new rulers were not necessarily local. For instance, Mit Singh Padhania,

---

[29] Foreign/Political Consultation, 29 December 1849, No. 49A. *DG Gurdaspur* (1883-84), 15. Lepel Griffin, *The Panjab Chiefs*, 197-98, 421 & 445.

[30] Griffin & Massy, *Chiefs and Families of Note in the Panjab*, II, 524. Foreign/Political Proceedings, 7 January 1853, No. 288; 14 January 1853, No. 219; 27 May 1853, No. 202. Ram Sukh Rao, *Sṛi Fateh Singh Partap Prabhakar*, 154.

descendant of a *chaudharī* in the Bari Doab, was granted a *jāgīr* worth 12,000 rupees by Mahan Singh Sukarchakia.[31]

The Sukarchakias were not exceptional in inducing *chaudharīs* or *muqaddams* to take up service. Godh Singh, son of Chaudharī Bulaki, joined Hari Singh of Amritsar and received a large *jāgīr* of 40,000 rupees. Nodh Singh Sandhu, whose father Ladda was a *lambardār* of Chhichhah village under the Mughals, was taken into service by Gujjar Singh of Gujrat and granted six villages in *jāgīr*. Ram Singh, son of Karam Singh, a *jāgīrdār* under the Mughals, was taken into service by Gujjar Singh of Gujrat in 1765 and was granted a *jāgīr* in Lahore. Likewise, Ram Singh Dharvi, whose ancestors were *jāgīrdārs* of the Mughals since the time of Akbar, was granted ten villages worth 15,000 rupees in service *jāgīr* by Baghel Singh Karora Singhia. Some of the dispossessed *pattidārs* were also granted service *jāgīrs*. Kahn Singh Shergill was deprived of his territory by Haqiqat Singh Kanhiya but he was granted a service *jāgīr* worth 2,000 rupees by Sada Kaur.[32]

In some cases, service *jāgīrs* were given by the rulers to their relatives. For example, Dasaunda Singh, a Dhillon Jat of Jhabal was taken into service by his half-brother Baghel Singh Karora Singhia and given a *jāgīr*. Nodh Singh, who married the sister of Amar Singh Bagga, was given a *jāgīr* worth 2,500 rupees by his brother-in-law. Similarly, Jassa Singh Dulu married a daughter of Raja Singh of Panjwar, took his brother-in-law Ratan Singh into service and granted him a *jāgīr* worth 1,000 rupees. Sada Kaur granted Gilwali in Amritsar district to her nephew Gurdit Singh in *jāgīr* for service. Mahan Singh Sukarchakia granted to his cousin Didar Singh Sandhanwalia a large *jāgīr* in two villages.[33]

The *jāgīrdārs* who distinguished themselves in service could hope to receive larger and larger *jāgīrs*. In 1783, Mahan Singh Sukarchakia took over the territories of the Chatthas, and assigned to Diwan Singh, his *jāgīrdār*, an additional allowance of 1,000 rupees per annum from the salt duties. Likewise, Pahar Singh Man, who showed great gallantry in various campaigns against the Chatthas, was granted an additional *jāgīr* of 11,000 rupees by Mahan Singh Sukarchakia. Kaur Singh

---

[31] Foreign/Political Proceedings, 7 January 1853, No. 288. Lepel Griffin, *The Panjab Chiefs*, 226-27, 308-12 & 423.

[32] Foreign/Political Proceedings, 14 January 1853, No. 232. Lepel Griffin, *The Panjab Chiefs*, 230-31, 406 & 421.

[33] Griffin & Massy, *Chiefs and Families of Note*, II, 164 & 417. Foreign/Political Consultation, 29 December 1849, No. 47A. *DG Amritsar* (1892-93), 21.

Kāliānwala was also given an additional *jāgīr* of 8,000 rupees by Mahan Singh. In 1765, Gujjar Singh Bhangi occupied Gujrat and added six villages to the *jāgīr* of Nodh Singh Chhichhawalia.[34]

In a few known cases, the rulers deprived the *jāgīrdārs* of their *jāgīrs* when they felt that the persons concerned were not performing their duties well. For example, Tegh Singh Kontal, a *jāgīrdār* of Jai Singh Kanhiya, lost a large part of his *jāgīr* because of his suspected involvement with Sansar Chand of Kangra. He was left with only six villages out of a total of fortyfive. Similarly, Nihal Singh Atariwala, at one time a powerful *jāgīrdār*, was totally deprived of his *jāgīrs* by Sahib Singh of Gujrat at the instance of Nihal Singh's cousins Tek Singh and Jodh Singh Atariwala.[35]

The service *jāgīrdārs* did not possess any hereditary rights over *jāgīrs*. But the rulers normally gave service to their descendants. That was why several families of *jāgīrdārs* continued to serve the rulers for more than one generation. On the death of Gaura Singh, a *jāgīrdār* of Sahib Singh of Gujrat, his son Nihal Singh was taken into service. Dasaunda Singh Randhawa and his descendants served Hari Singh of Amritsar and his successors for three generations. After the death of Dyal Singh Chhachhi, Mahan Singh Sukarchakia confirmed his son Jassa Singh in his *jāgīr*.[36]

Jāgīrdārs could lose or gain due to political changes. There are known instances of *jāgīrdārs* who suffered losses due to the subjugation of their masters by Ranjit Singh. Sobha Singh Bhakha, a *jāgīrdār* of 40,000 rupees under Haqiqat Singh Kanhiya, was left with a *jāgīr* of only 7,000 rupees. The Chhichhawalia family which was enjoying a large *jāgīr* of 40,000 rupees under Gujjar Singh of Gujrat was left with only a small *jāgīr* under Ranjit Singh. Some others of the former *jāgīrdārs* came to acquire large *jāgīrs* under Ranjit Singh: Deva Singh, son of Nodh Singh Majithia, a *jāgīrdār* of Buddh Singh Bagga; Ghaffur Khan Afghan, a *jāgīrdār* of Ahmad Khan Sial; Karam Singh Chahal, son of Katha Singh Chahal, a *jāgīrdār* of Lenha Singh of Lahore; Nihal

---

[34] Foreign/Political Proceedings, 29 December 1849, No. 49A. Lepel Griffin, *The Panjab Chiefs*, 151, 309 & 421.

[35] Aliuddin, *Ibratnāma* (Pbi. tr.), 259. Lepel Griffin, *The Panjab Chiefs*, 497. *DG Gurdaspur* (1883-84), 15. Foreign/Political Proceedings, 29 December 1849, No. 49A.

[36] Foreign/Political Proceedings, 29 December 1849, No. 49A. Lepel Griffin, *The Panjab Chiefs*, 59-60, 65-66, 217 & 406-07.

Singh Atariwala, a *jāgīrdār* of Sahib Singh of Gujrat, for instance.[37] It may be presumed that everyone in the service of a chief was not kept in employment by the subjugating chief.

There are known instances of *jāgīrdārs* who chose to stay with their old masters as *jāgīrdārs*. Ratan Singh of Panjwar was assigned a *jāgīr* worth 1,000 rupees by Jassa Singh Dulu in 1802 out of his own *jāgīr* of 60,000 rupees. In 1820, when Jassa Singh Dulu's *jāgīr* was decreased to 7,000 rupees, Ratan Singh received a *jāgīr* of only 500 rupees. Similarly, Khiwa Khan retired with Qutbuddin Khan of Qasur to Mamdot in 1807 and received a *jāgīr* worth 10,000 rupees for maintaining a small contingent of horsemen.[38]

The administrators who performed civil duties were also paid in *jāgīr*. Kamr Singh Nakkai gave *jāgīr* to his *diwān*, Tek Chand. Bagh Singh Hallowalia also gave service *jāgīrs* to his civil functionaries. The majority of the *qānūngos* were paid for their services through *jāgīrs*. Pahar Mal, for instance, was granted a *jāgīr* worth 340 rupees in Sujanpur by Amar Singh Bagga; at the same time he was allowed to collect 1/4 seer per maund of grain as fees of *qānūngoī*. Jassa Singh Ramgarhia granted half a village worth 190 rupees to a *qānūngo*, Narpat Rai. Jodh Singh Ramgarhia confirmed the grant in 1802 in favour of Narpat Rai's son, Gulab Rai. Jassa Singh Ramgarhia gave *jāgīr* to another *qānūngo* named Kishan Chand. Mangal Sein received a *jāgīr* from Mahan Singh Sukarchakia, and Buddhu Mal from Gujjar Singh of Gujrat.[39]

Several other categories of employees received *jāgīrs* for their personal services: *qāzīs*, *mallāhs*, cooks (*lāngarīs*), barbers and personal servants. Wazir Shah, a *lāngarī*, was granted a *jāgīr* worth 250 rupees by Mahan Singh Sukarchakia. The barber Fateh Chand and his brother Nand Ram were granted *jāgīr* worth three hundred rupees by Jodh Singh Ramgarhia. Some personal servants were also paid in *jāgīr*, like Mansukh Rai by Jassa Singh Ahluwalia, Siwaya Singh by Milkha Singh of Rawalpindi, and Pardhan Singh by Gurbakhsh Singh Dodia.[40]

---

[37] Foreign/Political Proceedings, 14 January 1853, No. 213. Lepel Griffin, *The Panjab Chiefs*, 303 & 421. *DG Multan* (1883-84), 58.

[38] Foreign/Political Proceedings, 29 December 1849, No. 47A. Lepel Griffin, *The Panjab Chiefs*, 259.

[39] Foreign/Political Proceedings, 16 April 1852, No. 55; 18 June 1852, No. 83; 31 March 1854, No. 232; 11 July 1856, No. 211; 8 August 1856, No. 207.

[40] Ibid., 13 August 1852, No. 49; 7 January 1853, No. 228; 5 September 1856, Nos. 110 & 114.

That the late eighteenth century Sikh chiefs gave *in'ām jāgīrs* to *chaudharīs* and *muqaddams* is evident from known instances. Chaudharī Nagalia was granted about twentytwo *bighas* of land by Jai Singh Kanhiya who gave hundred *ghumāons* of land, worth 100 rupees, to another *chaudharī*, Ghulam Khan. Jai Singh Kanhiya gave 160 *ghumāons* of land, worth 100 rupees, to Chaudharī Mian Khan, in addition to five per cent commission (*pachotra*) and two seers of grain per maund. Some other known grantees were Chaudharī Sultan Khan under Gurbakhsh Singh Kanhiya, Chaudharī Chet Ram under Amar Singh Bagga, Chaudharī Ikhlas Khan under Jodh Singh Veglia, Chaudharī Khudadad Khan under Suddh Singh Chhina, Chaudharī Amir Singh under Jodh Singh Wazirabadia, Chaudharī Mehr Singh under Nar Singh Chamiariwala, Chaudharī Muhammad Azim and Chaudharī Imam Bakhsh under Jassa Singh Ahluwalia.[41]

The Sikh chiefs gave *in'ām* to *lambardārs* also. Jai Singh Kanhiya, for instance, gave 150 *ghumāons* of land worth 90 rupees in Gurdaspur district to Sultan Ali, a *lambardār*. Gurbakhsh Singh Kanhiya granted fifty *ghumāons* of land to Mayya and Jiwan, the Gujjar *lambardārs* of the village Degowal. Begu Singh received a similar grant from Jassa Singh Ramgarhia; Kahan Singh, Natha Singh and Sukha Singh received grants from Fateh Singh Ahluwalia; Munim Khan, from Milkha Singh; Gulab Singh, from Gulab Singh of Amritsar; Muhammaduddin, from Lehna Singh of Lahore; and Sujan Khan, from Nizamuddin Khan.[42]

Land revenue was alienated by the Sikh chiefs in favour of the dispossessed chiefs and their dependants during the late eighteenth century. Tara Singh Dallewalia, for instance, took over Nakodar from Rai Ahmad Manj and granted him some land in subsistence *jāgīr*. In 1767, Charhat Singh occupied Pind Dadan Khan and granted a few villages to Sahib Khan Khokhar for subsistence. Mahan Singh Sukarchakia gave subsistence *jāgīr* worth 20,000 rupees to Sham Singh Man, the dispossessed chief of Mananwala in Amritsar district. He also granted five villages to the wife of Ghulam Muhammad Khan Chattha. When Milkha Singh Thepuria occupied Rawalpindi in 1767, he allowed Mansur Khan and Shadman Khan, the sons of Muqarrab Khan Gakkhar,

---

[41] Ibid., 8 August 1856, No. 207; 3 June 1853, No. 119; 17 April 1857, No. 603; 5 September 1856, Nos. 111, 113-14.

[42] Ibid., 5 September 1856, Nos. 111, 113-14, 212-13; 9 January 1857, No. 230.

to retain Pharwala in subsistence *jāgīr*. The most notable tribes of Rawalpindi were allowed to retain 192 villages in *jāgīr*.[43]

III

The tradition of giving grants of revenue-free land to religious persons and institution of different faiths was an old one in India.[44] This practice continued under the new rulers of the Punjab. The term commonly used for such grants in Mughal India was *madad-i-ma'āsh*.[45] What was granted through *madad-i-ma'āsh* was the revenue due to the government. It is well known that all the Sikh chiefs used to give revenue-free grants by way of *dharmarth*.[46] However, what is generally not realized is that the non-Sikh chiefs of the hills as well as the plains also alienated land revenue by way of charity.

Among the non-Sikh chiefs who are known to have given charitable grants were Ranjit Dev and his successor Brij Raj Dev of Jammu, Sansar Chand of Kangra, Umed Singh of Chamba, Amrit Pal of Basohli, Mahan Chand of Kahlur, Ram Singh of Jaswan, Shuja Khan and Muzaffar Khan of Multan, Mubarak Khan, Bahawal Khan and Sadiq Khan of Bahawalpur, Muhammad Khan of Mankera, Walidad Khan, Inayat Ullah Khan, Kabir Khan and Ahmad Khan Sial of Jhang, Muqarrab Khan Gakkhar of Rawalpindi, Ahmad Khan Khokhar of Pind Dadan Khan, Nizamuddin Khan and Qutbuddin Khan of Qasur, Sa'adat Yar Khan Kharal of Kamalia, Murad Bakhsh and Jalal Khan Bhatti of Pindi Bhattian, Allahyar Khan of Sahiwal, Jān Muhammad Chattha and Ghulam Muhammad Chattha of Rasulnagar.

---

[43] Foreign/Political Consultation, 29 December 1849, No. 47A. Aliuddin, *Ibratnāma* (Pbi. tr.), 439. *DG Gujranwala* (1883-84), 16. *SR Rawalpindi* (1865), 67-68. 'Papers Relating to Gakkhar Tribe', *Selections from the Records of the Government of the Punjab and its Dependencies*, New Series, No. XXIII, 11-15.

[44] Revenue-free lands were given even before the advent of the Turks. The Turk, Afghan and the Mughal rulers had also given grants. For the grants of the Mughals, B.N. Goswamy & J.S. Grewal, *The Mughals and the Jogis of Jakhbar*, 17-46.

[45] *Ā'īn-i-Akbarī* (Eng. tr.), II, 278. B.N. Goswamy & J.S. Grewal, *The Jogis of Jakhbar*, 19-20. Irfan Habib, *Agrarian System of Mughal India*, 298.

[46] Indu Banga, *Agrarian System of the Sikhs*, 148-65.

The new rulers of the late eighteenth century confirmed the grants given by the Mughals as a matter of policy. Hari Singh Bhangi, for instance, confirmed the grant of half of the village Ratta in Amritsar district given initially by Aurangzeb to Pir Barkhurdar. Similarly, Hakumat Singh, Gurbakhsh Singh and Sada Kaur confirmed six grants given by the Mughal rulers to the Vaishnava establishment of Pindori in Gurdaspur district. Because of the religious sentiment associated with the grants, the chiefs of the late eighteenth century generally confirmed the grants given by the Mughals and their immediate successors. Jhanda Singh of Amritsar, for instance, confirmed the grant given to Abdul Qadir of Chiniot by Inayat Ullah Khan Sial for an educational institution when a part of the Chiniot territory was occupied by Jhanda Singh.[47]

The chiefs used to issue formal orders bearing their seals. These orders were generally addressed to the *'āmils* or the *kārdārs*, the *chaudharīs* and the village *zamindārs*. To cite one example, in an order of Gulab Singh of Amritsar, there is his seal and the order is addressed to the *kārdārs* of Ta'alluqa Nuruddin in Amritsar. It is stated in the order that Khalsaji (Gulab Singh) has given by way of *bhet* land attached to the well called Gulabwala in *mauza'* Tharu to Bhup Chand Bedi with effect from the *kharif* crop of Sammat 1852 (A.D. 1795). All concerned are instructed not to interfere with this arrangement.[48]

A comparison of the orders of the rulers of the late eighteenth century with those of the Mughal emperors and their functionaries makes it clear that the essential points concerning the grant of revenue-free land were the same.[49] The land given in *dharmarth* was generally given in terms of *ghumāons*, *bighas*, *kanāls* and *marlās*. There are references also to the fourth or third of a village and to half or the whole

---

[47] Foreign/Political Proceedings, 7 January 1853, No; 234; 16 December 1853, No. 189; 17 March 1854, Nos. 195-97; 31 March 1854, No. 233; 12 December 1856, No. 255. B.N. Goswamy & J.S. Grewal, *The Pindori Documents*, XVIII-XXI & XXVIII-XXXIX.

[48] Foreign/Political Proceedings, 1 May 1857, No. 419; 7 January 1853, No. 234; 14 January 1853, No. 213; 27 May 1853, No. 208; 4 July 1856, No. 153. B.N. Goswamy & J.S. Grewal, *The Pindori Documents*, XIX, XX, XXI, XXV, XXIX, XXX & XXXIX.

[49] For a comparison, Documents I-IX, XI-XVI, in B.N. Goswamy & J.S. Grewal, *The Jogis of Jakhbar* issued by the Mughal rulers and their functionaries and *The Pindori Documents*, XVIII-XXXIV issued by the Sikh chiefs of the late eighteenth century.

village in many of these grants.[50] As during the Mughal times, concessions other than the grant of land revenue were also given during the late eighteenth century. For instance, Sada Kaur exempted a Brahman grantee from the payment of water tax (*nahrāna*) on the revenue-free land granted to him in several villages. The grantees were also exempted from forced labour (*kār* and *begār*) or any payment in lieu thereof.[51]

In some cases, the grantee was asked indirectly to perform a small service for the state. Basti Ram, a *sādh*, who was given revenue-free land in *mauza*' Ramni Chak in Pargana Amritsar by Jodh Singh Ramgarhia was asked to collect the entire revenue of 925 rupees from the village, keep 825 rupees with himself and deposit the remaining one hundred in the state treasury.[52] There was a common practice during the Mughal times to follow the principle of half and half in giving revenue-free grants on the basis of which half of the land granted for the purpose was culturable waste.[53] When this waste was brought under cultivation by the grantee, it became his property, and if he himself got it cultivated, he was entitled to keep its entire produce. During the late eighteenth century also instances are known of grantees themselves getting the land cultivated and keeping the entire produce.[54]

In the reign of Aurangzeb, revenue-free lands were formally made hereditary.[55] During the late eighteenth century also, there was a tendency to treat the *dharmarth* grants as hereditary. There are many references to hereditary holders of grants who enjoyed the right over revenue-free land throughout the late eighteenth and the early nineteenth century and survived into the British period.

If there was any interference with the revenue-free grants from any quarters, and it was brought to the notice of the chief concerned, he tried to ensure that the grantee enjoyed without interference what was given to him. Gurbakhsh Singh, for example, ordered the *zamīndārs* of

---

[50] Foreign/Political Proceedings, 14 January 1853, Nos. 213 & 220; 4 July 1856, No. 151; 28 November 1856, No. 131 & 142; 1 May 1857, Nos. 414 & 419.

[51] Ibid., 14 January 1853, Nos. 213 & 216; 16 December 1853, No. 189. J.S. Grewal, 'Jakhbar Revisited', *Studies in Local and Regional History*, 44-49.

[52] Foreign/Political Proceedings, 27 June 1856, No. 86 C; 27 May 1853, No. 193.

[53] Irfan Habib, *Agrarian System of Mughal India*, 302.

[54] Foreign/Political Proceedings, 16 December 1853, No. 189.

[55] Irfan Habib, *Agrarian System of Mughal India*, 306.

a particular village not to interfere with the collection of the revenues by the grantee; they were ordered, in fact, to ensure that the entire quantity of grain already collected should be handed over to him.[56] In the case of a dispute, the chiefs used to appoint arbitrators. There is an interesting case of the time of Sahib Singh of Gujrat in which a village in Amritsar alienated by way of *dharmarth* by his predecessor Gujjar Singh was claimed by five persons on the basis of orders in their possession. Sahib Singh appointed Bhag Singh as an arbitrator to investigate into the claims of each party. It was finally decided that one Naichal Das was the genuine claimant and not Ratan Chand, Jaspat Rai, Nikka Singh or Badri Das. The village was confirmed by Sahib Singh in the name of Naichal Das.[57]

The example of the chiefs was followed by their *jāgīrdārs* who alienated portions of revenue from their own *jāgīrs* for charitable purposes. Prominent among such persons were those who were closely connected with the chief. There are instances of grants given by the wife of Hari Singh of Amritsar, the wife of Bagh Singh Hallowalia, the wife of Nar Singh Chamiariwala, the brother of Jassa Singh Ramgarhia, and the daughter of Ran Singh Nakkai. Among the *jāgīrdārs* alienating revenue by way of *dharmarth* figure the names of Nihal Singh Atariwala, Karam Singh Chahal, Jodh Singh Bhakka, Fateh Singh Kāliānwāla, Sham Singh Kunjahia, Kapur Singh, Dasaunda Singh, Pahar Singh Man and Churh Singh. The *diwāns* and the *kārdārs* also gave charitable grants. Diwan Dhanpat Rai, a *diwān* of Jaimal Singh Kanhiya, for instance, gave two *kanāls* of land to Chaman, a Brahman, for a *dharmsala*. Even the *ghurcharhas* are known to have alienated revenues from their own *jāgīrs*. Amir Singh, a *ghurcharha* of Nar Singh Chamiariwala, for instance, gave twenty *bighas* of land in Sialkot district for the maintenance of a *dharmsala*. Prem Singh and Kapur Singh, *ghurcharhas* respectively of Jassa Singh Ramgarhia and Jaimal Singh Kanhiya, gave similar grants.[58]

---

[56] B.N. Goswamy & J.S. Grewal, *The Pindori Documents*, XXVI; XIX, XXII, XXVIII & XXXIV. Foreign/Political Proceedings, 27 May 1853, No. 193; 4 July 1856, No. 153; 1 May 1857, No. 419.

[57] Foreign/Political Proceedings, 14 January 1853, No. 213. For a comparison with the Mughal times, B.N. Goswamy & J.S. Grewal, *The Jogis of Jakhbar*, Document X.

[58] Foreign/Political Proceedings, 21 February 1851, No. 142A; 14 November 1851, No. 54; 14 January 1853, Nos. 212-13, 219, 229 & 238; 27 May 1853, Nos. 196, 198-99, 202; 4 July 1856, No. 156; 12 December

A large number of *chaudharīs* and *muqaddams* too gave *dharmarth* grants. Chaudharī Nidhan Singh, Chaudharī Alam Khan, Chaudharī Jagir Khan and Chaudharī Afzal Khan, for instance, gave revenue-free grants for charitable purposes. The number of known instances of *muqaddams* giving charitable grants is larger than that of the *chaudharīs*: Hira Khan in Sayyadnagar, Fazil Khan in Bhoon Fazil, Wilayat Khan in Kot Burah, Khan Muhammad in Kot Qadir Bakhsh, Muhammad Khan in Kothi Mahin, Izzat Khan in Nangal Kamla, Karam Singh in Chachwal, and Sahib Khan in Musapur, for instance. Grants given by the *muqaddams* jointly are also known, like those of Nur Khan and Sultan Khan in Batala; Shahdad Khan and Bakhtawar Khan in Hafizabad and Buddhu and Puran in Pasrur.[59]

The largest number of grants were given to individuals and institutions belonging to the Sikh faith. The descendants of Guru Nanak, the Bedis, received the maximum grants. Nearly all the Sikh chiefs gave revenue-free lands to them. It is interesting to note that Mahan Chand of Kahlur, Walidad Khan Sial of Jhang, and Qutbuddin Khan of Qasur also gave grants to the Bedis. A large number of grants were given to the Bedis by *jāgīrdārs* and *ghurcharhas*, like Sham Singh Kunjahia under Charhat Singh Sukarchakia, Jodh Singh Bhakka under Haqiqat Singh Kanhiya, Kapur Singh under Jaimal Singh Kanhiya, Karam Singh Chahal under Lehna Singh of Lahore, Dharam Singh and Mohar Singh under Bagh Singh Miraliwala, Karam Singh and Diwan Singh under Jodh Singh Saurianwala, and Churh Singh under Jodh Singh Wazirabadia. The Bedis of Dera Baba Nanak received perhaps the largest number of grants.[60]

The descendants of Guru Ram Das, the Sodhis too were patronized by a large number of Sikh chiefs. Nearly twenty chiefs gave grants worth 8,000 rupees to a score of Sodhis. Mahan Singh Sukarchakia gave a grant worth 1,300 rupees to Sodhi Kiun Singh at Haranpur in Rawalpindi. Karam Singh Dulu granted the whole village of Salara worth 830 rupees in Pargana Chiniot to Sodhi Kesar Singh. Similarly, the descendants of Guru Amar Das, the Bhallas were given

---

1856, No. 255; 31 December 1858, No. 113. Foreign/Political Consultation, 18 June 1852, No. 182.

[59] Foreign/Political Proceedings, 9 January 1854, No. 221; 29 August 1856, Nos. 240-41; 27 March 1857, No. 197; 29 May 1857, Nos. 197 & 243; 31 December 1858, Nos. 318 & 1686.

[60] Ibid., 13 August 1852, No. 49; 14 January 1853, Nos. 213, 219-20 & 223; 23 June 1854, Nos. 202 & 205; 9 January 1857, Nos. 215-16; 1 May 1857, No. 419; 31 December 1858, Nos. 1069 & 1677.

revenue-free land in *dharmarth.* The first known grant is that of Haqiqat Singh Kanhiya who gave three-fourth of the village of Dulla in Pargana Shakargarh to Mohar Singh Bhalla in 1756. Brij Raj Dev of Jammu granted the whole of Chak Langa worth four hundred rupees in Pargana Sialkot to Dalpat Rai Bhalla.[61] There is no known instance but it is not unlikely that some Trehan descendants of Guru Angad also received *dharmarth* grants.

The Udasi centres known as Akharas, Deras, Darbars, Smadhs, and Dharmsalas were extensively patronized by the new chiefs of the Punjab. A large number of fresh grants were given to the newly founded Udasi centres which came into prominence during the late eighteenth century. There were half a dozen such centres in the city and district of Amritsar. The Akhara of Baba Santokh Das, known as Akhara Brahm Buta, was virtually within the Golden Temple complex. These Akharas were established in the city by Baba Pritam Das, Baba Ghamand Das, and Baba Ganga Ram. Two other Akharas in Amritsar which received *dharmarth* grants were Akhara Mastram and Akhara Bibeksar. Some of the other institutions which received *dharmarth* grants were the Dera of Mahant Sital Das in Gurdaspur district, known as Dera Tahli Sahib, the Dera of Baba Sant Ram in Dera Baba Nanak, the Asthan of Baba Nanak in Gujrat, the Darbar at Rori Sahib near Eminabad, and the Dera of Bhai Pheru on the road between Lahore and Multan. The chiefs who bestowed such grants were Ranjit Dev of Jammu, Bahawal Khan of Bahawalpur, Muzaffar Khan of Multan, Walidad Khan and Inayat Ullah Khan Sial of Jhang, Gurbakhsh Singh Kanhiya, Jhanda Singh and Ganda Singh of Amritsar, Nahar Singh, Gian Singh and Khazan Singh Nakkai, Buddh Singh Faizullapuria, Jassa Singh Ramgarhia, and Lehna Singh Bhangi. Some *zamindārs* and *jāgīrdārs* also gave grants to *udāsīs.* Like them the *nirmala sādhs* received revenue-free grants from Mahan Singh Sukarchakia, Bagh Singh Hallowalia, and Jodh Singh Saurianwala.[62]

Revenue-free lands were granted to various Gurdwaras. Prominent among these were Harmandar Sahib or the Golden Temple at Amritsar, the Darbar Sahib at Tarn Taran, the Gurdwara Shahidganj at Lahore, and Gurdwara Manji Sahib at Jandiala. The establishments like the Akal

---

[61] Ibid., 21 February 1851, Nos. 142A & 218A; 14 November 1851, No. 49; 16 April 1852, No. 49; 27 May 1853, Nos. 196 & 199; 11 July 1856, No. 208; 5 September 1856, No. 110; 27 May 1858, No. 199.

[62] Ibid., 12 March 1852, No. 98; 7 January 1853, No. 219; 14 January 1853, Nos. 229, 235 & 241; 27 May 1853, No. 202; 12 December 1856, No. 235; 31 December 1858, No. 1053.

Bunga and the Jhanda Bunga in the Harmandar Sahib complex at Amritsar received separate grants. It is interesting to note that the grants given by Jhanda Singh of Amritsar to religious institutions amounted to more than four thousand rupees. Some Gurdwaras in villages received revenue-free grants from Walidad Khan Sial, Bishambar Das of Jandiala, Bhag Singh Ahluwalia, Khazan Singh Nakkai, Jodh Singh Saurianwala, and Pahar Singh Man.[63] Revenue-free lands were given to *granthis, rāgīs, rabābīs,* and *dhādīs* attached to the Harmandar Sahib at Amritsar. Similar grants were enjoyed by those associated with the institutions at Kartarpur, Goindwal, Nankana Sahib, and Rori Sahib. It is interesting to note that Ahmad Khan Sial gave revenue- free land to Bhai Darbari Singh, a Khatri of Maghiana, for reading the Granth.[64]

The new chiefs of the Punjab gave revenue free grants for temples dedicated to various deities. Karam Singh Dulu, for instance, gave land to Jiwan Ram, a Brahman, for the upkeep of a temple. Buddh Singh Faizullapuria and Jaimal Singh Kanhiya gave grants to the Devidwaras at Patti and Shakargarh, respectively. Similarly, Ahmad Khan Sial of Jhang gave a grant of ten rupees to one Bhola Bhagat of Shorkot for a Devidwara. Revenue-free grants were given to halting places for travellers, known as *dharmsalas*, generally connected with temples. Walidad Khan Sial, for instance, gave fourteen *bighas* of land to Prem Das for a *dharmsala*. It is interesting to note that similar grants were given to temples by *jāgīrdārs, ghurcharhas, zamīndārs* and *muqaddams*.[65]

Purohits and Brahmans were patronized by a large number of chiefs: Sansar Chand of Kangra, Amrit Pal of Basohli, Walidad Khan Sial, Muzaffar Khan, Fateh Singh Ahluwalia, Sahib Singh of Gujrat, Lehna Singh of Lahore, Gulab Singh of Amritsar, Jassa Singh

---

63 Foreign/Political Consultation, 12 March 1852, No. 98; 22 April 1859, No. 45. Foreign/Political Proceedings, 14 November 1851, No. 49; 16 April 1852, No. 49; 10 June 1853, No. 218; 29 August 1856, No. 250; 28 November 1856, Nos. 112 & 152; 9 January 1857, Nos. 221 & 235; 31 December 1858, Nos. 1113 & 3315.

64 Foreign/Political Proceedings, 23 August 1850, No. 35C; 20 August 1852, No. 141; 7 January 1853, No. 222; 14 January 1853, Nos. 226, 235, 238 & 241; 23 June 1854, No. 205; 4 July 1856, No. 151; 28 November 1856, No. 142; 9 January 1857, No. 298; 13 February 1857, No. 288.

65 Ibid., 30 August 1852, No. 141; 27 May 1853, No. 202; 31 March 1854, Nos. 232-33; 22 March 1856, No. 133; 8 August 1856, No. 206; 29 August 1856, No. 242; 12 December 1856, No. 253; 9 January 1857, No. 414; 29 May 1857, No. 197; 31 December 1858, No. 318.

Ramgarhia, his successor Jodh Singh Ramgarhia, and Sada Kaur for instance. It is interesting to note in this connection that the Sikh chiefs of Rawalpindi, Milkha Singh and his son Jiwan Singh, gave grants of six hundred acres worth about one thousand rupees. Fateh Singh Kāliānwāla, a *jāgīrdār* of Mahan Singh Sukarchakia, granted a whole village in Pargana Tarn Taran worth three hundred rupees to Pandit Harnam Das of Lahore.[66]

The Vaishnava Maths, Thakurdwaras, Deras, Smadhs and Dharmsalas received revenue-free grants from the new rulers of the Punjab. The establishment at Pindori in Gurdaspur district received the largest number of grants and became one of the most venerated institutions of this period. The old grants coming down from the Mughal times were confirmed by the Sikh rulers as a matter of principle. Six such grants were confirmed by Hakumat Singh, Jai Singh and Gurbakhsh Singh. Sada Kaur too confirmed grants given initially to the Pindori establishment by Jahangir in the villages of Pindori, Bhagwanpur, Jairam, and Maharajpur worth 2,300 rupees in all. Jai Singh Kanhiya granted the village of Lahri Gosain to this establishment in 1773. Amar Singh Bagga granted land with a well and an orchard in 1789. Ram Singh of Jaswan granted three villages to the establishment at Pindori. The consideration shown by the rulers to the Mahants of Pindori comes out clearly in their orders to the *'āmils*, *kārdārs*, *zamīndārs*, *jāgīrdārs* and the *panches*, in which they repeatedly instruct them not to allow any interference with the collection of revenue by the Mahant of Pindori.[67]

The establishments at Dhianpur, Dhamtal and Datarpur also received grants from Jai Singh Kanhiya, Sada Kaur, Amar Singh Bagga, and Tara Singh Pathankotia. Jalal Khan Bhatti of Pindi Bhattian gave revenue-free land to the *smādh* of Baba Lal at Datarpur. Some of the other establishments patronized were the *smādh* of Chatar Das Bairagi at Amritsar, a *smādh* founded by Atma Ram in Amritsar and another by

---

[66] B.N. Goswamy & J.S. Grewal, 'Some Religious Land Grants in Kangra', *The Historian's Punjab: Miscellanous Articles*, 92-106. Vogel, *Catalogue of Bhuri Singh Museum*, 11. Foreign/Political Proceedings, 14 November 1851, No. 49; 6 August 1852, No. 130A; 7 January 1853, Nos. 225 & 242; 14 January 1853, Nos. 213 & 238; 27 May 1853, Nos. 202, 205 & 211; 27 June 1856, No. 86C; 8 August 1856, No. 218; 31 December 1858, Nos. 1102 & 1104.

[67] Foreign/Political Proceedings, 21 February 1851, No. 218A; 16 April 1852, Nos. 59-60. B.N. Goswamy & J.S. Grewal, *The Pindori Documents*, XIX-XXIII, XXVI-XXIX & XXXIV.

Sahaj Ram in Talwandi, the Thakurdwara of Hari Har in Qasur and the Thakurdwaras at Badoke in Sialkot, at Fatehgarh in Gurdaspur, and at Pariharan in Hoshiarpur. Individual Bairagis also received grants from the late eighteenth century chiefs. Buddh Singh Faizullapuria, for instance, gave patronage to Mahant Sharda Ram; Gujjar Singh Bhangi to Mahant Gopal Das; Sahib Singh of Gujrat to Mahant Lachhman Das; Jodh Singh Ramgarhia to Mahant Thakur Das; Jaimal Singh Kanhiya to Mahant Mukand Das; Bagh Singh Hallowalia to Mahant Amar Das of Zafarwal, Mahant Lachhman Das of Mirzapur, and Mahant Baldev Das of Devli.[68]

The Jogis associated with several Shaiva establishments called Shivdwaras or Shivalas, received revenue-free grants from the Sikh and non-Sikh chiefs of the Punjab. Among them were Shiv Das, Rasak Nath, Amir Nath, Dyal Nath, Daya Nath, Hadayat Nath, Shahamat Puri and Lalpuri Gosain. The earliest known grant given to a Shaiva Jogi is that of Jalal Khan Bhatti, given to Daya Nath in 1749 for a Shivala in Pargana Hafizabad. The other non-Sikh chiefs who gave similar grants were Sansar Chand of Kangra, Walidad Khan Sial, Mubarak Khan of Bahawalpur, and his brother Ghulam Hussain Khan. The Jogi establishment at Jakhbar in the upper Bari Doab received a grant from Amar Singh Bagga, the Sikh chief of Sujanpur, who granted revenue-free land in *mauza*' Panjar to Daya Nath.[69]

Muslim individuals and institutions were also patronized by the new rulers of the Punjab. They received grants not only from Muslim chiefs but also from others. The Sikh chiefs confirmed the imperial grants, and gave fresh ones to *sayyads*, *shaikhs*, *jogīs*, *mirāsīs*, and *bhatts*.[70] The *khānqahs*, *takiyas*, *masjids*, and shrines received a number of grants from both Sikh and non-Sikh chiefs. These grants were given

---

[68] Foreign/Political Consultation, 18 June 1852, No. 182. Foreign/Political Proceedings, 5 December 1856, No. 217; 12 December, 1856, No. 255; 9 January 1857, No. 221; 17 April 1857, No. 503; 29 May 1857, No. 197; 10 September 1858, No. 226; 31 December 1858, Nos. 321, 1053 & 1670; 8 April 1859, No. 65. *DG Hoshiarpur* (1883-84), 67.

[69] Foreign/Political Consultation, 18 June 1852, No. 182; Foreign/Political Proceedings, 18 June 1854, No. 232; 12 December 1856, No. 255; 19 December 1856, No. 172; 28 November 1856, No. 131; 1 May 1857, No. 413.

[70] Foreign/Political Proceedings, 7 January 1853, No. 234; 14 January 1853, No. 213; 31 March 1854, No. 233; 11 July 1856, No. 208; 28 November 1856, No. 135; 9 January 1857, No. 274; 27 March 1857, No. 246. *DG Multan* (1883-84), 52 & 55.

for the maintenance of these establishments and for their attendants. Several Muslim chiefs confirmed the imperial grants and gave fresh grants of their own. Ranjit Dev of Jammu also gave four such grants. *Chaudharīs*, *muqaddams*, *zamīndārs* and *jāgīrdārs* gave similar grants.[71]

In a few cases, revenue-free land was granted for a specific purpose like distribution of medicines to the poor or for daily distribution of food. Inayat Ullah Khan Sial made a grant of 75 rupees in favour of Kesho Das, a Brahman, for the purpose of teaching. Similarly, Jhanda Singh of Amritsar, and Gujjar Singh and Sahib Singh of Gujrat gave revenue-free lands in support of educational establishments. A grant of Gulab Singh of Amritsar is also on record in which he gave six *bighas* of land worth 14 rupees a year to one Dharam Singh to maintain a *chhabīl* in summers at Gilwali gate in Amritsar for providing free drinking water.[72]

It may be added that state patronage during the late eighteenth century was not confined to the grants of revenue-free land. Grants were sometimes made in cash. In such cases, the source from which the grantee was to collect his share used to be explicitly stated in the order. Walidad Khan Sial, for instance, made a cash grant on the date groves of Jhang in favour of Asa Nand of Shorkot for oil for the lamps of a *masjid*. In a few other cases, *dharmarth* grants were made in kind. The articles given were *dāl*, *ghee*, wheat or flour, woollen clothes, blankets, and the like.[73] Tolls and customs were also remitted sometimes. Jai Singh Kanhiya, remitted transit duty on the produce of the Pindori establishment crossing the river Beas. Similarly, Bhag Singh Bagga remitted the octroi duty on articles purchased for the Jogis at Jakhbar.[74]

---

[71] Foreign/Political Proceedings, 4 October 1850, No. 45; 31 March 1854, Nos. 232-33; 27 June 1856, No. 86A; 4 July 1856, Nos. 152-54; 26 September 1856, No. 238; 28 November 1856, Nos. 113, 131, 135 & 139; 5 December 1856, Nos. 210-11; 25 June 1858, No; 275; 25 February 1859, No. 173 & 176.

[72] Ibid., 20 August 1852, No. 141; 7 January 1853, No. 238; 31 March 1854, No. 233; 13 February 1857, No. 289; 1 May 1857, No. 416; 31 December 1858, No. 1104. Foreign/Political Consultation, 4 June 1858, No. 142.

[73] Foreign/Political Proceedings, 14 November 1851, Nos. 54-56; 20 August 1852, Nos. 140-41; 7 January 1853, No. 241; 27 May 1853, No. 196; 30 April 1852, No. 100; 6 August 1852, No. 130A; 31 March 1854, No. 232. Foreign/Political Consultation, 18 June 1852, No. 182.

[74] B.N. Goswamy & J.S. Grewal, *The Pindori Documents*, XXV; *The Jogis of Jakhbar*, XVII.

IV

In retrospect we can see that there was hardly anything in the last quarter of the eighteenth century in the Punjab which should necessarily have resulted in the decline of agriculture. The evidence which we have on administrative units and their functionaries, the methods and rates of assessment, and the attitude of the new rulers towards the cultivators gives an indication that agricultural production did not suffer. There are no revenue figures comparable with those of the Mughal times but figures by themselves would not prove any point, because the rate of assessment was a crucial factor in the situation. About the early nineteenth century it is maintained that there was certainly a revival of agriculture even if the revenue figures are smaller than those of the seventeenth century. If there was a decline in agricultural production during the eighteenth century, it may be true of the middle decades of the century. In any case, before the century ended, cultivation appears to have been on the increase.

Not only the Sikh but also the non-Sikh chiefs of the Punjab alienated land-revenue in favour of those who served them in military or civil capacity. The chiefs gave *in'ām jāgīrs* by way of reward; subsistence *jāgīrs* were given to dispossessed chiefs and their relatives. These *jāgīrs* were generally hereditary. Some of the former chiefs and *pattīdārs* and their dependants were taken into service by the new rulers. Even in the case of the Sikh chiefs, it appears that they encouraged *chaudharīs* and *muqaddams* to take service under them. The alienation of revenue took place on a large scale.

Some of those who served the new rulers received very large *jāgīrs*. A single *ghurcharha* sometimes was given a whole village. The *jāgīrdārs* who performed meritorious service were encouraged by additions to their *jāgīrs*. At the same time there are examples of *jāgīrs* being reduced owing to the inefficiency or disloyalty of the *jāgīrdārs*. Service *jāgīrs* by their very nature were precluded from being hereditary, but the competent heirs and close relatives of *jāgīrdārs* were inducted into service as a matter of policy. Political change could affect the fortune of the *jāgīrdārs* for better or worse. In the light of all this information on the *jāgīrdārī* system in the Punjab during the late eighteenth century, it is safe to suggest that the system was no different from what we find in the early nineteenth century under Maharaja Ranjit Singh. It was very much similar to the system prevalent under the Mughals. It is obvious, therefore, that the *jāgīrdārī* system survived the political upheaval of the eighteenth century. Furthermore, it accounted for much of the social change and, paradoxically, for a certain degree of political stability.

State patronage during the late eighteenth century was not confined to the co-religionists of the rulers. Rather, they gave grants to religious institutions and individuals of all faiths. This was partly because of their catholic outlook. But their self-interest too was involved. Through charitable grants, they tended to increase their power and influence as if in a spirit of competition. To enlist the support of influential individuals by giving them grants was to enlist the support of their followers at the same time.

7

MANUFACTURES AND TRADE

Twentieth century historians have written very little about manufactures and trade in the Punjab during the late eighteenth century. This has been due partly to lack of easily available information on the subject. However, as the works of N.K. Sinha and H.R. Gupta indicate, there are references to manufactures and trade during the late eighteenth century in the writings of the contemporary Europeans.[1] Furthermore, there is evidence of the existence of towns and cities in the Punjab during this period, and their existence could not be totally unconnected with trade and manufactures. The available evidence on the early nineteenth century situation can also be helpful for knowing something about the late eighteenth century, particularly if compared also with the information available for the Mughal times.

For direct evidence on the late eighteenth century, we have the contemporary works of A.L.H. Polier, George Forster, James Browne, John Griffiths and William Francklin. Among the near contemporary travellers and writers were an (anonymous) officer of the Bengal army, Baron Charles Hugel, C. Grey and Lepel H. Griffin. The district gazetteers of Kangra and Montgomery and the *Calcutta Gazette* also contain direct statements about the late eighteenth century. Among the Persian and Gurmukhi writers who refer to the late eighteenth century Punjab are Tahmas Khan, Ram Sukh Rao, Sohan Lal Suri and Ganesh Das.

I

George Forster writing in the 1780s, provides the best though limited evidence on trade. He refers to 'the collector of the customs' at Bilaspur where he also saw a caravan of the agents of some merchants on its way to Delhi and Lucknow. The brother of the Bilaspur collector was 'the

---

[1] N.K. Sinha, *Rise of the Sikh Power*, 112-14. H.R. Gupta, *History of the Sikhs*, IV, 379-81.

manager of the Kangra custom house'. When Forster reached Nadaon, he was a little surprised that in spite of the troubled state of the country, the collector of customs at Nadaon came out of the town to receive 'a toll duty of a few pence'. At Chenini, later, he had to pay one rupee 'for permission to cross the Chenab'. Between Bilaspur and Kangra, Forster discovered that a coin of inferior value was more acceptable than the Mughal Alam Shahi rupee. Near Nurpur, he saw another caravan of traders bound for Delhi. The boatman at the ferry of Basohli demanded a much higher rate than the usual before some Sikh horsemen told him to reduce the demand.[2]

Forster observed that before Nadir Shah's invasion of India, the trade route from Delhi to Kashmir passed through Sarhind, Lahore and Bhimber but after the Afghan invasions and particularly after the occupation of territories by the Sikhs, the merchants felt unsafe to use that route. They now used the Bilaspur, Kangra and Jammu route to Kashmir. Though this alternative route was safer, it was more tedious and involved larger expense. One important result of this change in the trade route, according to Forster, was the great prosperity of Jammu. Ranjit Dev encouraged traders of all communities, including Muslims for whom he allotted a certain quarter of the city which came to be known as Mughalpura, and built a mosque for them. His judicious administration made Jammu 'a place of extensive commercial resort where all descriptions of men experienced in their persons and property, a full security'.[3]

Between Jammu and Kashmir, the articles of merchandize were carried by men, generally Kashmiris, each of whom carried a load amounting to half the load of a strong mule. Horses or mules, according to Forster, were not used in transportation because of the absence of adequate paths and the steepness of mountains. The rate of hire was fixed at four rupees a carrier. The shawls from Kashmir were carried packed in oblong bales, contained in hides. In the 1780s, commerce in Jammu was not so prosperous as around 1770. This was partly due to the sack of Jammu by Mahan Singh Sukarchakia and partly due to the more rigorous demands of Ranjit Dev's successor on local and foreign traders. Nevertheless, Forster could easily contact his banker and

---

[2] *A Journey from Bengal to England*, I, 243-44, 252-53, 260, 267, 271 & 345.

[3] Ibid., I, 283-86.

immediately got his *hundī* encashed. He also observed that the income of the Jammu state still came largely from 'import and export duties'.[4]

Forster was never able to visit the Punjab plains but he carried the impression that an extensive and valuable commerce was carried on in the territories of the Sikh chiefs and 'extended to distant quarters of India', particularly to the provinces of Bihar and Bengal, where many Sikh merchants had taken up residence. Forster also observed: 'Merchants of every nation or sect, who may introduce a traffic into their territories, or are established under their Government, experience a full protection, and enjoy commercial privileges in common with their own subjects. At the same time it must be noticed, that such immunities are granted only to those who remain amongst them, or import wares for the immediate supply of the Sicque markets. But the foreign traders, or even travellers, who attempt to pass through the Punjab are often plundered and usually ill-treated'.[5]

In addition to what we have in Forster's work, there is very meagre information on trade and manufactures in the hills. In the *Tahmas Nāmā*, there is a reference to the levying of transit duty on the Ravi near Shahpur; it is also added that Tahmas Khan himself was exempted from this duty on the basis of a letter of the Raja of Jammu.[6] In the *Rājdarshinī*, there is a reference to bankers in Jammu during the reign of Ranjit Dev. The author of the *Rājdarshinī* also gives the names of some Khatri millionaires of Jammu: Badri Das, Jawala Das, Jawala Mal, Hira Nand, Gouri Shah, Jog Das, Shahzada Mal, Milkhi Shah, and Badar Bahadur Singh Badhera. The number of shops in the *bazar* of Jammu from one end to the other was about ten thousand.[7] Hugel repeats Forster about Jammu as the great entrepot for trade with Kashmir till it was plundered by Mahan Singh and adds that shawl trade was distributed to other places, notably Amritsar and Lahore.[8] Whereas Forster does not refer to any manufactures in the hills, Grey refers to the manufacture of 'arms, ordnance and accountrements of all descriptions', but these were got manufactured by William O'Brien, the European officer in the

---

[4] Ibid., I, 281-82, 285 & 290.

[5] Ibid., I, 337-38.

[6] Tahmas Khan, *Tahmas Nāmā* (Eng. tr.), 103.

[7] Ganesh Das, *Rājdarshinī* (Eng. tr.), 9-10.

[8] Baron Charles Hugel, *Travels in Kashmir and the Panjab* (tr. & ed. J.B. Jervis), 274.

employment of Sansar Chand of Kangra.[9] In the *District Gazetteer of Kangra*, there is a reference to Kashmiri immigrants who had settled in Nurpur and who manufactured shawls and other woollens.[10] Francklin refers to the exchange of cloths, matchlocks and horses from the plains for commodities sent out from the hills.[11]

The major items of export from the Punjab plains, according to Francklin, were horses, camels, rice, sugar, white cloth, matchlocks, swords, bows and arrows. In addition to rice, sugar and white cloth, wheat and indigo were exported to Kashmir and to the countries west of the Indus. The items of import from there were swords, horses, fruit, lead and spices; and from Kashmir, shawls, saffron, fruit and a variety of cloths.[12] From the Gujarat side, the items of import to the Punjab plains were pearls, gold-thread, elephant's teeth, broad cloths, nutmegs, cloves, dry dates, coconut, iron, lead, copper, vermilion, and drugs.[13] From the Deccan, the imports consisted of iron, sulphur, salt, lead, indigo, coarse broad cloth, and spices.[14] Sohan Lal Suri and Ganesh Das refer to the extraction of salt from the mines of the Salt Range, and its trade during the late eighteenth century.[15]

On the basis of contemporary evidence, H.K. Naqvi suggests that a certain degree of stability in the trade at Lahore was achieved in the 1770s. Goods from Murshidabad came to Lahore through Patna and generally consisted of raw silk, cotton fabrics, silken stuffs and Chinaware. In 1777, for instance, the total cargo forwarded from Patna to Lahore consisted of '1662 maunds 20 seers of raw silk, 11,813 pieces of cotton goods and 9,656 pieces of silken stuffs; there were 3 maunds of vermilion but no Chinaware'.[16]

Contemporary writers also refer to the manufactures of the Punjab plains during the late eighteenth century. According to James Browne, the principal manufactures of the Punjab were fine cloths made at

---

[9] C. Grey, *European Adventurers of Northern India, 1785 to 1849*, 64. Kulu was known for iron mines and Suket and Mandi for copper: Hutchison & Vogel, *Hill States*, II, 482.

[10] *DG Kangra* (1883-84), 252-53.

[11] Ganda Singh (ed.), *Early European Accounts of the Sikhs*, 105.

[12] Ibid., 105-06.

[13] Ibid., 93.

[14] Ibid., 105.

[15] Sohan Lal, *Umdat-ut-Tawārīkh* (Pbi. tr), II, 11. Ganesh Das, *Early Nineteenth Century Panjab* (Eng. tr.), 72.

[16] Hameeda Khatoon Naqvi, *Urban Centres and Industries in Upper India 1556-1803*, 49.

Lahore and also arms which he thought were the best in Hindustan.[17] Griffiths refers to the manufacture of shawls and blankets, white cloths and fine and coarse piece goods at Lahore. He refers also to the manufacture of piece goods, white cloths and *chintz* of all sorts at Multan, and to the manufacture of swords and matchlocks at Gujrat.[18] The principal manufactures of the Punjab noticed by William Francklin towards the end of the eighteenth century were swords, matchlocks, cotton cloths, and coarse and fine silks.[19] According to Polier, the Punjab was known for a breed of the best horses in northern India and, according to Francklin, the Sikh territories were said to contain prodigious quantities of cattle, oxen, cows and sheep as well as horses.[20]

Francklin carried the impression that the trade which the Punjab at one time had with the rest of northern India was no longer there in the late eighteenth century. It did not mean, however, that there was no trade. Commercial intercourse between the Punjab and Hindustan was still there. The merchants who wanted to conduct trade in the territories of the Sikh chiefs had to get passports to enter their territories, but such passports were issued almost as a matter of routine. In the new political situation, new routes of trade had come into use. An important route within the Punjab was from Amritsar to Patiala, by way of Machhiwara. From Patiala, there was a trade route to Rajasthan by way of Hansi and also through Kaithal, Jind and Dadri. There was also a trade route from Patiala to Delhi through Karnal.[21]

As in the hills so in the plains, traders had to pay custom duties. James Browne refers to the partition of Lahore amongst three chiefs, each of whom received a certain share of the revenues from imposts and duties.[22] According to Lepel Griffin, Chaudhari Chhaju Mal reduced the amount of custom duties by more than a half to attract merchants and traders to take up residence in the *katra* founded in Amritsar by Jai Singh Kanhiya.[23] There were bankers and money lenders in the plains as in the hills during the late eighteenth century. In the *District Gazetteer of Montgomery*, besides a general reference to Khatris and Aroras as traders and money lenders, it is explicitly stated that many Aroras repopulated deserted villages under the Nakkai chiefs; many

---

[17] Ganda Singh (ed.), *Early European Accounts of the Sikhs*, 17.

[18] Ibid., 89-90.

[19] Ibid., 102.

[20] Ibid., 66.

[21] Ibid., 105.

[22] Ibid., 16.

[23] *The Panjab Chiefs*, 46.

Khatris also settled in the district during that time.[24] According to Griffin, Gurmukh Singh Lamma's father Pardhan Singh was a money changer in the small town of Khiwa on the right bank of the river Jehlam, opposite Jalalpur, in the time of Mahan Singh Sukarchakia.[25]

An officer of the Bengal army who visited Lahore in the first decade of the nineteenth century observed that as a result of the invasions of Zaman Shah in the late 1790s, the principal bankers and merchants of Lahore had shifted to Amritsar.[26] In spite of the existence of bankers and manufactures even in small towns, Francklin carried the impression that because of the scarcity of precious metals in the Sikh territories, trade was 'chiefly carried on by barter system especially in the manufacturing towns'.[27] Nevertheless, the contemporary writers mention prices in cash.

The information on prices relates only to the extraordinary years of famine and scarcity. Tahmas Khan, for instance, refers to the famine that occured in the Punjab around 1760 and mentions that the price of wheat in Sialkot, Lahore and Jalandhar was more than five and half rupees per maund.[28] During the famine of 1783, grain was sold in Batala at about four and a half rupees a maund; in Lahore, the price of grain was ten rupees a maund; in Gujrat, more than eleven rupees; in Jehlam and Jammu, more than thirteen rupees; and in Sialkot, it was twenty rupees a maund.[29] Ram Sukh Rao, on the other hand, states that during the reign of Bhag Singh Ahluwalia, in 1783, the price of grain was only two rupees per maund.[30] During Zaman Shah's invasion in 1797, the price of wheat is given as 17 seers per rupee, that of *ghee* as 2 seers, of oil 4 seers and of barley as 20 seers a rupee.[31] In the year following, wheat was sold at 20 seers a rupee, rice at 12 seers, pulses at 15 seers, raw sugar at 14 seers, better quality sugar at 3 seers, and *ghee* at two

---

[24] *DG Montgomery* (1884), 69-70.

[25] Lepel Griffin, *The Panjab Chiefs*, 540.

[26] 'A Tour to Lahore (in 1808) by an Officer of the Bengal Army', *Asiatic Annual Register* (1811), 433.

[27] Ganda Singh (ed.), *Early European Accounts of the Sikhs*, 99.

[28] Tahmas Khan, *Tahmas Nāmā* (Eng. tr.), 107. *SR Jhang* (1882), 37.

[29] Extract of a letter dated 13 May 1784, W.S. Setton Carr, *Selections from Calcutta Gazettes*, 14. Krishna Dyal Bhargava, *Browne Correspondence* (Indian Records Series), 310. *SR Sialkot* (1865), 54. *SR Lahore* (1873), 37. *SR Gujrat* (1874), 173. *SR Jehlam* (1883), 99.

[30] Ram Sukh Rao, *Jassa Singh Binod* (ms), f. 249b.

[31] Foreign/Political Consultation, 20 February 1797, No. 15.

and half seers a rupee.[32] These prices were unusual but even so there is no suggestion that cash nexus was absent or even unimportant.

II

The existence of towns and cities in the late eighteenth century Punjab may be regarded as an index of the existence of manufactures and trade. It is necessary to underline, therefore, that many urban centres of the Mughal times were revived by the new rulers of the Punjab during the late eighteenth century. Lahore, for instance, had been utterly ruined during the continuous invasions of Ahmad Shah Abdali. When Gujjar Singh, Lehna Singh and Sobha Singh occupied the city in 1765, they paid much attention to its rehabilitation. They issued a proclamation that whosoever would oppress the subjects, would be punished. Gujjar Singh built Qila Gujjar Singh and invited people to reside there. He laid forty wells for the supply of water and got constructed 15 shops and 150 houses.[33]

Several other chiefs are known to have revived towns. Kamr Singh Nakkai, for instance, rebuilt Satghara which had been sacked around 1745 and abandoned by its inhabitants. He built a brick wall around the town.[34] Gujrat, situated on the imperial road, had been a prey to the advancing and retiring armies of Ahmad Shah. When Gujjar Singh occupied it in 1765, he rebuilt the fort and invited traders and others to reside inside. He spared no efforts to induce the people to settle down to peaceful occupations.[35] Similarly, Sialkot was repopulated by Jiwan Singh, Mohar Singh, Sahib Singh and Natha Singh; Bhera, by Dhanna Singh Kalalwala; Batala, by Jai Singh Kanhiya; Jalalpur, by Rahmat Khan Waraich; and Jhang, by Walidad Khan Sial.[36]

It is true that some of the urban centres of the Mughal times declined, or vanished altogether during the late eighteenth century but the number of those which came up was larger. The development of Ramdaspur, now called Amritsar, is well known. The Golden Temple which was blown up by Ahmad Shah Abdali in 1762 was reconstructed

---

[32] Foreign/Political Proceedings, 11 January 1799, No. 33.

[33] *DG Lahore* (1883-84), 161.

[34] *DG Montgomery* (1933), 36.

[35] *SR Gujrat* (1861), 4-5. A.C. Elliot, *The Chronicles of Gujrat*, 31.

[36] *SR Montgomery* (1874), 36. *SR Shahpur* (1866), 47. *SR Jhang* (1882), 35. Ganesh Das, *Early Nineteenth Century Panjab* (Eng. tr.), 29, 68 & 83. Aliuddin, *Ibratnāma* (Pbi. tr.), 82.

by the Sikh chiefs. They also built their *bungas* around the Golden Temple.[37] Besides the central township, the Sikh chiefs built about a dozen *katras* around, encouraging traders and craftsmen to reside in them. These *katras* provided all the security its inhabitants needed. Every *katra* had its own administration.[38] Some of the chiefs built forts as well, like Jassa Singh Ahluwalia, Jassa Singh Ramgarhia and Mahan Singh Sukarchakia, besides Hari Singh who adopted the town as his capital.[39] Thus, a cluster of townships came to develop around Ramdaspur during the late eighteenth century. There were some other new towns. Dera Baba Nanak developed into an urban centre during the late eighteenth century. Pilgrims started visiting it, especially during the fairs of Baisakhi, Diwali and Kartik Purnima. Traders and craftsmen were added to its population.[40] Rawalpindi was a small village before it was occupied by Milkha Singh Thepuria in 1767. He fortified the place, constructed a number of new buildings, employing a large number of workers. He invited traders from Bhera, Miani, Pind Dadan Khan and Chakwal to settle in Rawalpindi. It became a large town under his administration.[41] Gujranwala under Charhat Singh Sukarchakia, Fatehabad and Kapurthala under Fateh Singh Ahluwalia, Rahon under Tara Singh Dallewalia, Hallowal under Bagh Singh Hallowalia, Phillaur under Tara Singh Kang, Sujanpur under Amar Singh Bagga, Sayyadwala under Kamr Singh Nakkai, and Nur Mahal under Charhat Singh Nur Mahilia

---

[37] J.S. Grewal, *The Reign of Maharaja Ranjit Singh*, 17. *DG Amritsar* (1892-93), 150. Madanjit Kaur, 'The Harmandir', *The City of Amritsar, An Introduction* (ed. Fauja Singh), 36-37. Anand Gauba, *Amritsar: A Study in Urban History, 1849-1947*, 4 & 370.

[38] J.S. Grewal, 'Historical Development of Amritsar', *The City of Amritsar* (ed. Fauja Singh), 377. *DG Amritsar* (1892-93), 150. Ahmad Shah, *Tārīkh-i-Panjab* (Pbi. tr.), 41. Aliuddin, *Ibratnāma* (Pbi. tr.), 76-87. Giani Gian Singh, *Tāwarīkh Sri Amritsar* (ed. Gurdit Singh), 19-20.

[39] The forts were Qila Ahluwalia, Qila Ramgarhia, Qila Sukarchakia and Qila Bhangian: J.S. Grewal, 'Ramdaspur to Amritsar', *Studies in Urban History* (ed. J.S. Grewal & Indu Banga), 120. Anand Gauba, *Amritsar:A Study in Urban History, 1849-1947*, 6.

[40] Indu Banga, 'Polity, Economy and Urbanization in the Upper Bari Doab (1700-1947)', *Studies in Urban History* (ed. J.S. Grewal & Indu Banga), 196.

[41] *DG Rawalpindi* (1895), 52 & 255. Ganesh Das, *Early Nineteenth Century Panjab* (Eng. tr.), 42.

were some of the other places which grew up as urban centres during the late eighteenth century.[42]

Urban centres developed at some altogether new places. Haqiqat Singh Kanhiya, for instance, founded Fatehgarh and Narot Jaimal Singh. His brother Mehtab Singh founded Chittaurgarh.[43] Qila Sobha Singh and Qila Suba Singh were built respectively by Sobha Singh and Suba Singh, sons of Bagh Singh Hallowalia.[44] Nidhan Singh Hattu built Daska.[45] Shuja Khan of Multan built Shujabad, with a fort and a palace. His son Muzaffar Khan founded the town of Muzaffarbad in 1794. His daughter, Khan Bibi, built the fort and the town of Khangarh, while his son founded Ghazanfarabad.[46] Nur Muhammad Chattha, likewise, built Rasulnagar and his son Pir Muhammad, Alipur, Naiwala and Fatehpur.[47] Muhammad Yar Bhatti built Jalalpur Bhattian.[48] Ghamand Chand of Kangra founded Sujanpur. His grandson Sansar Chand built a palace at Tira and the place came to have the double name Tira-Sujanpur.[49] Basohli was enlarged by Raja Amrit Pal and his successor Mohinder Pal.[50] Although many of the towns and cities were founded or revived to serve as administrative centres, this was not their only function. It is impossible to think of the economic activity of the Punjab during the late eighteenth century without its towns and cities.

---

[42] *DG Gujranwala* (1895), 170. Ganesh Das, *Early Nineteenth Century Panjab* (Pbi. tr.), 76, 105, 175. Ganesh Das, *Chār Bāgh-Panjab* (Pbi. tr.), 128. Aliuddin, *Ibratnāma* (Pbi. tr.), 363. *DG Jullundur* (1904), 3-5 & 33. Lepel Griffin, *The Panjab Chiefs*, 512.

[43] Ahmad Shah, *Tārīkh-i-Panjab* (Pbi. tr.), 56.

[44] Munshi Amin Chand, *A History of the Sialkot District*, 150. *DG Sialkot* (1895), 174. Ganesh Das, *Early Nineteenth Century Panjab* (Eng. tr.), 76-77.

[45] Munshi Amin Chand, *A History of the Sialkot District*, 150.

[46] Foreign/Secret Consultation, 7 July 1797, No. 3. *SR Muzaffargarh* (1882), 49-50. F.W. Skemp (tr.), *Multani Stories*, 23.

[47] *DG Gujranwala* (1895), 178. Ganesh Das, *Early Nineteenth Century Panjab* (Eng. tr.), 106-07. J.S. Grewal, *Maharaja Ranjit Singh*, 17. Lepel Griffin, *The Panjab Chiefs*, 403.

[48] Ganesh Das, *Early Nineteenth Century Panjab* (Eng. tr.), 108.

[49] *DG Kangra* (1883-84), 254. Hutchison & Vogel, *Hill States*, I, 176.

[50] Hutchison & Vogel, *Hill States*, II, 591, 608 & 611.

III

Evidence from the nineteenth century on manufactures and trade relates to about forty towns and cities. As may be expected, the majority of these were in the upper Doabs. In fact, later evidence on manufactures and trade in the lower Doabs relates only to ten towns and cities. The most important of these centres were Multan, Mankera, Leia, Kusak, Jhang, Sahiwal, Malka Hans, Pakpatan, Qabula and Kamalia.

There are numerous references to the manufactures and trade of Multan not only in its *District Gazetteer* but also in the *Umdat-ut-Tāwarīkh* and in the work of travellers like Masson and Burnes and in some other records and publications of the early nineteenth century. These references confirm the impression gathered from contemporary accounts that Multan was an important centre of manufactures and trade during the late eighteenth century. The items of manufacture mentioned in these sources are silk and cotton cloth particularly the richer sort of *lungis*, *chintzes*, *gulbadan*, brocades, tissues, wollen carpets, shoes, pottery, ivory stuffs and saddles.[51] There are references also to *hundīs* of large amounts submitted to Ranjit Singh by the chiefs of Multan from time to time.[52] Masson noticed that the Lohani Afghan merchants had an extensive trade between Multan and Afghanistan.[53]

For the lower Sindh Sagar Doab, there are references to transit duties which could not be a new development of the early nineteenth century.[54] Similarly, when Sohan Lal Suri refers to *lungīs*, *gulbadan* and *chintzes* coming from the chief of Mankera to Maharaja Ranjit Singh as tribute in 1817, we may be sure that all these articles were not imported into the territories of the Mankera chief from outside and all of these were not manufactured only in the early decades of the nineteenth century.[55] There is a reference by Masson to transit duties collected on

---

[51] Sohan Lal, *Umdat-ut-Tawārīkh* (Pbi. tr.), II, 64, 164, 178, 199, 202 & 224. Mountstuart Elphinstone, *An Account of the Kingdom of Caubul*, I, 28. Alexander Burnes, *Travels Into Bokhara Containing the Narrative of a Voyage on the Indus From the Sea to Lahore*, I, 95. Foreign/Secret Consultation, 24 August 1840, No. 116. *DG Multan* (1883-84), 106-08.

[52] Sohan Lal, *Umdat-ut-Tawārīkh* (Pbi. tr), II, 117, 130, 164, 199 & 241.

[53] Charles Masson, *Narrative of Various Journeys*, I, 395.

[54] *SR Muzaffargarh* (1882), 83.

[55] Sohan Lal, *Umdat-ut-Tawārīkh* (Pbi. tr), II, 239.

merchandize in the territories of Mankera.[56] Leia is mentioned as a good market for indigo, sugar, *ghee*, grain, cotton, wool, iron and copper.[57] Like Leia, Dera Ismail Khan across the Indus was known for its transit trade.[58]

According to Sohan Lal Suri, the Janjua chief of Kusak used to collect 2 *annas* a rupee as duty on the value of salt extracted from the mines in his territory.[59] Mohan Lal estimated in the 1840s that duty on salt amounted to about two lacs of rupees. In the late 1840s, salt was excavated from the mines of Khewra at the rate of twenty maunds a rupee and sold to merchants at the rate of two rupees. The yearly amount of salt extracted was six lacs of maunds.[60] This concrete information gives a fair idea of the position in the late eighteenth century when the quantities and rates involved could be different but not radically different. According to Ganesh Das, Sahiwal was famous for its *salu*, a piece of dyed red cloth, generally used by brides to cover their heads.[61] Vessels of copper and brass were manufactured there; it was also known for its turners in ivory and wood.[62] Jhang and Maghiana on the eastern bank of the Chenab were known for white cotton cloth which was exported to Afghanistan.[63] Good blankets were made at Malka Hans and Qasur was known for its leather work, particularly shoes and harness.[64] Lungīs and *dohars* manufactured at Pakpatan were carried to Amritsar, Lahore and Multan; *ghee* from Kamalia and Qabula found markets in Multan and Amritsar.[65]

There are several references in the nineteenth century sources to the manufactures and trade of the Jalandhar Doab. In the *Asiatic Annual Register* of 1806, for instance, there is a reference to the famous *chandeli* of Nakodar and other similar kinds of cloth which was carried to Multan, Peshawar and Kabul. At this time, Nakodar was under Tara

---

56 Forrest (ed), 'Masson's Journals', *Selections*, 146-47.

57 Edward Thornton, *A Gazetteer of the Countries Adjascent to India*, II, 22-23.

58 Forrest (ed.), 'Masson's Journals', *Selections*, 146-47.

59 *Umdat-ut-Tawārīkh* (Pbi. tr), II, 118.

60 *Journal of a Tour*, 23. For its position during the Mughal times, *Ā'īn-i-Akbarī* (Eng. tr.), II, 319.

61 Ganesh Das, *Early Nineteenth Century Panjab* (Eng. tr.), 73.

62 *SR Shahpur* (1866), 48.

63 Edward Thornton, *A Gazetteer of the Countries Adjascent to India*, II, 46. *SR Jhang* (1882), 55.

64 *DG Montgomery* (1883-84), 143. *DG Lahore* (1883-84), 197.

65 *DG Montgomery* (1883-84), 143.

Singh Dallewalia.[66] In the *Asiatic Annual Register* of 1809, there is a reference to several kinds of coarse cloth being manufactured at Phagwara.[67] There are references to the manufacture of coarse cloth and *chintzes* at Sultanpur in the *District Gazetteer of Kapurthala State* published in 1904. We may be sure that this was not a new development because Sultanpur was famous for its *chintzes* and quilts during the Mughal times.[68] The later references to the manufacture of sugar not only in Kapurthala but also in the Jalandhar Doab as a whole would not be a new development, because the Jalandhar Doab was known for its manufacture of sugar during the sixteenth and seventeenth centuries.[69] The other agricultural produce of the Doab which entered the market included rice, oil, tobacco, and fruit.[70] There are references also to non-agricultural manufactures in the Jalandhar Doab: brass, copper and bell metal utensils in Phagwara; bows and arrows, silver wire and laces in Jalandhar.[71]

In the Bari Doab, the city of Lahore was the most important centre of manufactures and trade during the Mughal period, known for its fine calico, striped silk, shawls, satin, embroidery, coarse woollen stuffs, turbans, carpets, swords, leather, shoes, boats, bows and arrows, indigo, and sugar. It was connected with the markets of Delhi, Kabul, Kashmir and Multan.[72] Ganesh Das who refers to the revival of Lahore during the late eighteenth century, also refers to the crowding of communities both Hindu and Muslim in the city. Before the end of the eighteenth century, when Lahore was revived as an urban centre, Amritsar had become its rival in manufactures and trade. In the *Asiatic*

---

[66] Maulavi Abdul Qadir, 'Memorandum of the Route between Delhi and Qabul', *Asiatic Annual Register* (1806), 10. There is a general reference to the *sahukārs* of Nakodar in Sohal Lal, *Umdat-ut-Tawārīkh* (Pbi. tr), II, 71.

[67] 'A Tour to Lahore (in 1808) by an Officer in the Bengal Army', *Asiatic Annual Register*, (1811), 427.

[68] Sujan Rai Bhandari, *Khulāsat-ut-Tawārīkh* (Pbi. tr.), 77. Irfan Habib, *An Atlas of the Mughal Empire*, 4B, 12- 13. *DG Kapurthala State* (1904), 45.

[69] Sujan Rai, *Khulāsat-ut-Tawārīkh* (Pbi. tr.), 77. *DG Jalandhar* (1883-84), 46. *SR Hosiarpur* (1885), 97. *DG Kapurthala State* (1904), 21.

[70] *SR Jullundur* (1852), 3. *SR Hoshiarpur* (1885), 97.

[71] *DG Jalandhar* (1883-84), 46. *DG Kapurthala State* (1904), 21.

[72] *Ā'īn-i-Akbarī* (Eng. tr.), I, 98. W.H. Moreland, *India at the Death of Akbar: An Economic Study*, 147, 164 & 166. Irfan Habib, *An Atlas of the Mughal Empire*, 13. Hameeda Khatoon Naqvi, *Urban Centres and Industries in Upper India 1556-1803*, 23, 46-47, 70-71.

Annual Register of 1809, Amritsar is mentioned as the grand emporium of trade for shawls and saffron from Kashmir and a variety of other commodities from the Deccan and from the eastern parts of India. Some coarse kind of cloth and inferior silks were manufactured in Amritsar itself.[73] The district gazetteers of Lahore and Amritsar confirm the impression that enough of the trade and manufacturing activity of Lahore and Amritsar continued into the British period.[74]

The district gazetteer of Gurdaspur suggests a continuation of trade and manufactures in the towns of Batala, Dinanagar, Pathankot, Sujanpur, Dera Baba Nanak and Sri Hargobindpur. The items of manufacture and trade in these towns were *lois*, shawl-weaving, coarse pashmina, leather work, wood carving, and dying of fabrics.[75] In the settlement reports of Gogera and Montgomery, there is a reference to the export of grains from Gogera to Multan and Sirsa. Good cloth was made in Sayyadwala and grain was exported from here to the Rachna Doab while cotton seeds were sent to Jhang and Firozpur.[76]

Sialkot in the Rachna Doab was known for its paper, embroidered muslin, quilts, brocades, daggers and spears.[77] Ganesh Das refers to four categories of fine quality paper in Sialkot.[78] According to the district gazetteer of Sialkot, since much of the Sialkot paper during the Mughal times was exported to other places, its manufacture declined during the late eighteenth century.[79] The statement made by Ganesh Das does suggest, however, that the manufacture of paper in Sialkot survived the political change. In addition to paper, he refers to fine *susi*, *lachas* and *lungīs* as the specialities of Sialkot.[80] The village of Kotli Loharan near Sialkot was known for the manufacture of guns in the late eighteenth century as much as in the early nineteenth.[81] Chiniot was known for its

---

[73] 'A Tour to Lahore (in 1808) by an Officer of the Bengal Army', *Asiatic Annual Register*, (1811), 430. *DG Amritsar* (1892-93), 117.

[74] *DG Lahore* (1883-84), 97. *DG Amritsar* (1892-93), 117.

[75] *DG Gurdaspur* (1883-84), 59, 74, 100 & 103. Rita Grewal, 'Polity, Economy and Urbanization: Early Nineteenth Century Punjab', M.Phil Dissertation, Guru Nanak Dev University, Amritsar, 1985, 65.

[76] *SR Googaira* (1860), 38-39. *SR Montgomery* (1878), 67.

[77] Sujan Rai, *Khulāsat-ut-Tawārīkh* (Pbi. tr.), 83-84. Irfan Habib, *An Atlas of the Mughal Empire*, 13.

[78] Ganesh Das, *Early Nineteenth Century Panjab* (Eng. tr.), 85.

[79] *DG Sialkot* (1895), 167.

[80] Ganesh Das, *Early Nineteenth Century Panjab* (Eng. tr.), 85. *SR Sialkot* (1865), 19.

[81] Sohan Lal, *Umdat-ut-Tawārīkh* (Pbi. tr.), II, 19.

bow makers, wood-carvers, painters and masons.[82] Gujranwala was known for its brass vessels, jewellry, shawl edgings and silk and cotton scarves.[83] Wazirabad, which was famous for its boat building activity during the Mughal period, retained its name for boat building in the nineteenth century in addition to the manufacture of a variety of hardware, metal ware and knives.[84]

In the Chaj Doab, there were only two towns in addition to Sahiwal, which were known for trade and manufactures, namely Gujrat and Bhera. Gujrat was known for its manufacture of matchlocks, swords and daggers, and also for its shawls, embroidry, brass vessels, wood work and shoes.[85] Bhera was known for its excellent stone cutters and its manufacture of arms, cutlery and felt. Some of the other items of trade in Bhera were cotton cloth, iron, rice and sugar.[86]

In the upper Sindh Sagar Doab, Rawalpindi was by far the most important centre of trade and manufactures. Mohan Lal refers to its brass and copper articles.[87] Some of the other places known for their manufactures in the upper Sindh Sagar Doab were Pindi Gheb, Fatehjang and Dangli. The items of manufacture were cloth, blankets, packing bags, saddles, lacquered legs for bed steads and low chairs.[88] Pind Dadan Khan served as a market for salt extracted from the Salt Range.[89]

IV

Looking at the evidence coming from the contemporary observers, we get an unmistakable impression that there was a considerable trade activity in the principalities of the new chiefs of the Punjab during the period under discussion. The contemporary evidence on manufactures of Lahore, Multan and Gujrat is also significant. The first two were the

---

[82] Ibid., 109. *SR Jhang* (1882), 52.

[83] *SR Gujranwala* (1860), 19.

[84] Irfan Habib, *An Atlas of the Mughal Empire*, 13.

[85] Ganesh Das, *Early Nineteenth Century Panjab* (Eng. tr.), 62. Shahamat Ali, *The Sikhs and the Afghans*, 63. *DG Gujrat* (1883-84), 115.

[86] *SR Shahpur* (1866), 47-48. David Ross, *Land of the Five Rivers*, 155.

[87] *Journal of a Tour*, 330.

[88] Ibid., 12. *DG Rawalpindi* (1895), 191-92.

[89] Edward Thornton, *A Gazetteer of the Countries Adjascent to India*, II, 103-04.

most important manufacturing and trade centres of the Punjab during the Mughal period and their revival, however partial during the late eighteenth century, was important. Gujrat too was a manufacturing centre during the Mughal period. It is interesting to note that there is considerable continuity in the manufacturing activities of urban centres from the sixteenth to the eighteenth century. Towards the end of the sixteenth century, the items of manufacture in Lahore were fine calico, striped silk, shawls, carpets, coarse woollen stuffs, felts, swords and bows and arrows.[90] Towards the end of the eighteenth century, the items were fine cloths, arms, shawls and blankets, white cloths and fine and coarse piece-goods. For Multan, during the Mughal period, the items manufactured were woollen and cotton carpets, *chintz* and bows. During the late eighteenth century, the items were piece-goods, white cloths and *chintz*. In Gujrat, the items in the Mughal period were swords and daggers. In the late eighteenth century, the items were swords and matchlocks.

Looking at the evidence for urbanization, there is hardly any doubt that some of the towns and cities of the Mughal period suffered a decline and a few of them lost their status as urban centres. It is more important, however, that many of the important urban centres were revived, not only the capital cities of Lahore and Multan but also the important towns like Gujrat, Sialkot, Batala, Jalandhar, Dipalpur, Wazirabad and Rahon. Even more important is the fact that some important urban centres grew up all afresh. The most important of these was Amritsar. Some of the other important examples were Rawalpindi, Gujranwala and Kapurthala. It is equally to the point that if the size of some of the former towns and cities became smaller during the late eighteenth century, the number of urban centres increased very considerably. Most of the towns and cities of the late eighteenth century served not only as centres of administration but also as centres of distribution, trade and manufactures.

Turning to the nineteenth century sources, we come upon occasional statements about the late eighteenth century. For instance, salt mines continued to be worked during the time of the Janjua chiefs.

---

90 The information on the items of manufactures in Lahore, Multan and Gujrat has been taken from Irfan Habib, *An Atlas of the Mughal Empire*, 4B.

Secondly, the evidence coming from the first decade of the nineteenth century is almost contemporary. In Phagwara, coarse cloth was manufactured.[91] Besides coarse cloth inferior silks were manufactured in Amritsar. Furthermore, when Sohan Lal Suri mentions the items coming from Mankera in the second decade of the nineteenth century, it may not be unsafe to assume that manufacture of these items was not altogether a new development. Lastly, there is much more evidence relating to the trade activity and manufactures of a large number of towns and cities in the area under consideration to argue that this activity was not entirely new, particularly when we know that many of these towns and cities were coming up in the late eighteenth century. Thus, when we combine the nineteenth century information with contemporary evidence, we get the impression that what we know in concrete terms is really much less than what was actually there.

On the whole, we may conclude that if manufactures and trade in the Punjab declined during the middle decades of the eighteenth century, there was a visible revival before its end. However, in the absence of concrete and detailed data, it is not possible to institute a quantitative comparison between the situation during the early and the late eighteenth century, or between the situation during the late eighteenth century and the early nineteenth. Nevertheless, the available evidence leaves the dominant impression that the economy of the Punjab during the early nineteenth century was not so much a fresh development as a continuation of the development in witness during the late eighteenth century.

Lest it should appear that we have come to an exceptional kind of conclusion about the urban economy of the Punjab during the late eighteenth century, we may quote the observations of G.D. Sharma about the urban economy in Western India during the late eighteenth century: 'By the middle of the eighteenth century, the Mughal empire in many parts of the Indian subcontinent was replaced by regional states. The absence of central political control did not, however, necessarily imply any serious disruption in regional economies. The financial policies of the Marathas and the Rajputs were dictated by their immediate requirements, and their methods resulted in a process of commercialisation in which merchant capital played a vital role.

---

[91] Maulavi Abdul Qadir, 'Memorandum of the Route Between Delhi and Qabul', *Asiatic Annual Register* (1806), 10. 'A Tour to Lahore (in 1808) by an Officer of the Bengal Army', *Asiatic Annual Register* (1811), 427.

Consequently, not only the cities but also the *pargana* towns became centres of trade and commerce which in turn strengthened merchant capital'.[92]

---

[92]'Urban Economy in Western India in late Eighteenth Century', *The City in Indian History* (ed. Indu Banga), Manohar Publications, Delhi, 1991, 99.

8

CONCLUSION

What strikes us first in the politics of the Punjab during the late eighteenth century is the large number of political units, numbering in fact about one hundred and twentyfive. Nearly forty of these were in the hills, and they were not exactly new principalities. Even so, the number of new principalities was very large: seventeen in the Bist Jalandhar Doab, thirtythree in the Bari Doab, twenty in the Rachna Doab, three in the Chaj Doab and fourteen in the Sindh Sagar Doab. The average area of a principality in the plains was about 800 square miles. In the upper Doabs of the Punjab which covered an area of about 40,000 square miles, there were nearly seventy principalities, the average area of a principality coming to about 600 square miles. In the lower Doabs, where seventeen principalities covered about 30,000 square miles, the average area of a principality was more than 1,750 square miles.

None of the new principalities was really large. In terms of revenue from land, only about half a dozen of them had the annual income of more than ten lacs of rupees a year. The number of principalities with an annual income of five to ten lacs of rupees was less than a dozen. Nearly a dozen principalities had a yearly income of two and a half to five lacs of rupees. The annual income of over a score of principalities ranged from one to two and a half lacs. There were nearly forty principalities with an annual income of less than one lac of rupees. A few of these could collect only about 20,000 rupees a year. Thus, though all the principalities were small, the difference between the largest and the smallest was rather considerable. Similarly, in terms of area, the range between the largest and the smallest principality was rather large though the area even of the largest principality was much less than the area of two average districts of the British Punjab.

Turning to the religious affiliation of the rulers, we find that the majority of the rulers were Sikh. However, the combined number of Hindu and Muslim chiefs in the area under study was larger than that of the Sikh chiefs. The Hindu chiefs were mostly in the hills, numbering about thirty. Of the Muslim chiefs, there were only ten in the hills, but twentyseven in the plains. The total number of Sikh principalities in the plains was about sixty. In terms of their racial background, nearly all the chiefs of the hills were Rajput. They were divided into several branches. Several of the chiefs in the plains also claimed Rajput status, like the Gakkhars of Rawalpindi, the Khokhars of Pind Dadan Khan, the Janjuas of Kusak and Malot, the Jodrahs of Pindi Gheb, the Sials of Jhang, the Bhattis of Kapurthala and Jalalpur Bhattian, the Manj of Talwan and Nakodar, the Kharals of Kot Kamalia, the Ghebas of Kot, and the Tiwanas of Nurpur.

The number of Jat rulers was equally large. More than eighty per cent of the Sikh rulers were Jat, belonging to the clans of Sandhu, Randhawa, Gill, Man, Virk, Sidhu, Kahlon, Kang, Dhillon, Dhaliwal, Bajwa, Khaira, Ghumman, Bhangu, Chhina and Waraich. The largest number came from amongst the Sandhus; as many as nine chiefs belonged to this clan. Five of the Jat chiefs were Randhawa; three each were Gill, Man and Virk; two each were Sidhu, Kahlon and Kang; and one each was Dhillon, Dhaliwal, Bajwa, Khaira, Ghumman, Bhangu, Chhina, and Waraich. In some cases at least there was a correlation between the number of chiefs and the strength of their clans. However, all the Jat chiefs were not Sikh: the Wattus, the Hans, the Chatthas, the Niranjanias, for example. The number of non-Jat and non-Rajput rulers was rather small. The most important among them were the Afghan chiefs of Multan, Mankera and Qasur. Similarly, there were three Baloch chiefs in Leia, Shahpur and Khushab. There were two important principalities established by individuals belonging to the lower castes of the traditional varna order, namely the Ramgarhias of Sri Hargobindpur who were carpenters and the Ahluwalias of Kapurthala who were originally Kalals, the distillers of liquor. It has been possible to identify two Khatri chiefs during the late eighteenth century, one with his headquarters at Banga in the Jalandhar Doab and the other at Makhad in the Sindh Sagar Doab.

The late eighteenth century rulers of the Punjab came from different political backgrounds. The non-Sikh chiefs who established themselves in the hills were actually the members of dynasties older than the Mughals. They had lost their independence during the Mughal rule and were paying regular tribute to their suzerains and serving them with contingents when required. When Ahmad Shah Abdali supplanted the Mughals in the province of Lahore, he tried to exercise suzerain rights over the hill chiefs. With the removal of the Mughal and the Afghan authority from the Punjab, the majority of the hill chiefs became independent.

The non-Sikh chiefs of the plains belonged to three categories: the former Afghan governors who became independent due to political upheavals in Afghanistan, like the Saddozai rulers of Multan and Mankera; influential individuals belonging to different religious groups who became involved in politics, raised forces, acquired territories, collected revenues and became chiefs, like the Niranjanias of Jandiala, the Sayyads of Hujra Shah Muqim, and the Chishti Shaikhs of Pakpatan; the rest of them were the former *jāgīrdārs* and intermediary *zamindārs* under the Mughals. During the eighteenth century, when the hold of the Mughal government weakened, these intermediaries started keeping the revenues with themselves. They acquired more resources and power. When Ahmad Shah Adbali invaded India, they paid tribute to him, if necessary, to be confirmed in their possessions. Thus, when Ahmad Shah Abdali or his successor was unable to come to the Punjab, the autonomous chiefs had only to withhold tribute and to defend themselves against their neighbours to become independent.

The political background of the Sikh chiefs of the Punjab during the late eighteenth century was different from that of the Hindu and Muslim chiefs. Whereas, the chiefs in the hills became independent rulers in the absence of the political framework of the Mughal empire, and the Muslim chiefs could take advantage largely of its administrative framework, the first generation of the Sikh chiefs had actually been descendants of ordinary subjects of the Mughal empire belonging to the cultivating class or to the classes associated with it. They set aside the Mughal politico-administrative framework altogether and they had to wage a long struggle for establishing their principalities. What enabled them to wage a long political struggle and to emerge as rulers was essentially the institutions they evolved, like the *gurmata*, *dal khālsā*, *rakhī* and the *misl*.

The information available on the individual chiefs of the Punjab during the late eighteenth century enables us to know something of the political process after their principalities were founded. It is interesting to note first of all that several of the Sikh chiefs occupied territories at a time when Ahmad Shah Abdali was supposed to be ruling over the Punjab. Some of these Sikh chiefs could rightly claim that they had founded their principalities in the 1750s. This, incidentally, throws an interesting light on the Sikh-Afghan struggle. It was not the question of Ahmad Shah Abdali trying to persecute or extirpate the Sikhs; it was a struggle for territorial occupation. While Ahmad Shah Abdali was try-

trying to establish his effective control over the territories wrested from the Mughals, the leaders of the Khalsa were trying to wrest from Ahmad Shah Abdali as much of the territory as they could. Their common aspiration imparted cohesion and solidarity to their enterprize. It was not an accident, therefore, that the Sikhs evolved their characteristic institutions during this struggle.

However, once the Sikh leaders had established their principalities, they became more and more like the other chiefs of the region. They started joining opposing sides in battles, fighting in fact a few battles of their own. In this, they were not different from the chiefs of the hills, or the chiefs of the lower Doabs. In this whole process, in any case, several of the newly established principalities were wiped out, like Bangahal, Kutlehr and Shahpur in the hills, Kapurthala, Nakodar, Qadian, Rasulnagar, Pind Dadan Khan, Ahmadabad, and Rawalpindi in the upper Doabs, and Malka Hans and Haveli in the lower Doabs. It is more significant, however, that the majority of the late eighteenth century principalities survived into the early nineteenth. Their survival may be attributed largely to the fact that none of the new chiefs possessed adequate resources for aggrandizement at the cost of others, and the more powerful chiefs were not prepared to combine their resources against the others.

Nevertheless, the relative position of the late eighteenth century chiefs did not remain the same throughout the period. In the hills, the chiefs of three principalities came successively into prominence: the chiefs of Jammu, Chamba and Kangra. In the lower Doabs, the most promiment chiefs were those of Multan, Jhang, Bahawalpur and Leia. By the last decade, however, the chief of Leia had been replaced by the ruler of Mankera, and Multan was still the most prominent principality. The chiefs of Jhang suffered loss of territory, and therefore in power and prestige. Bahawalpur became independent of Multan but eventually to become subordinate to the British on the south of the Satlej and to Ranjit Singh in the north. In the upper Doabs of the Punjab, the important chiefs before 1775 were Charhat Singh, Hari Singh, Gujjar Singh, Jassa Singh Ahluwalia, Jassa Singh Ramgarhia and Jai Singh Kanhiya. Charhat Singh was able to take over Pind Dadan Khan worth over six lacs of rupees a year, and Gujjar Singh took Rawalpindi worth over three lacs of rupees a year. By the last decade of the eighteenth century, the successors of Hari Singh and Jassa Singh Ramgarhia had suffered loss in resources and prestige. Thus, there were only four prominent chiefs: Ranjit Singh, Fateh Singh Ahluwalia, Sada Kaur and Sahib Singh of Gujrat. By'the first decade of the eighteenth century, Fateh

Singh Ahluwalia and Sada Kaur had joined hands with Ranjit Singh, which may largely account for his success and the downfall of Sahib Singh among a host of other chiefs, both Sikh and non-Sikh.

In the administrative organization of the principalities during the late eighteenth century, there was hardly any change in the hills, understandably because the vassal chiefs were always autonomous in the internal administration and they did not feel the need of introducing any change on becoming independent. In the lower Doabs, however, the change in administrative organization was quite appreciable. There were no provincial governors because their position was occupied by the chiefs themselves. Some of the chiefs appointed *wazīrs* to assist them in the affairs of government and administration. However, there was no *sadr* to look after the administration of justice and charitable grants. His counterpart now was a *qāzī* at the court who was appointed by the chief. The *qāzīs* outside the capital continued to function as before. The chiefs appointed their own *dīwāns*, *faujdārs* and *thānadārs*. At the *pargana* level, the *'āmils* continued to function as before, occasionally called *kārdārs* and assisted by *qānūngos*, *chaudharīs* and *muqaddams*. Thus, the change was confined largely to the top. The arrangements at the *pargana* level were not affected by the political change.

In the upper Doabs, the chief headed the civil and military administration, assisted by a *dīwān* or *dīwāns* at his headquarters. The *pargana* became synonymous with *ta'alluqa* as the most important unit of administration under a *kārdār* who was responsible for its entire administration under the supervision of the chief. He was assisted by *qānūngos*, *chaudharīs* and *muqaddams*. The size of the *ta'alluqa* in many cases remained the same, while in others it became either larger or smaller. At several places, the *qāzī* too continued to function now as before. Thus, in the upper Doabs also the important change took place at the top but not at the *ta'alluqa* level.

The armies of the chiefs of the late eighteenth century were understandably rather small. Even under the chief of some consequence the number of troops ranged from 5,000 to 15,000. The proportion of the troops directly under the chief (*fauj-i-khās*) was even smaller. The majority of the troops were provided by the *jāgīrdārs* under their own command. There were no war elephants, no heavy artillery, though some of the chiefs had a few small cannons. Swivels and matchlocks were in use, but not on a large scale. The most important wing of the army was the cavalry. The highest ambition of a brave man was to be a *ghurcharha*. Infantry was used for garrison duty as well as on the field of battle. Forts and fortresses were constructed for the purposes of defence.

In the absence of effective equipment for siege, the attacker depended on bribery or long siege. The commanders of artillery were generally Muslim under all the chiefs who had any artillery worth the name. In the early nineteenth century, Sansar Chand of Kangra employed a European as a gunner, becoming thus a forerunner of Ranjit Singh in this respect.

The political process by which the new principalities were established during the late eighteenth century ensured the predominance of some ethnic or religious groups in the government and administration of the principalities. Both in the civil administration and in the army, important assignments were given to the members of the same group. However, there were some significant exceptions. The artillery commanders, as we noticed above, were generally Muslim. Similarly, the *dīwāns* in all the principalities were generally Hindu, mostly *khatrīs*. The *qāzīs* also continued to function in several non-Muslim principalities. Similarly, there was hardly any change in the traditional composition of the *qānūngos*, *chaudharīs* and *muqaddams*. On a small scale, thus, in a sense, the tradition of the Mughal administration was kept up. There were changes in the personnel and even designations but no significant change in the basic framework and functions.

The late eighteenth century polity in the Punjab was characterized by a system which can be referred to as monarchical, with the suzerain-vassal relationship as its important feature. As a successor of the Mughals, Ahmad Shah Abdali had tried to assert his suzerain rights over the old and new chiefs of the Punjab but with a limited success. Only a few chiefs of the Punjab recognized the suzerainty of his successors, and that too for a limited period. This did not mean, however, that every chief in the Punjab was an independent monarch. In the hills, for example, Ranjit Dev of Jammu, Raj Singh of Chamba and Sansar Chand of Kangra established their suzerain rights over a large number of principalities in the hills. In the lower Doabs, the chief of Mankera claimed suzerain rights over half a dozen principalities. In the upper Doabs, there is hardly any example of a Sikh chief asserting suzerain rights over another Sikh chief, but there are many known instances of Sikh chiefs asserting suzerain rights over non-Sikh chiefs in the hills as well as the plains. Important among such overlords were Jassa Singh Ahluwalia, Charhat Singh, Hari Singh, Gujjar Singh, Jassa Singh Ramgarhia and Jai Singh. The principalities which they subordinated in the hills were Jammu, Akhnur, Bhimber, Khari Khariali, Guler, Jaswan, Siba, Datarpur, Kangra, Nurpur, Mandi, Suket, Chamba and Bhadarwah. In the plains, their vassal territories were Kapurthala,

Phagwara, Talwan, Rasulnagar, Pindi Gheb, Kot, Shamsabad, Jhang and Pind Dadan Khan. These lists do not exhaust the number of vassal territories, or of the Sikh overlords. It may also be pointed out that the overlordship did not necessarily last long, partly because some of the vassal territories were eventually annexed by the overlords themselves. Thus, we can see that the suzerain-vassal relationship was important not only for polity but also for the political process. Nevertheless, in one sense it was certainly less important now than in the Mughal times. The only condition insisted upon by the overlord now generally was the payment of tribute.

The historians of the Punjab have looked upon Sikh polity as different from the polity of the rest of the region. In this connection, what J.D. Cunningham referred to as 'theocratic, confederate, feudalism' has been interpreted in ways which underline the importance of the *sarbat khālsā*, the *gurmata*, the *dal khālsā*, the *rakhī* and the *misl*, attaching at the same time a special significance to the Sikh coins. On closer examination it becomes clear that Sikh doctrine which played a significant role in the context of the eighteenth century was the doctrine of Guru-Panth. It enabled the Sikh leaders and their followers to meet as a community and to take decisions on common issues of importance. Since the majority of these decisions related to armed action, they brought the combined forces of the Sikh leaders into action, constituting the *dal khālsā*. Thus, the *sarbat khālsā*, the *gurmata* and the *dal khālsā* were different aspects of a single situation. The action of the *dal khālsā* related to territorial occupation, and *gurmatas* were not extended to the realm of administration and government. Under the *rakhī* system, the Sikh leaders or the chiefs could levy a part of the land revenue from an unoccupied territory on the theoretical assurance that no one else would be allowed to collect the rest of the revenue, or taxes. The *misl* was a voluntary combination of Sikh leaders and their followers for the purpose of conquest and territorial occupation. On many occasions, thus, a combination of the *misls* constituted the *dal khālsā*. There is no doubt whatsoever that all these 'institutions' were extremely important for territorial occupation but none of them had any direct bearing on government and administration.

The Sikh coins are looked upon not only as a declaration of independence by the Sikhs but also as the symbol of their collective sovereignty. The basic argument is that the inscriptions on these coins refer to political power as derived from Guru Nanak or from God. The name of any individual chief does not appear on the coins. There are numerous examples, however, of the seals of the Sikh chiefs bearing their names and invoking God for help. Even the epithet *khālsāji* is often used for the individual chief. Therefore, it may be safely inferred that the coins current in the dominions of the Sikh chiefs, declaring the common derivation of their power from the Guru or God, ensured the sovereignty of each individual. This was in consonance with the fact that no Sikh chief acknowledged the overlordship of another, whether Sikh or non-Sikh. The sovereignty of the individual Sikh chief was unambiguously expressed in his relations with other chiefs and his undivided and unqualified control over his territories.

Unlike Prinsep, the contemporary European observers of the Punjab during the late eighteenth century gathered the impression that the cultivation in the dominions of the Sikhs was in a good state and the condition of the peasantry too was better than elsewhere. This impression appears to be justified from other information about the land revenue administration. In the whole of the Punjab, in fact, *batāī* and *kankūt* were far more important than *zabt* as the methods of assessment; the former two were always more welcome to the cultivators than the third. In the case of *zabt*, collection was always made in cash but in the case of *kankūt* and *batāī*, the officials could turn the revenue collected in kind into cash by selling the commodity on their own initiative. Some cesses also were collected from the cultivators. Extension of cultivation was encouraged by giving grants of revenue-free land. There was no appreciable change in the pattern of crops and there was no change in the administration at the *pargana* level. Thus, there is hardly any evidence, direct or indirect, to support Prinsep's assumption that no class could find happiness, contentment or rest in a country ruled by seventy thousand sovereigns.

Although, we have more information on *jāgīrs* in the upper Doabs of the Punjab during the late eighteenth century, there is hardly any doubt that the system as such was prevalent in the hills and the lower Doabs as well. In fact, the pattern of *jāgīrs* appears to be close to what was there under the Mughals. There are instances of *jāgīrs* given for military service, some of which were pretty large. There are instances of *jāgīrs* given to single horsemen. *Jāgīrs* were given to individuals for performing services in the civil administration, to *dīwāns*, *qāzīs*, and *qānūngos*. There are instances of *jāgīrs* given to several other categories of individuals, like *lāngarīs* and *mallāhs*. *In'ām jāgīrs* were given as a reward for acts of gallantry and other meritorious acts as well as for bringing waste land under cultivation. Subsistence *jāgīrs* were given to close relations by the chiefs to enable them to live in accordance with their social status. No exact figures are available but there is enough evidence to infer that generally about half of the revenues were alienated in *jāgīrs*. From the two known instances of *jāgīrs* given to outsiders by Sansar Chand of Kangra, we get the impression that the chiefs of the hills were not always reluctant to give *jāgīrs* for service. The *jāgīrdārī* system during the late eighteenth century accommodated social change, and thereby introduced a certain element of political stability.

As is the case of *jāgīrdārs*, so in the case of the grantees, the pattern during the late eighteenth century remained very much similar to the pattern existing earlier under the Mughals. Almost all the chief confirmed old grants as a matter of routine and gave fresh grants of their own. Formal orders were issued which were essentially similar to the orders of the Mughal times in their operative part. There was a tendency among the chiefs to treat *madad-i-ma'āsh* or *dharmarth* grants as hereditary. The example of the chiefs was followed by *jāgīrdārs*, and even by *chaudharīs* and *muqaddams*. The largest proportion of fresh grants went to the co-religionists of the chiefs but the others were not ignored. It is interesting to note in this connection that the descendants of Guru Nanak were given grants not only by Sikh but also by Hindu and Muslim chiefs. We get the impression that the Sikh chiefs gave more grants to individuals and institutions belonging to faiths other than their own. But this was partly because the proportion of non-Sikh religious personages and institutions in the dominions of the Sikh chiefs was very large. This was not the pattern of demographic distribution in either the hills or the lower Doabs. In any case, grants were given to religious personages and institutions of all faiths throughout the Punjab during the late eighteenth century. To complete the picture, it may be added that grants were given for the distribution of medicine, or food or water. Grants were given also in cash. It is possible to maintain that the pattern of state patronage remained very similar to what was there before.

There is evidence of deurbanization in the Punjab during the late eighteenth century in the sense that some of the urban centres of the Mughal times either went out of existence or became merely villages. However, many of them continued to exist, or they were revived. Furthermore, several new urban centres were founded. If the size of the cities became smaller, the number of urban centres became much larger. Nearly all of them were administrative centres, but not merely administrative centres. There was varying degree of trade or manufacture in all of them. Not only in terms of survival, but also of trade and manufacturing activities, there was a significant continuity in the case of

Lahore, Multan, Sialkot, Gujrat, Batala and Jalandhar. Several new urban centres came to be known for their specialities. This indirect evidence of trade and manufacture from the growth of urbanization is supported by direct evidence of contemporary and near contemporary records. The possibility of a relative shift from the upper Doabs to the hills and the lower Doabs can be postulated, but the revival of trade and manufactures in the upper Doabs before the end of the eighteenth century is not in doubt. The correlation that is generally assumed by historians between political disintegration and economic decline does not get support from what we know of the Punjab during the late eighteenth century.

Already known and fresh information has enabled us to answer many questions which provide better understanding of the late eighteenth century Punjab. We may now consider the significance of this understanding in the context of Mughal and Sikh history, the two major contexts for the history of the Punjab during the eighteenth century. We have seen that the holders of formal positions in the administrative framework of the Mughal or the Afghan empire as vassal chiefs, governors, *jāgīrdārs*, *zamīndārs*, and holders of large *madad-i-ma'āsh* grants took advantage of the declining control of the central and provincial authorities to carve out principalities for themselves either directly or through a phase of suzerain-vassal relationship. This enables us to see the decline of the old and the rise of the new powers as two aspects of the same process. In the case of the Sikh chiefs, who rose into power by discarding the Mughal administrative framework, there is another point to consider. Irfan Habib's suggestion that peasant discontent could be channelized into revolt by the cohesive force of a common religious bond has to be expanded further by suggesting that religious doctrines had to be translated into political institutions for a successful struggle as exemplified by the Sikhs.

The political process which brought new rulers into power resulted in significant changes but the institutions of the Mughal times survived the overthrow of the Mughals. The institutional continuity is most clearly visible in the suzerain-vassal relationship, the *jāgīrdārī* system, the system of charitable grants, and the revenue administration at the *pargana* level. Indeed, the resilience of institutions is evident also from the developments of the early nineteenth century when the entire Punjab came under the political authority of a single ruler. Furthermore, the urban and agrarian economy of the Punjab during the early nineteenth century was a continuation of the developments during the late eighteenth. Even more significant was the way in which the pattern of state patronage was reinforced during the early nineteenth century.

We have already suggested that in the context of the late eighteenth century polity the Sikh chief was no different from the other chiefs of the Punjab. He was a monarch in the sense that he held undivided authority over the territories under his control, a position which he could bequeath to one of his heirs. It is interesting to note that Ranjit Singh, the second successor of Charhat Singh and therefore the third chief of the dynasty, has been looked upon as the first Sikh monarch of the Punjab. But the only difference in his position before and after 1800 was that of the scale of his dominions. He was indeed a successor of Prinsep's seventy thousand sovereigns.

There are historians of the Sikhs who have tended to present Ranjit Singh as a representative of the Sikh Panth. It is argued that he issued no coin in his own name and he referred to his government as the *sarkār-i-khālsā*. This view is based on the erroneous impression that the inscriptions on the Sikh coins symbolized collective sovereignty of the Khalsa and that *sarkār-i-khālsā* refers to the government of the Khalsa Panth. We have seen that the terms *sarkār* and *khālsāji* were used for many individual chiefs of the late eighteenth century. Ranjit Singh's position was no different from their position. It may be mentioned in this connection that on a slab over the entrance to the Golden Temple, Ranjit Singh refers to himself as 'Maharaja'.

Lastly, we may consider the situation during the early nineteenth century when the Punjabis, that is the people of the region itself, came to have the largest share in the political power and economic resources of the region. In the employment of Ranjit Singh, there were some foreigners and some non-Punjabis. But the bulk of the ruling class at the higher rungs and the whole of the ruling class at its lower rungs was Punjabi. The essential similarity of this pattern with that of the late eighteenth century did not appear to be so evident earlier as now when we know that in the region as a whole during the late eighteenth century, the political power nearly at all levels was in the hands of the people of the region. It has been suggested that Punjabi identity as it was expressed in Punjabi literature was the result partly of the emergence of a ruling class which was predominantly Punjabi. This was not a development of the early nineteenth but of the late eighteenth century. It should not come to us as a surprise if the creative writers of the Punjab started giving expression to Punjabi regional sentiment much before Ranjit Singh appeared on the scene.

APPENDIX

THE CHIEFS

Basic information on the bulk of the principalities discussed in the body of this work has been tabulated here. The first known chief of each principality figures in alphabetical order. In the third entry, the headquarters of the principality is given first, followed by other identified territories shown on the map. The years of temporary possession are given in brackets in some cases. Territories on the other side of the Satlej are also shown in brackets. The resources of a principality are given in rupees, wherever information was available. In the column of succeeding chiefs, the names of the successors are given with the years of their rule (and not of life) in brackets. All other columns are rather self-explanatory.

The Chiefs

Sl. No.	*First known chief*	*Territories and revenues (in rupees)*	*Racial background*	*Religious affiliation*	*Succeeding chiefs*	*Position in relation to the contemporary chiefs*	*Position in relation to Ranjit Singh*
1	2	3	4	5	6	7	8
1.	Ahmad Khan	Nakodar; worth 1 lac.	Rajput (Manj)	Muslim	—	Lost territories to Tara Singh Dallewalia in 1767 and received subsistence *jāgīr*.	—
2.	Alam Khan	Akhnur; worth 50,000.	Rajput (Akhnuria)	Muslim	—	Paid tribute to Ranjit Dev of Jammu and Mahan Singh Sukarchakia.	Lost territories in 1812.
3.	Amar Singh Bagga	Sujanpur; Sukalgarh,	Jat (Man)	Sikh	Bhag Singh (1805-08),	—	Made subordinate in 1805; lost

		Dharmkot, Narot, Behrampur, Shakargarh, Bhagowal.			Buddh Singh (1808-09).		territories in 1809; received *jāgīr*.
4.	Arbel Singh	40 villages around Sidhu in the Bari Doab	Jat (Sidhu)	Sikh	Bhup Singh, Kahn Singh.	—	Lost territories; received service *jāgīr*.
5.	Azmat Dev	Mankot (Ramkot); worth 50,000.	Rajput (Mankotia)	Hindu	Dalel Singh, Achar Singh.	Paid tribute to Ranjit Dev of Jammu.	Made subordinate in 1809; lost territories in 1820; received subsistence *jāgīr*.
6.	Bagh Singh Hallowalia	Zafarwal; Hallowal, Bal, Dhodha, Saukanwind, Changi-Changa, Qila Sobha Singh, Qila Suba Singh, Gulmohar, Alwalpur, Wadala, Talwandi; worth 1,50,000.	Jat	Sikh	—	—	Made subordinate in 1804; lost territories in 1810; received subsistence *jāgīr*.

1	2	3	4	5	6	7	8
7.	Bahadur Singh	Kirmchi (Bhoti); worth 20,000.	Rajput (Bhotial)	Hindu	—	Paid tribute to Ranjit Dev of Jammu.	Made subordinate in 1809; lost territories in 1834; received subsistence *jāgīr*.
8.	Bandu Khan	Khari Khariali; Mangla; worth 1 lac.	Rajput (Chib)	Muslim	Umar Khan, Akbar Ali Khan.	Paid tribute to Ranjit Dev of Jammu, Gujjar Singh and Sahib Singh.	Made subordinate and lost territories in 1810; received subsistence *jāgīr*.
9.	Bikram Sen	Suket; worth 70,000.	Rajput (Suketia)	Hindu	Ranjit Sen, Bikram Sen II (1790-1838), Ugar Sen (1838-76).	Paid tribute to Jassa Singh Ramgarhia from 1770 to 1775; to Jai Singh Kanhiya from 1775 to 1786; to Sansar Chand from 1786 to 1809.	Made subordinate in 1809; lost territories in 1840.

10.	Charhat Singh	Gujranwala; Eminabad, Qila Didar Singh, Qila Sahib Singh, Sayyadpur, Chakwal, Jalalpur, Jehlam, Rohtas, Salt Range, Kotli Loharan, Pind Dadan Khan, Ahmadabad, Naushehra, Daulatnagar, Daud Khel, Dallur, Kunjah, Kuthala, and Manchar; worth 13 lacs.	Jat	Sikh	Mahan Singh (1774-90), Ranjit Singh (1790-1839).	Received tribute from the chiefs of Pindi Gheb, Kot, Shamsabad, Malot, Rasulnagar, Jammu and Akhnur.	—
11.	Charhat Singh Sangatpuria	28 villages in Amritsar and Gurdaspur district; worth 40,000.	Jat (Sandhu)	Sikh	Sardul Singh, Nar Singh & Didar Singh.	—	Lost territories in 1805; received service *jāgīr*.
12.	Churh Mal	Phagwara; worth 50,000.	—	—	—	Paid tribute to Jassa Singh Ahluwalia and his successors	Lost territories in 1804; received subsistence *jāgīr*.

1	2	3	4	5	6	7	8
13.	Dal Singh Akalgarhia	Akalgarh; Ahmadabad, Chawinda, Adamke; worth 2 lacs.	Jat (Gill)	Sikh	—	—	Lost territories in 1804; received subsistence *jāgīr*.
14.	Daud Khan	Dipalpur; worth 35,000.	Pathan	Muslim	Jalaluddin Khan (1772-1804), Giasuddin Khan (1804-1807).	Paid tribute to Ran Singh Nakkai.	Lost territories in 1807; received service *jāgīr*.
15.	Devi Chand	Kahlur (Bilaspur); and the territories on the south of the Satlej; worth 70,000.	Rajput (Kahluria)	Hindu	Mahan Chand (1778-1824).	Lost Fathpur, Bahadurpur and Ratanpur to the chief of Nalagarh.	Made subordinate in 1809.
16.	Dhanna Singh Kalalwala	Bhera; Kalalwala, Panwana, Chaubara, Maharajke.	Jat (Bajwa)	Sikh	Jodh Singh (1793-1806).	—	Lost Bhera in 1803 and other territories in 1806; received service *jāgīr*.

17.	Dharm Das	Jodhanagri; and 40 villages; worth 35,000.	—	—	Ram Chand, Lachhman Das.	Paid tribute to Jassa Singh Ahluwalia and his successors.	Lost territories in 1804; received subsistence *jāgīr*.
18.	Dharm Singh Amritsaria	Banga	Khatri	Sikh	—	—	Made subordinate in 1804; lost territories in 1806; received service *jāgīr*.
19.	Dhian Singh	Kotla; worth 20,000.	Rajput	Hindu	—	Paid tribute to Sansar Chand of Kangra.	Made subordinate in 1809; lost territories in 1812; received service *jāgīr*.
20.	Fateh Khan	Leia; Karor, Dera Din Panah, Fatehpur, Sanawan, Mahmudkot, Mankera.	Baloch (Jaskani)	Muslim	Hayat Khan	Lost territories to Abdul Nabi Kalhora in 1788.	—

1	2	3	4	5	6	7	8
21.	Fateh Muhammad Khan	Kusak; Khewra, Makhiala, Girjakh, Choa Saidan Shah.	Rajput (Janjua)	Muslim	—	—	Lost territories in 1810; received subsistence *jāgīr*.
22.	Ghamand Chand	Kangra; Nadaon, Daulatpur, Bajwara, Mahal Morian, Jawalamukhi, Tira-Sujanpur; worth 7 lacs.	Rajput (Katoch)	Hindu	Tegh Chand (1774-75), Sansar Chand (1775-1823), Anirudh Chand (1823-31), Ranbir Chand & Parmod Chand.	Received tribute from Guler, Kotla, Siba, Datarpur, Mandi, Suket, Nurpur, Kulu, Jaswan and Kahlur.	Made subordinate in 1809; lost territories in 1828; Anirudh Chand sought British protection; recalled in 1833 and given subsistence *jāgīr*
23.	Govardhan Chand	Guler; Kotla; worth 1,40,000.	Rajput (Guleria)	Hindu	Parkash Chand (1760-90), Bhup Chand (1790-1820).	Lost Kotla in 1785; paid tribute to Jassa Singh Ramgarhia from 1770 to 1775, to Jai Singh Kanhiya from 1775 to 1786;	Made subordinate in 1809; lost territories in 1813; received subsistence *jāgīr*.

						to Sansar Chand from 1786 to 1809.	
24.	Gujjar Singh	Gujrat; 1/3 of Lahore, Daulatanagar, Dinga, Bahlolpur, Manawar, Sodhra, Jalalpur, Pothohar, Sarai Kala, Mirpur, Bajwat, Nangal Duna Singh; worth 13 lacs.	Jat (Sandhu)	Sikh	Sahib Singh (1788-1810).	Received tribute from the chiefs of Akhnur, Bhimber and Khari Khariali.	Made subordinate in 1807; lost territories in 1810; received subsistence *jāgīr*
25.	Gul Muhammad	Qadian	Sayyad	Muslim	Atta Muhammad	Lost territories to Jassa Singh Ramgarhia in 1770.	Family recalled; granted *jāgīr*.
26.	Gulab Singh Khaira	Adinanagar; Khadur; worth 1 lac.	Jat (Khaira)	Sikh	—	—	Made subordinate in 1803; lost territories

1	2	3	4	5	6	7	8
							in 1809; received subsistence *jāgīr*.
27.	Gurbakhsh Singh Dodia	Doda; Sandhanwal, Ranjrur, Jassar, Jamke, Bhopalwala, Dera Baba Nanak Khas; worth 80,000.	Jat (Randhawa)	Sikh	Sudha Singh (1795-1813), Gajja Singh (1813).	—	Lost territories in 1813; received service *jāgīr*.
28.	Gurbakhsh Singh Wazirabadia	Wazirabad; Ghirthal, Gojra, Mitranwala.	Jat (Waraich)	Sikh	Jodh Singh (1776-1809), Ganda Singh (1809).		Made subordinate in 1809; lost territories in 1810; received subsistence *jāgīr*.
29.	Haibat Khan	Darband	Afghan (Hindwal Tanaoli)	Muslim	Hashim Ali (1803-04), Nawab Khan (1804-18), Painda Khan (1818 onwards)	—	Made subordinate in 1824; lost territories in 1842; received service *jāgīr*.

30.	Haqiqat Singh	Fatehgarh Churian; Miankot, Narot Jaimal Singh and Kalanaur.	Jat (Sandhu)	Sikh	Jaimal Singh (1782-1812).	—	Lost territories in 1812; received subsistence *jāgīr*.
31.	Hari Singh	Amritsar; Chaprar, Gondal, Rangpur, Bahadurpur, Roras, Begowala, Goindke, Ban-Bajwa, Kul-Bajwa, Ugoke, Badoke, Adamke, Bhagowal, Muradpur, Chittie Sheịkhan, Bhagwal, Qasur (1790-94) & Multan (1772-80); worth 10 lacs.	Jat (Gill)	Sikh	Jhanda Singh (1765-74), Ganda Singh (1774-75), Charhat Singh (1775 only), Desa Singh (1775-82), Gulab Singh (1782-1800), Gurdit Singh (1800-05).	Received tribute from the chiefs of Jhang, Jammu and Pind Dadan Khan.	Lost territories in 1805; received subsistence *jāgīr*.
32.	Hira Singh Nakkai	Chunian; Satghara, Khudian, Faridabad, Malka Hans, Kamalia (1781-	Jaṭ (Sandhu)	Sikh	Nahar Singh (1766-67), Ran Singh (1767-81), Bhagwan Singh (1781-1789),	Received tribute from the chief of Dipalpur.	Lost territories in 1810; received service *jāgīr*.

1	2	3	4	5	6	7	8
		90s), Sayyadwala (1770-81); worth 3 lacs.			Gian Singh (1789-1807), Kahn Singh (1807).		
33.	Inder Dev	Bandralta (Ramnagar); worth 1,25,000.	Rajput (Bandral)	Hindu	Bhupindar Dev	Paid tribute to Ranjit Dev of Jammu.	Made subordinate in 1809; lost territories in 1822; received subsistence *jāgīr*.
34.	Jafar Khan	Khushab; worth 1 lac.	Baloch	Muslim	—	—	Made subordinate in 1804; lost territories in 1810; received subsistence *jāgīr*.
35.	Jai Singh Kanhiya	Batala; Gurdaspur, Kahnuwan, Panjgiraian, Thoba, Chawinda,	Jat (Sandhu)	Sikh	Sada Kaur (1789-1822).	Received tribute from the chiefs of Kangra,	Made subordinate in 1808; lost territories in

		Ajnala, Uthian, Bulaki, Mukerian, Hajipur, Nangal, Bhagwanpur, Maharajpur, Sayyidana, Talibpur, Bianpur, Chak-Sharif, Degowal, Malikpur, Faridnagar, Sohian and Mirthal.				Guler, Jaswan, Siba, Datarpur, Mandi, Nurpur, Suket, Basohli, Chamba and Bhadarwah.	1821; received service *jāgīr*.
36.	Jassa Singh Ahluwalia	Kapurthala; Fatehabad, Balachaur, Jalalabad, Nur Mahal, Sathiala, Goindwal, Vairowal, Sarhali, Sharaqpur, Jhabal, Tarn Taran (Mallanwala, Makhu, Kot Isa Khan); worth 12 lacs.	Kalal	Sikh	Bhag Singh (1783-1801), Fateh Singh (1801-36), Nihal Singh (1836 onwards).	Received tribute from the chiefs of Kapurthala, Phagwara, Talwan, Jandiala and Jodhanagri.	Made subordinate in 1809; lost territories in the Bari Doab in 1825; retained rest of the territories as a vassal.

1	2	3	4	5	6	7	8
37.	Jassa Singh Daskewala	Daska; Akbar, Gilotean, Dhamoke; worth 1,60,000.	—	Sikh	Nidhan Singh	—	Made subordinate in 1807; lost territories in 1810; received service *jāgīr*.
38.	Jassa Singh Ramgarhia	Sri Hargobindpur; Qadian, Kalanaur, Dhariwal, Ichhogil, Pindori, Ghuman, Begowal, Dasuya, Garhdiwala, Naya Nangal, Urmar, Tanda, Talwara; worth 7 lacs.	Tarkhan	Sikh	Jodh Singh (1803-16), Vir Singh (1816).	Received tribute from the chiefs of Kangra, Guler, Jaswan, Siba, Datarpur, Mandi, Nurpur, Suket, Basohli, Chamba and Bhadarwah.	Lost territories in 1816; received subsistence *jāgīr*.
39.	Jhanda Singh	Kathgarh; and the villages around; worth 1 lac.	—	Sikh	Tara Singh (1797).	—	Allowed to retain territories as service *jāgīrdār*.

40.	Jit Pal	Basohli; Lakhanpur; worth 75,000.	Rajput (Balauria)	Hindu	Amrit Pal (1757-76), Vijay Pal (1776-1806), Mahinder Pal (1806-13), Bhupinder Pal (1813-34).	Lost Bhalai and Jund to Raja Ugar Singh of Chamba in 1758 and Lakhanpur to Prithi Singh of Nurpur in 1785; paid tribute to Ranjit Dev of Jammu.	Made subordinate in 1809; lost territories in 1834; received subsistence *jāgīr*.
41.	Jiwan Singh	1/4 of Sialkot	Jat (Ghumman)	Sikh	—	—	Lost territories in 1807; received subsistence *jāgīr*.
42.	Kamr Singh Nakkai	Gogera; Harrapa, Kabirwala, Chichawatni, Sayyadwala, Pakka-Sidhar, Brahmpur Kamalia (1767-81).	Jat	Sikh	Wazir Singh (1780-90), Mehr Singh (1790).	—	Lost territories in 1804; received service *jāgīr*.

1	2	3	4	5	6	7	8
43.	Kapur Singh Faizullapuria	Jalandhar; Patti (Bharatgarh, Banur, Sarhind); worth $5\frac{1}{2}$ lacs.	Jat (Virk)	Sikh	Khushal Singh (1753-95) Buddh Singh (1795-1811).	—	Made subordinate in 1805; lost territories in 1811; sought British protection.
44.	Kapur Singh Saurianwala	Saurian; Karial; worth 1,50,000.	Jat (Sidhu)	Sikh	Jodh Singh, Amir Singh, Sukha Singh (1825).	—	Made subordinate in 1799; lost territories in 1825; received service *jāgīr*.
45.	Karam Singh	Povind; worth 8,000.	—	Sikh	Gulab Singh.	—	Lost territoties in 1805; received service *jāgīr*.
46.	Karam Singh Chhina	Firozke; Chhina, Nigran, Lalu, Bajra; worth 70,000.	Jat (Gill)	Sikh	—	—	Lost territories in 1806; received service *jāgīr*.

47.	Karam Singh Dulu	Chiniot; part of Amritsar; worth 1,50,000.	Jat	Sikh	Jassa Singh (1800-02).	Lost Chiniot in 1778, but recovered in 1787.	Lost territories in 1802; received subsistence *jāgīr*.
48.	Karam Singh Mananwala	Mananwala; with some villages near Amritsar.	Jat (Man)	Sikh	Ram Singh (1779-88), Sham Singh (1788-90).	Lost a part of the territories to Mahan Singh Sukarchakia in 1790.	Allowed to retain Mananwala worth 20,000 rupees as service *jāgīrdār*.
49.	Karora Singh	Hariana; Hoshiarpur, Basian, Sham-Chaurasi, Pandorian, Bhunga, and the territories across the river Satlej; worth 5 lacs.	Jat (Sandhu)	Sikh	Baghel Singh Dhaliwal (1761-1805).	Received tribute from the chief of Talwan.	Lost territories in 1809.

1	2	3	4	5	6	7	8
50.	Kirpal Das	Jandiala; worth 50,000.	Jat	—	Dyal Das, Saran Das, Bishambar Das.	Paid tribute to Jassa Singh Ahluwalia and his successors.	Lost territories in 1812.
51.	Lakha Wattu	Haveli Lakha Wattu; and the territory on the south of the Satlej; worth 80,000.	Rajput (Wattu)	Muslim	Ahmad Yar Khan (1760).	Lost Haveli Lakha Wattu to Lehna Singh Bhangi in 1767; retired to his territories across the river Satlej.	Lost territories in 1807; received service *jāgīr*.
52.	Lal Singh Miraliwala	Miraliwala; with 150 villages.	Jat (Virk)	Sikh	Bagh Singh	—	Lost territories in 1805; received service *jāgīr*.

53.	Lal Singh Shamkotia	Kanganpur	—	Sikh	—	—	Lost territories in 1807.
54.	Lehna Singh	One-third of Lahore; Shahdara, Fazlabad, Talwandi, Haveli Lakha Wattu.	Jat (Kahlon)	Sikh	Chait Singh (1797).	—	Lost territories in 1799; received service *jāgīr*.
55.	Mahmud Khan	Talwan; Nur Mahal; worth 2 lacs.	Rajput (Manj)	Muslim	Shahbaz Khan	Paid tribute to Baghel Singh Karora Singhia for some time.	Lost territories in 1806; received subsistence *jāgīr*..
56.	Majja Singh Khundawala	Naoshehra; Zafarwal, Khunda.	Jat (Randhawa)	Sikh	Prem Singh	Lost a part of the territories to Sada Kaur in 1795.	Lost territories in the first decade of the 19th century; received service *jāgīr*.
57.	Malik Aulia Khan	Pindi Gheb; Chakwal.	Rajput (Jodrah)	Muslim	Malik Amanat Khan, Ghulam Muhammad.	Paid tribute to Charhat Singh Sukarchakia.	Lost territories in 1813; received *chahāramī* rights.

1	2	3	4	5	6	7	8
58.	Man Pal	Bangahal; Bara Bangahal, Chhota Bangahal.	Rajput (Bangahalia)	Hindu	—	Lost a part of his territory to Ghamand Chand in the 1760s; subsistence *jāgīr* given by Raj Singh of Chamba to Man Pal's widow.	—
59.	Mehtab Singh	Wadala	Jat (Sandhu)	Sikh	Sham Singh & Nidhan Singh.	Lost Wadala to Nidhan Singh.	Lost territories in 1810; received service *jāgīr*.
60.	Milkha Singh Thepuria	Rawalpindi; Kahuta, Hasan Abdal, Syadpur; worth 3 lacs.	—	Sikh	Jiwan Singh (1804-15), Anand Singh (1815).	Received tribute from the chiefs of Khanpur, Sarai Niamat Khan and Mari.	Made subordinate in 1802; lost territories in 1815; received service *jāgīr*.
61.	Mirza Singh	10 villages; worth 15,000 rupees .	Jat (Shergill)	Sikh	Kahn Singh & Jit Singh.	Lost a part of his territories	Lost territories in 1805;

					in 1787.	to Jaimal Singh of Fatehgarh Churian.	received service *jāgīr*.
62.	Mohar Singh Atariwala	1/4 of Sialkot	Jat	Sikh	—	—	Lost territories in 1807; received subsistence *jāgīr*.
63.	Mubarak Khan	Lodhran; Mailsi, Dunyapur, Chota Jalalpur, Jatoi, Alipur, Sitpur, Rawani, Shahr Sultan, Bahadurpur, Khairpur, Mubarkpur.	Afghan (Daudputra)	Muslim	Bahawal Khan II (1772-1809), Sadiq Khan II (1802-26), Bahawal Khan III (1826 onwards).	Paid tribute to the rulers of Kabul till 1793.	Made subordinate in 1811; lost territories in 1831; continued to rule over territory on the south of the Satlej.
64.	Mubark Khan	Sahiwal; Shahpur, Bhera; worth 1,50,000.	Baloch	Muslim	Muhammad Khan	Lost Bhera to Jhanda Singh Bhangi in 1771.	Made subordinate in 1804; lost territories in 1810; received service *jāgīr*.

1	2	3	4	5	6	7	8
65.	Muhammad Azim Khan	Malka Hans; Qabula, Pakka Sadhar; worth 50,000.	Jat (Hans)	Muslim	Muhammad Hayat	Lost territories to Bhagwan Singh Nakkai in 1790.	—
66.	Muhammad Khan	Mankera; Morad Ali, Leia, Bhakkar, Khanpur, Sanawan, Dera Ismail Khan, Khangarh, Mahmudkot, Kahlur Kot, Darya Khan, Kirrai Kot Nawankot, Koreshi, Pir Abdul Rahman; worth 10 lacs.	Afghan (Saddozai)	Muslim	Sher Mohammad Khan (1816-21).	Received tribute from the chiefs of Kalabagh, Isa Khel, Kulachi, Kirri, Mangal and Marwat.	Made subordinate in 1816; lost territories in 1821 and 1836; received subsistence *jāgīr*.
67.	Muhammad Nasim Khan	Shamsabad; Talagang, Reshan.	Rajput (Awan)	Muslim	—	Paid tribute to Charhat Singh Sukarchakia.	Lost territories in 1813; received service *jāgīr*.

68.	Muhammad Yar	Pindi Bhattian; Jalalpur, Hafizabad, Chak Bhatti; worth 1,50,000.	Rajput (Bhatti)	Muslim	Jalal Khan	—	Lost territories in 1802; received service *jāgīr*.
69.	Muhammad Yar Khan	Kamalia; Khanpur, Kharal, Faridabad, Rahimabad, Satghara; worth 3 lacs.	Rajput (Kharal)	Muslim	Sa'adat Khan II	Lost territories on both sides of the river Ravi except Kamalia to Hira Singh and Kamr Singh Nakkai around 1763.	Lost territories in 1804; received service *jāgīr*.
70.	Muhiyudin Khan	Qasur; Hardo Shaikh Sadh, Mamdot; worth 3 lacs.	Pathan	Muslim	Hamid Khan (1763-80), Nizamuddin Khan (1780-1802), Fatehuddin Khan (1802-07).	Paid tribute to Jhanda Singh Bhangi.	Made subordinate in 1801; lost territories in 1807; received service *jāgīr*.
71.	Muqarrab Khan	Rawalpindi; Gujrat, Pharwala, Dangli, Syadpur, Hasan Abdal,	Rajput (Gakkhar)	Muslim	Mansur Khan, Shadman Khan, Mehdi Ali Khan.	Lost Gujrat to Gujjar Singh Bhangi in 1765 and Rawalpindi	Lost territories in 1818; received subsistence

1	2	3	4	5	6	7	8
		Rohtas; worth 9 lacs.				to Gujjar Singh Bhangi and Charhat Singh Sukarchakia in 1767; left with Pharwala alone.	*jāgīr*.
72.	Nand Chand	Datarpur; worth 50,000.	Rajput (Dadwal)	Hindu	Gobind Chand	Paid tribute to Jassa Singh Ramgarhia from 1770 to 1775; to Jai Singh Kanhiya from 1775 to 1786; to Sansar Chand from 1786 to 1809.	Made subordinate in 1809; lost territories in 1818; received *jāgīr*.
73.	Narain Pal	Chauki Kutlehr; worth 25,000.	Rajput (Kutlehria)	Hindu	—	Territories taken over by Ghamand Chand and Sansar Chand from 1758 to	Made subordinate in 1809; lost territories in 1825; received

						1786; recovered with the help of the Gurkhas in 1806.	service *jāgīr*.
74.	Natha Singh Shahid	1/4 of Sialkot	Jat	Sikh	—	—	Lost territories in 1807; received subsistence *jāgīr*.
75.	Nur Muhammad	Rasulnagar; Alipur, Manchar, Sayyadpur, Ahmadnagar.	Jat (Chattha)	Muslim	Pir Muhammad (1760-74), Ghulam Muhammad (1774-83), Jan Muhammad (1783).	Lost territories to Mahan Singh Sukarchakia in 1783 and given subsistence *jāgīr*.	—
76.	Prit Singh	Jaswan; worth 1,25,000.	Rajput (Jaswal)	Hindu	Umed Singh	Paid tribute to Jassa Singh Ramgarhia from 1770 to 1775, to Jai Singh Kanhiya from	Made subordinate in 1809; lost territories in 1816; received service *jāgīr*.

1	2	3	4	5	6	7	8
						1775 to 1786; to Sansar Chand from 1786 to 1809.	
77.	Prithi Singh	Nurpur; Shahpur; worth 4 lacs.	Rajput (Pathania)	Hindu	Bir Singh (1789-1846).	Paid tribute to Jassa Singh Ramgarhia from 1770 to 1775; to Jai Singh Kanhiya from 1775 to 1786; to Sansar Chand from 1786 to 1809.	Made subordinate in 1809; lost territories in 1816; sought British protection.
78.	Puran Pal	Bhadu; worth 50,000.	Rajput (Bhadwal)	Hindu	Prithi Pal, Jai Pal	Paid tribute to Ranjit Dev of Jammu.	Made subordinate in 1809; lost territories in 1820; received subsistence *jāgīr*.

79.	Rai Ibrahim	Kapurthala; Sultanpur, Dhaliwal, Dhilwan, Hamira, Lohian; worth 3 lacs.	Rajput (Bhatti)	Muslim	—	Lost territories to Jassa Singh Ahluwalia in 1780 and given subsistence *jāgīr*.	—
80.	Rai Jalal	Kot; Khunda, Western half of Fatehjang.	Rajput (Gheba)	Muslim	Rai Muhammad Khan	Paid tribute to Charhat Singh Sukarchakia.	Lost territories in the first decade of the 19th century; received sevice *jāgīr*.
81.	Ranjit Dev	Jammu; Manawar, Kathua, Hamidgarh, Samba, Gondal, Chaprar, Chawinda, Karianwala, Daulatanagar, Bahlolpur; worth 5 lacs.	Rajput (Jamwal)	Hindu	Brij Raj Dev (1781-86), Sampuran Dev (1786-97), Jit Dev (1797-1815).	Received tribute from Jasrota, Bandralta, Mankot, Bhadarwah, Bhadu, Chenini, Khari Khariali, Akhnur, Samba, Riasi, Kirmchi, Bhau, Dalpatpur and Tirikot.	Made subordinate in 1809; lost territories in 1815; received subsistence *jāgīr*.

1	2	3	4	5	6	7	8
82.	Rattan Dev	Jastora; worth 1,25,000.	Rajput (Jasrotia)	Hindu	Ajaib Singh, Lal Singh,	Paid tribute to Ranjit Dev of Jammu.	Made subordinate in 1809; lost territories in 1824; received susbsistence *jāgīr*.
83.	Ruhulla Khan	Ahmadabad	Rajput (Khokhar)	Muslim	—	Lost Ahmadabad to Charhat Singh Sukarchakia in 1767.	—
84.	Saeed Khan	Shahpur	Rajput (Pathania)	Muslim	—	Territories taken over in 1781 by Tara Singh of Pathankot, Amar Singh of Sujanpur and Prithi Singh of Nurpur.	—
85.	Sahaj Singh	14 villages near Phagwara; worth 20,000.	Jat (Bhangu)	Sikh	Dyal Singh	—	Allowed to retain territories as service *jāgīrdār*.

86.	Sahib Khan	Pind Dadan Khan; worth $6\frac{1}{2}$ lacs.	Rajput (Khokhar)	Muslim	—	Lost territories to Charhat Singh Sukarchakia in 1767 and given subsistence *jāgīr*.	—
87.	Sahib Singh	Taragarh; Wachhoya.	Jat (Veglia)	Sikh	Jodh Singh, Vir Singh, Amir Singh, Kahn Singh.	—	Lost territories in 1812; received subsistence *jāgīr*.
88.	Sahib Singh	30 villages near Kathu Nangal.	Jat (Randhawa)	Sikh	Jit Singh & Buddh Singh.	—	Allowed to retain territories as service *jāgīrdār*.
89.	Sahib Singh	Shaikhupura; worth 1,60,000.	Jat (Virk)	Sikh	Amir Singh	—	Made subordinate in 1795; lost territories in 1808; received service *jāgīr*.
90.	Sahib Singh Sialkotia	1/4 of Sialkot	—	Sikh	—	—	Lost territories in 1807.

1	2	3	4	5	6	7	8
91.	Sampat Pal	Bhadarwah; worth 50,000.	Rajput (Bhadrawahia)	Hindu	Fateh Pal (1770-90), Daya Pal (1790-1810), Pahar Chand (1810-20).	Paid tribute to Ranjit Dev of Jammu and the chief of Chamba.	—
92.	Sanwal Singh Chamiariwala	Pasrur; Ajnala, Chamiari, Ghaniwal, Narowal, Lal, Sankhtara, Dhamtal, Bajwa; worth 2 lacs.	Jat (Randhawa)	Sikh	Nar Singh	—	Made subordinate in 1804; lost territories in 1806; received subsistence *jāgīr*.
93.	Sayyad Sadruddin	Hujra Shah Muqim; Bashirpur; worth 75,000.	Sayyad	Muslim	Sayyad Qutb Ali	—	Lost territories in 1807.
94.	Shabt Khan	Malot; Kahan.	Rajput (Janjua)	Muslim	Ghulam Muhiyyuddin Khan	Paid tribute to Mahan Singh Sukarchakia.	Lost territories in the first decade of the 19th century.

95.	Shaikh Muhammad Abdus Subhan	Pakpatan; with some territory on the south of the Satlej; worth 30,000.	Shaikh	Muslim	Shaikh Ghulam Rasul, Shaikh Muhammad Yar.	—	Made subordinate in 1815; lost territories in 1825; received subsistence *jāgīr*.
96.	Shakar Khan	Multan; Khangarh, Garh Maharaja, Shujabad, Sarai Sidhu, Sher Shah, Soman, Abdul Rahman, Dera Din Panah, Mubarik, Kojah, Syar Miani, Rangpur, Muzaffargarh; worth 9 lacs.	Afghan (Saddozai)	Muslim	Shuja Khan (1766-74), Muzaffar Khan (1774-1818).	Lost Multan to Jhanda Singh in 1772 but recovered in 1780. Paid tribute to the rulers of Kabul from time to time.	Made subordinate in 1803; lost territories in 1818; received subsistence *jāgīr*.
97.	Shamsher Chand	Chenini; worth 30,000.	Rajput (Hantal)	Hindu	Kishore Chand, Tegh Chand, Dyal Chand.	Paid tribute to Ranjit Dev of Jammu.	Made subordinate in 1809; lost territories in 1822; received subsistence *jāgīr*.

1	2	3	4	5	6	7	8
98.	Shamsher Sen	Mandi; worth 4 lacs.	Rajput (Mandial)	Hindu	Surma Sen (1781-88), Ishwari Sen (1788-1826), Zalim Sen (1826-39), Balbir Sen (1839-40)	Lost a part of his territory to the chiefs of Kangra, Kulu and Suket in 1792.	Made subordinate in 1809; lost territories in 1840; received *chāharamī* rights.
99.	Sher Jang Khan	Bhimber; worth 1,50,000.	Rajput (Chib)	Muslim	Sultan Khan	Paid tribute to Gujjar Singh Bhangi.	Made subordinate in 1810; lost territories in 1812; received service *jāgīr*.
100.	Sher Khan	Nurpur; Miththa Tiwana.	Rajput (Tiwana)	Muslim	Khan Mohammad Khan (1767-1804), Ahmad Yar Khan (1804-17).	—	Made subordinate in 1803; lost territories in 1817; received service *jāgīr*.

101. Sher Singh	Siba; worth 20,000.	Rajput (Sibaia)	Hindu	Gobind Singh	Lost territories to Bhup Chand of Guler in 1808.	Lost Siba in 1813; received subsistence *jāgīr* in 1820 through the influence of Dhian Singh.
102. Sobha Singh	One-third of Lahore, Nawankot, Sarai Amanat Khan, Khanpur, Niazbeg, Begowal.	Jat (Sandhu)	Sikh	Mohar Singh (1797-99).	—	Lost territories in 1799.
103. Suba Khan	Sarai Niamat Khan (lower Darband).	Afghan (Pallal Tanaoli)	Muslim	Gul Sher Khan, Ahmad Ali Khan, Akbar Ali Khan, Sarbuland Khan.	Paid tribute to Milkha Singh of Rawalpindi.	Made subordinate in 1821; lost territories in 1824.
104. Sultan Jafar Khan	Khanpur	Rajput (Gakkhar)	Muslim	—	Paid tribute to Milkha Singh of Rawalpindi.	Made subordinate in 1821; lost territories in 1831; received

1	2	3	4	5	6	7	8
							subsistence *jāgīr* in 1837.
105.	Tara Singh	Phillaur; Kang.	Jat (Kang)	Sikh	Koer Singh (1790-95), Sadda Singh, Megh Singh.	—	Lost territories in 1809; received service *jāgīr*.
106.	Tara Singh Dallewalia	Rahon; Kang, Dalla, Sarai Dakhni, Nawan Shahr (Dharmkot, Mahitpur, and Ghungrana); worth 4 lacs.	Jat (Kang)	Sikh	Jhanda Singh, Dasaunda Singh, (1807).	—	Made subordinate in 1805; lost territories in 1807; received service *jāgīr*.
107.	Tara Singh Pathankotia	Pathankot; Shahpur; worth 60,000.	Jat (Sandhu)	Sikh	—	—	Lost territories in 1807; received subsistence *jāgīr*.
108.	Tedhi Singh	Kulu; Sultanpur, Chhota Bangahal,	Rajput (Kaulua)	Hindu	Pritam Singh (1767-1806),	Paid tribute to Sansar Chand	Made subordinate in 1809;

		Bara Bangahal; worth 1,30,000.			Bikrama Singh (1806-16), Ajit Singh (1816-40).		lost territories in 1840; received *jāgīr*.
109.	Tehil Singh Chhachi	Makhad	Khatri (Kohli)	Sikh	Fateh Singh & Sher Singh.	—	Allowed to retain territories as service *jāgīrdārs*.
110.	Umed Singh	Chamba; worth 3.5 lacs.	Rajput (Chambial)	Hindu	Raj Singh (1764-94), Jit Singh (1794-1808), Charhat Singh (1808-44).	Received tribute from Bhadarwah, Kashtwar, Bhadu, Basohli and Bandralta.	Made subordinate in 1806; lost Fatehgarh and Rihlu in 1820.
111.	Walidad Khan	Jhang; Chiniot, Maghiana, Khiwa, Jalalpur, Shorkot, Masson, Pipalwala, Karianwala; worth 8,50,000.	Rajput (Sial)	Muslim	Inayat Ullah Khan (1747-87), Sultan Khan 1787), Sahib Khan (1787-90), Kabir Khan (1790-1801), Ahmad Khan (1801-16).	Lost Chiniot in 1760, recovered in 1778 but lost again in 1787.	Made subordinate in 1803; lost territories in 1816; received service *jāgīr*.

BIBLIOGRAPHY

BIBLIOGRAPHY

I. PERSIAN

Ā'īn-i-Akbarī	Abul Fazl Allami, *Ā'īn-i-Akbarī* (tr. H.S. Jarrett), Oriental Books Reprint Corporation, Vol. I, New Delhi, 1977, Vols. II & III, New Delhi, 1978.
Akbar Nāmā	Abul Fazl, *Akar Nāma* (tr. H. Beveridge), Rare Books, Vols. I & II, Delhi 1972, Vol. III, Delhi, 1973.
Akhbārāt	Garrett, H.L.O & G.L Chopra, (tr. & ed), *Events at the Court of Ranjit Singh (1810-17)* (translation of Persian news letters of the Darbar of Maharaja Ranjit Singh), The Punjab Government Record Office Publication, Monograph No. 17, Punjab Languages Department, Patiala, 1970 (reprint).
Asrar-i-Samadi	*Asrar-i-Samadi* (tr. & ed. Janak Raj & Gurbakhsh Singh), Punjabi University, Patiala, 1978.
Bābur-Nāma	Zahiru'd-din-Muhammad Bābur Padshāh Ghazi, *Bābur-Nāma* (tr. A.S. Beveridge), 2 Vols., Oriental Books Reprint Corporation, New Delhi, 1970 (reprint).
Chār Bāgh-i-Panjab	Ganesh Das, *Chār Bāgh-i-Panjab* (tr. Amarwant Singh, in typescript), Guru Nanak Dev University, Amritsar.
	Grewal, J.S. & Indu Banga (tr. & ed), *Early Nineteenth Century Panjab* (a part of Ganesh Das's *Chār Bāgh-i-Panjab*), Guru Nanak University, Amritsar, 1975.
Farmans, Parwanās, Baināmas etc. (Pindori Documents)	Goswamy, B.N. & J.S. Grewal (tr. & ed.), *The Mughal and Sikh Rulers and the Vaishnavas of Pindori* (A Study of 52 Persian Documents from the Pindori

Collection), Indian Institute of Advanced Study, Simla, 1969.

Farmāns, Parwānas, Baināmas etc. (Jakhbar Documents) — Goswamy, B.N. & J.S. Grewal (tr. & ed.), *The Mughals and the Jogis of Jakhbar* (A study of 16 Persian Documents of the Jakhbar Collection), Indian Institute of Advanced Study, Simla, 1967.

Gulābnāma — Kirpa Ram, *Gulābnāma* (tr. Sukhdev Singh Charak), Light & Life Publishers, New Delhi, 1977.

Ibratnāma — Aliuddin Mufti, *Ibratnāma* (tr. Gurbakhsh Singh, in typescript), Punjabi University, Patiala.

Jangnāma — Qazi Nur Muhmmad, *Jangnāma* (tr. & ed. Ganda Singh), Sikh History Research Centre, Khalsa College, Amritsar, 1939.

Khulāsat-ut-Tawārīkh — Sujan Rai Bhandari, *Khulāsat-ut-Tawārīkh* (tr. Ranjit Singh Gill, ed. Fauja Singh), Punjabi University, Patiala, 1972.

Ma'āsir-al Umarā' — Nawab Samsām-ud-Daula Shāh Nawāz Khan, *Maāthir-ul-Umara* (tr. H Beveridge), 2 Vols., Janaki Prakashan, Patna, 1979 (reprint).

Muntakhab ut-Tawārīkh — Abdu-l-Qādir Ibn-i-Muluk Shāh & Al-Badaoni, *Muntakhabu-t Tawārīkh* (tr. & ed. W.H. Lowe), 2 Vols., Academica Asiatica, Patna, 1973.

Rājdarshinī — Ganesh Das, *Rājdarshinī*, (English translation in typescript with Professor Indu Banga), Guru Nanak Dev University, Amritsar.

Tahmas Nāma — Tahmas Khan, *Tahmas Nāma* (tr. P. Setu Madhava Rao), Popular Prakashan, Bombay, 1967.

Tamassukat — Grewal, J.S. (tr. & ed.), *In the By-Lanes of History: Some Persian Documents from a Punjab Town*, Indian Institute of Advanced Study, Simla, 1975.

Tārīkh-i-Ālamgir Sānī — (anon.)*Tārīkh-i-Ālamgir Sānī* (tr. Jadunath Sarkar, in typescript), Punjab State Archives, Patiala.

Tārīkh-i-Hind — Ahmad Shah Batalia, *Tārīkh-i-Hind* (the part translated by Gurbakhsh Singh as *Tārīkh-i-Panjab*), Punjabi University, Patiala, 1972.

Tārīkh-i-Sikhān — Khushwaqat Rai, *Tawārīkh-i-Sikhān* (tr. Milkhi Ram Khushan, in typescript), Punjabi University, Patiala.

Tuzuk-i-Jahāngīrī — Jahangir, Emperor, *The Tuzuk-i-Jahāngīrī* or *Memoirs of Jahangir* (tr. Alexander Rogers, ed. Henry Beveridge), 2 Vols., Munshiram Manoharlal, Delhi, 1968 (2nd ed.).

Umdat-ut-Tawārīkh — Sohan Lal Suri, *Umdat-ut-Tawārīkh* (tr. Amarwant Singh, ed. J.S. Grewal & Indu Banga), Daftar II, Guru Nanak Dev University, Amritsar, 1985.

Zafarnāma-i-Ranjit Singh — Diwan Amar Nath, *Zafarnāma-i-Ranjit Singh* (tr. Kirpal Singh), Punjabi University, Patiala, 1983.

II. PUNJABI

Bhangu, Ratan Singh, *Prachin Panth Parkash*, Wazir-i-Hind Press, Amritsar, 1962 (4th ed.).

Giani Gian Singh, *Tawārīkh Guru Khālsa*, Vol. II, Khalsa Tract Society, Amritsar, 1878.

————, *Raj Khalsa*, Vol. III of *Tawārīkh Guru Khālsa*, Punjab Languages Department, Patiala, 1970 (reprint).

————, *Tawārīkh Sri Amritsar*, Kendri Singh Sabha Commitee, Amritsar, 1977.

Ram Sukh Rao, *Jassa Singh Binod* (ms), M/771, Punjab State Archives, Patiala.

————, *Sri Fateh Singh Partap Prabhakar* (ed. Joginder Kaur), Patiala, 1980.

III. URDU

Amin Chand, Munshi, *Tawārīkh-i-Sialkot* (tr. Charles A. Roe), Lahore, 1874.

Debi Parsad, *Gulshan-i-Panjab* (tr. Harminder Singh, ed. Fauja Singh), Punjabi University, Patiala, 1979.

Kali Rai, *Sair-i-Panjab* (tr. Giani Lal Singh, ed. Fauja Singh), Punjabi University, Patiala, 1971.

Kanhiya Lal, *Tārīkh-i-Panjab* (tr. Jit Singh Seetal), Punjabi University, Patiala, 1968.

IV. CONTEMPORARY/NEAR CONTEMPORARY ACCOUNTS

Abdul Kadir, 'Memorandum of the Route between Delhi and Cabul', *Asiatic Annual Register (1806)*, London, 1809.

Anon., 'A Tour to Lahore (in 1808) by an Officer of the Bengal Army', *Asiatic Annual Register*, *(1809)*, London, 1811.

Browne, James, *History of the Origin and Progress of the Sikhs* (India Tracts), London, 1788.

————, *Browne Correspondence* (ed. K.D. Bhargava), India Records Series, New Delhi, 1960.

Burnes, Alexander, *Travels into Bokhara Containing the Narrative of a Voyage of the Indus from the Sea to Lahore*, 3 Vols., London, MDCCCXXXIX.

Campbell, George, *Memoirs of My Indian Career*, 2 Vols., London, 1893.

Cunningham, Joseph Davey, *A History of the Sikhs from the Origin of the Nation to the Battles of the Sutlej*, S. Chand & Co., New Delhi, 1972 (reprint, first published in 1849).

Drew, Frederic, *The Jummoo and Kashmir Territories*, Oriental Publishers, Delhi, 1971 (reprint, first published in 1875).

Elphinstone, Mountstuart, *An Account of the Kingdom of Caubul*, Vol. I, London, 1842 (reprint, first published in 1815).

————, *The History of India*, London, 1911 (9th ed. first published in 1841).

Forrest, George, W. (ed.), *Selections from the Travels and Journals Preserved in the Bombay Secretariat*, Bombay, 1906.

Forster, George, *A Journey from Bengal to England through the Northern Part of India, Kashmire, Afghanistan and Persia and into Russia by the Caspian-Sea*, 2 Vols., Punjab Languages Department, Patiala, 1970 (reprint, first published in 1808).

Francklin, W., *The History of the Reign of Shaw Aulum*, London, 1798.

———— (comp.), *Military Memoirs of George Thomas*, London, 1805.

Ganda Singh (ed.), *Early European Accounts of the Sikhs*, Indian Studies: Past and Present, Calcutta, 1962 (reprint).

Garrett, H.L.O. (ed.), *The Punjab-A Hundred Years Ago, as Described by V. Jacquemont and A.Soltykoff*, The Punjab Government Record Office Publication, Monograph No. 18, Lahore, 1935.

Grey, C., *European Adventurers of Northern India 1785 to 1849* (ed. H.L.O. Garrett), Government Printing, Lahore, 1929.

Griffiths, John, 'A Memorandum of the Panjab and Kandhar' (A letter written to Alexander Adamson dated Surat, 17th February 1794), *Early European Accounts of the Sikhs* (ed. Ganda Singh), Indian Studies: Past & Present, Calcutta, 1962 (reprint).

Hugel, Baron Charles, *Travels in Kashmir and the Panjab* (tr. & ed. T.B. Jervis), London, 1845.

Lawrence, H.M., *Adventures of an Officer in the Service of Ranjit Singh*, 2 Vols., London, 1845.

Malcolm, John, *Sketch of the Sikhs*, London, 1812.

Masson, Charles, *Narrative of Various Journeys in Beluchistan, Afghanistan and the Punjab*, Vol. I, London, 1842.

M'Gregor, W.L., *The History of the Sikhs: Containing the Lives of the Gooroos: the History of the Independent Sirdars, or Missuls and the Life of the Great Founder of the Sikh Monarchy, Maharajah Runjeet Singh*, Vol. I, London, 1846.

Mohan Lal, Munshi, *Journal of a Tour through the Punjab, Afghanistan, Turkistan, Khorasan and Part of Persia*, Calcutta, 1834.

Moorcraft, W. & G.Trebeck, *Travels in the Himalayan Provinces of Hindustan and the Punjab, in Ladak and Kashmir, in Peshawar, Kabul and Kunduz and Bokhora from 1819 to 1825*, Punjab Languages Department, Patiala, 1970 (reprint, first published in 1837).

Polier, Colonel, A.L.H., 'The Siques', *Early European Accounts of the Sikhs* (ed. Ganda Singh), Indian Studies: Past & Present, Calcutta, 1962 (reprint).

Prinsep, Henry T., *Origin of the Sikh Power in the Panjab and Political Life of Maharaja Ranjit Singh*, Punjab Languages Department, Patiala, 1970 (reprint, first published in 1834).

Shahamat Ali, *Picturesque Sketches in India: History of Bahawalpur*, London, 1848.

————————, *The Sikhs and the Afghans*, Punjab Languages Department, Patiala, 1970 (reprint, first published in 1847).

Smyth, Major G. Carmichael (ed.), *A History of the Reigning Family of Lahore, with some Account of the Jummoo Rajahs, the Seik Soldiers and their Sirdars*, Calcutta, 1847.

Thornton, Edward, *A Gazetteer of the Countries Adjascent to India on the North-West including Sind, Afghanistan, Beloochistan, Punjab*, Vol. II, London, 1844.

Vigne, G.T., *A Personal Narative of a Visit to Ghuzni, Kabul and Afghanistan*, London, 1840.

V. OFFICIAL PUBLICATIONS

(i) *District Gazetteers*

Amritsar (1883-84 & 1892-93); Attock (1883-84); Bahawalpur (1904); Chenab Colony (1904); Dera Ghazi Khan (1883-84); Dera Ismail Khan (1883- 84); Firozpur (1883-84); Gujranwala (1883-84, 1895 & 1935); Gujrat (1883- 84); Gurdaspur (1883-84); Hazara (1883-84); Hoshiarpur (1883-84); Jhelam (1883-84); Jhang (1883-84); Jullundur (1883-84); Jullundur and Kapurthala (1904); Kangra (1883-84); Lahore (1883-84); Montgomery (1883-84); Multan (1883-84); Muzaffargarh (1919); Rawalpindi (1895 & 1907); Shahpur (1883- 84); Sialkot (1895 & 1921).

(ii) *Settlement Reports*

Anderson, A., *Report on the Land Revenue Settlement of the Siba Jagir in the Kangra District of the Punjab (1881-82)*, Lahore, 1882.

Barnes, G.C. & C.J. Christian, *Report on the Revised Settlement of the Oonah, Hushiarpur, Gurshunkur and Harriana Purgunahs of the Hushiarpur District in the Trans-Sutlej States*, Lahore, 1860.

Barnes, G.C. & J.B. Lyall, *Report of the Land Revenue Settlement of the Kangra District*, Lahore, 1889.

Carriot, Major J.G., *Report on the Settlement of the Rawalpindi District (1865)*, Lahore, 1865.

Creathed, R., E.A. Prinsep, R. Temple and Others, *Report on the Revised Settlement of Purgunah Narowal Tulwandee of the Umritsar District in the Umritsar Division*, Lahore, 1860.

Davies, R.H. & M. Blyth, *Report on the Revised Settlement of the Umritsar, Saurian and Turn-Taran Purganahas of the Umritsar District in the Umritsar Division*, Lahore, 1860.

Elphinstone, N.W., *Report on the Revised Settlement of the Googaira District in the Mooltan Division*, Lahore, 1860.

Lyall, J.B., *Report of the Land Revenue Settlement of the Kangra District (1865-72)*, Lahore, 1874.

Meckenzie, Capt. Hector, *Report on the Revised Settlement of the Goojrat District in the Rawalpindi Division*, Lahore, 1861.

Moncktov, C.S., *Report on the Settlement of the Jhung District (1860)*, Lahore, 1860.

Montgomery, Capt. J.A.L., *Final Report of the Revised Settlement of Hoshiarpur District (1879-84)*, Calcutta, 1885.

Nisbet, R.P., *Report on the Revision of the Land Revenue Settlement of the Gujranwala District (1866-67)*, Lahore, 1874.

O'Brien, Edward, *Report on the Land Revenue Settlement of the Muzaffargarh District (1873-80)*, Lahore, 1882.

Ousley, G. & W.G. Davies, *Report on the Revised Settlement of the Shahpoor District in the Rawalpindi Division (1866)*, Lahore, n.d.

Prinsep, E.A., *Report on the Revised Settlement of Sealkote District in the Amritsur Division*, Lahore, 1865.

Roe, C.A., & W.E. Purser, *Report on the Revised Land Revenue Settlement of the Montgomery District (1874)*, Lahore, 1878.

Saunders, L.S., *Report on the Revised Settlement of the Lahore, District (1865-69)*, Lahore, 1873.

Smith, Capt. J. Dunlop, *Final Report on the Revised Settlement of Sialkot District (1885-95)*, Lahore, 1895.

Steedman, E.B., *Report on the Revised Settlement of the Jhang District (1874-80)*, Lahore, 1882.

Temple, R., *Report on the Settlement under Regn IX of The District of Jullundur in the Trans-Satluj States*, Lahore, 1852.

Thomson, R.G., *A Report of the Second Regular Settlement of the Land Revenue of the Jehlam District in the Rawalpindi Division of the Punjab*, Lahore, 1883.

Walker, G.C., *Final Report on the Revision of Settlement of the Lahore District*, Lahore, 1894.

Waterfield, W.G., *Report on the Second Regular Settlement of the Gujrat District (1866-68)*, Lahore, 1874.

(iii) *Other Official Publications*

Calender of Persian Correspondence, 5 Vols., Calcutta, 1911-30.

Hamilton, G.W., 'On the Tirnee Tax of Jhung', *Selections from the Public Correspondence of the Administration for the Affairs of the Punjab*, Vol. I, No. 9, Lahore, 1853, 103-11.

Imperial Gazetteer of India, Vol. XV, Claredon Press, Oxford, 1908.

Imperial Gazetteer of India (Punjab), Provincial Series, 2 Vols., Calcutta, 1908.

Journals and Diaries of the Assistants to the Agent, Governor-General, North West Frontier and Resident at Lahore, 1846-49, Vol. IV, Pioneer Press, Allahabad, 1911.

Political Diaries of Lieut. H.B. Edwardes Assistant to the Resident at Lahore, 1847-49: Lahore Political Diaries, Punjab Government Records, Vol. V, Pioneer Press, Allahabad, 1911.

Poona Residency Correspondence, Vols. I & II, Bombay, 1936, Vols. VIII & IX, Bombay, 1943.

Press Lists of the Old Records in the Punjab Secretariat- Delhi, Residency, Ludhiana & Karnal Agencies, 1804-16, Vol. II, Lahore.

Press Lists of Old Records in the Punjab Secretariat-Ludhiana, Karnal and Ambala Agencies, 1809-40, Vol. III, Lahore.

Ruling Princes and Chiefs, Notables and Principal Officials of the Punjab Native States, Government Printing, Punjab, Lahore, 1918.

Sandeeman, Hugh David, *Selections from Calcutta, Gazetteer of the Years 1806 to 1815 inclusive*, Vol. IV, Government Printing, Calcutta, 1868.

Selections from Note-Books Kept by Captain G. Birch (Assistant to Agent to the Governor General Karnal Agency), 1818-21, Vol. IX, Government Printing, Lahore, 1921.

Selections from the Records of the Government of the Punjab and its Dependencies, New Series No. XXIII, Papers relating to the Gakhar Tribe, Punjab Government Press, Lahore, 1887.

Setton Karr, W.S., *Selections from Calcutta Gazettes of the Years 1784, 1785, 1786, 1787 and 1788, Showing the Political Condition of the English in India*, Calcutta, 1864.

'The Administration of the Punjab', *The Calcutta, Review*, Vol. XXI, July-December 1853, Calcutta, 1853, 225-84.

The Land of the Five Rivers (Being Vol. I of the Punjab Administration Report 1921-22), Government Printing, Lahore, 1923.

VI. UNPUBLISHED OFFICIAL RECORDS

National Archives of India, New Delhi,.

(i) Foreign/Secret Consultation Files (1776-1849).

(ii) Foreign/Secret Proceedings Volumes (1800-1847).
(iii) Foreign/Political Consultation Files (1796-1858).
(iv) Foreign/Political Proceedings Volumes (1799-1859).

VII. BOOKS

Ahsan Raza Khan, *Chieftains in the Mughal Empire During the Reign of Akbar*, Indian Institute of Advanced Study, Simla, 1977.

Athar Ali, M., *The Mughal Nobility Under Aurangzeb*, Aligarh Muslim University, Aligarh, 1970 (reprint).

Bajwa, Fauja Singh, *Military System of the Sikhs* (1799-1849), Motilal Banarsidass, Delhi, 1964.

———— (ed.), *The City of Amritsar, : A Study of Historical, Cultural, Social and Economic Aspects*, Oriental Publishers & Distributors, New Delhi, 1978.

Banga, Indu, *Agrarian System of the Sikhs : Late Eighteenth and Early Nineteenth Century*, Manohar Publications, Delhi, 1978.

Bhagat Singh, *Sikh Polity in the Eighteenth and Nineteenth Centuries*, Oriental Publishers & Distributors, New Delhi, 1978.

Chopra, G.L., *The Punjab as a Sovereign State*, V.V. Research Institute, Hoshiarpur, 1960.

Datta, V.N., *Amritsar:Past and Present*, Municipal Committee, Amritsar, 1967.

Douie, J.M., *The Punjab, North West Frontier Province & Kashmir*, Seema Publications, Delhi, 1974.

Elliot, A.C., *The Chronicles of Gujrat*, Punjab Languages Department, Patiala, 1970 (reprint, first published in 1902).

Fagan, P.J., *Land Revenue : Its Origin and Development with special Reference to the Punjab*, Punjab Government Branch Press, Simla, 1921.

Ganda Singh, *A Bibliography of the Panjab*, Punjabi University, Patiala, 1966.

————, *Ahmad Shah Durrani*, Asia Publishing House, Bombay, 1959.

————, *Baba Banda Singh Bahadur : His Life and Achievements and the place of his Execution*, Sirhind Historical Research Society, Sirhind, 1976.

————, *Maharaja Ranjit Singh : First Death Centenary Memorial Volume* (edited in collaboration with Prof. Teja Singh), Khalsa College, Amritsar, 1939.

——————, *Sardar Jassa Singh Ahluwalia*, Punjabi University, Patiala.

Goulding, H.R. & T.H. Thornton, *Old Lahore*, Civil and Military Gazette Press, Lahore, 1924.

Grewal, J.S., *From Guru Nanak to Maharaja Ranjit Singh : Essays in Sikh History*, Guru Nanak University, Amritsar, 1972.

——————, *Historian's Punjab : Miscellaneous Articles*, Guru Nanak University, Amritsar, 1972.

——————, *The Reign of Maharaja Ranjit Singh : Structure of Power, Economy and Society*, Punjabi University, Patiala, 1981.

——————, *Maharaja Ranjit Singh*, Guru Nanak Dev University, Amritsar, 1983.

——————, *The Sikhs of the Punjab*, Cambridge University Press, Cambridge, 1991.

Griffin, Lepel, *Law of Inheritance to Chiefship as observed by the Sikhs before the Annexation of the Punjab*, Lahore, 1869.

——————, *Ranjit Singh*, S. Chand & Co., Delhi, 1967 (reprint).

——————, *The Panjab Chiefs : Historical and Biographical Notices of the Principal Families in the Territories under the Punjab Government*, Lahore, 1865.

Griffin, Lepel H. & C.F. Massy, *Chiefs and Families of Note in the Punjab* (revised by W.L. Conran & H.D. Craik), Vol. I, Government Printing, Lahore, 1909.

——————, *Revised Pedigree Tables of the Families mentioned in the Revised edition of the Chiefs and Families of Note of the Punjab*, Government Printing Press, Lahore, 1940.

Gupta, Hari Ram, *History of the Sikhs*, Munshiram Manoharlal, Vol.. II, New Delhi, 1978, Vol. IV, New Delhi, 1982.

——————, *Studies in the Later Mughal History of the Panjab (1707-93)*, The Minerva Book Shop, Lahore, 1944.

Hasrat, Bikramajit, *Life and Times of Ranjit Singh*, Published by the Author, Nabha, 1977.

Hutchison, J. & J. Ph. Vogel, *History of the Panjab Hill States*, 2 Vols., Department of Languages and Culture, Simla, 1982 (reprint).

Ibbetson, Denzil, *Panjab Castes*, Neeraj Publishing House, Delhi, 1934 (reprint).

Ibn Hasan, *The Central Structure of the Mughal Empire*, Munshiram Manoharlal, Delhi, 1970 (reprint).

Irfan Habib, *An Atlas of the Mughal Empire, Political and Economic Maps with Detailed Notes, Bibliography and Index*, Oxford, University Press, New Delhi, 1982.

————, *The Agrarian System of Mughal India (1526-1707)*, Asia Publishing House, Bombay, 1963.

Irvine, William, *The Later Mughals* (ed. Jadunath Sarkar), 2 Vols., M.C. Sarkar & Sons, Calcutta, 1982 (reprint).

Karam Singh, *Baba Ala Singh*, Parkash Publications, Patiala, 1918.

Kirpal Singh, *An Historical Account of Bhai Vasti Ram and Bhai Ram Singh*, Khalsa College, Amritsar, n.d.

————, *Life of Maharaja Ala Singh of Patiala, and His Times*, Khalsa College, Amritsar, 1954.

Kohli, Sita Ram, *Catalogue of Khalsa Darbar Records*, 2 Vols., Lahore, 1919 & 1927.

————, *Maharaja Ranjit Singh* (Pbi.), Atma Ram and Sons, Delhi, 1953.

————, *Sunset of the Sikh Empire* (ed. Khushwant Singh), Orient Longmans, New Delhi, 1967.

Latif, Syad Muhammad, *Early History of Multan*, Civil & Military Gazette Press, Lahore, 1891.

————, *History of the Panjab*, Eurasia Publishing House, New Delhi, 1964 (reprint, first published in 1889).

Massy, Charles Francis, *Chiefs and Families of Note in the Delhi,, Jalandhar, Peshawar and Derajat Divisions of the Punjab*, Pioneer Press, Allahabad, 1890.

Moreland, W.H., *From Akbar to Aurangzeb*, Oriental Reprints, Delhi, 1972.

————, *India at the Death of Akbar : An Economic Study*, Atma Ram & Sons, Delhi, 1962 (reprint).

————, *The Agrarian System of Moslem India*, Oriental Books Reprint Corporation, Delhi, 1968 (reprint).

Naqvi, Hameeda Khatoon, *Urban Centres and Industries in Upper India 1556-1803*, Asia Publishing House, Bombay, 1968.

Nayyar, Gurbachan Singh, *Sikh Polity and Political Institutions*, Oriental Publishers & Distributors, New Delhi, 1979.

Qureshi, Ishtiaq Hussain, *The Administration of the Mughal Empire*, N.V. Publications, Patna, n.d.

Randhawa, Mohinder Singh, *Basohli Paintings*, Publication Divisions, Government of India, Delhi, 1954.

Rose, H.A., *A Glossary of Tribes and Castes of the Punjab and North West Frontier Province of India*, 3 Vols., Punjab Languages Department, Patiala, 1970 (reprint).

Saran, P., *The Provincial Government of the Mughals (1526-1658)*, Asia Publishing House, Bombay, 1973 (2nd ed.).

Ross, David, *Land of the Five Rivers*, Punjab Languages Department, Patiala, 1970 (reprint, first published in 1883).

Sarkar, Jadunath, *Fall of the Mughal Empire*, Vol. II, Orient Longman, Calcutta, 1966.

————, *Mughal Administration*, M.C. Sarkar & Sons, Calcutta, 1952 (4th ed.).

Satish Chandra, *Parties and Politics at the Mughal Court (1707-40)*, People's Publishing House, New Delhi, 1972 (2nd ed.).

Siddiqi, Noman Ahmad, *Land Revenue Administration Under the Mughals (1700-1750)*, Aligarh Muslim University, Aligarh, 1970.

Sinha, N.K., *Ranjit Singh*, A. Mukherjee & Co., Calcutta, 1968 (3rd ed.).

————, *Rise of the Sikh Power*, A Mukherjee & Co., Calcutta, 1960 (3rd ed.).

Skemp, F.W. (collected and translated), *Multani Stories*, Government Printing, Punjab, Lahore, 1917.

Teja Singh, *Sikhism : Its Ideals and Institutions*, Longmans, Green & Co., Bombay, 1937.

———— (ed.), *Tales from the Sikh History of the Rawalpindi, Attock & Peshawar Districts : The Sikh Folk-Lore Series*, No. I, Model Electric Press, Lahore, 1917.

Teja Singh & Ganda Singh, *A Short History of the Sikhs*, Orient Longmans, Bombay, 1950.

Trevaskis, Hugh Kennedy, *Land of Five Rivers : An Economic History of the Punjab from the Earliest Times to the year of Grace, 1890*, Oxford, 1928.

Vogel, J. Ph., *Catalogue of the Bhuri Singh Museum at Chamba*, Calcutta, 1909.

Waheedudin, Fakir Syed, *The Real Ranjit Singh*, Punjabi University, Patiala, 1981.

Whitehead, R.B., *Catalogue of Coins in the Punjab Museum, Lahore*, Vols. II & III, Oxford, 1914 & 1934.

Wilson, H.H., *A Glossary of Judicial and Revenue Terms*, Munshiram Manoharlal, Delhi, 1968 (reprint).

VIII. ARTICLES

Ahsan Raza Khan, 'Kinship and Political Power: Tribal to Territorial : A Historical Perspective from 16th Century North-Western India', *Proceedings Punjab History Conference*, Patiala, 1979, 86-94.

Bajwa, Fauja Singh, 'The Misaldari Period of Sikh History', *Panjab Past and Present*, Vol. XI (1977), 88-92.

Banga, Indu, 'Ahmad Shah Abdali's Designs over the Punjab', *Proceedings Indian History Congress*, Patiala, 1968, 85-90.

————, 'Polity, Economy and Urbanization in the Upper Bari Doab (1700- 1947)', *Studies in Urban History* (ed. J.S. Grewal & Indu Banga), Guru Nanak Dev University, Amritsar, 1981, 192-206.

————, 'Presidential Address (Medieval Section)', *Proceedings Punjab History Conference*, Patiala, 1980, 83-95.

————, 'Sikh Revenue Administration : The Framework', *Studies in Local and Regional History* (ed. J.S. Grewal), Guru Nanak Dev University, Amritsar, 1974, 55-85.

————, 'The Nature of Sikh Rule', *Proceedings Punjab History Conference*, Patiala, 1972, 60-73.

————,'The Sikh Polity During the Eighteenth Century', *Proceedings Punjab History Conference*, Patiala, 1982, 105-10.

Chetan Singh, 'Riverine Transport in Punjab and the Decline of Trade in Multan during the second half of the 17th century', *Proceedings Punjab History Conference*, Patiala, 1981, 80-86.

Grewal, J.S., 'Historical Development of Amritsar, in Retrospect', *The City of Amritsar*, (ed. Fauja Singh), Oriental Publishers & Distributors, New Delhi, 1978, 373-85.

————, 'Historical Geography of the Punjab,' *Journal of Regional History*, I (1980), 1-15.

————, 'Jakhbar Revisited', *Studies in Local and Regional History* (ed. J.S. Grewal), Guru Nanak University, Amritsar, 1974, 37-54.

————, 'Legacies of the Sikh Past for the Twentieth Century', *Sikh History and Religion in the Twentieth Century* (ed. Joseph T.O' Connell *et al*), University of Toronto, 1988, 18-31.

————, 'Literary Evidence : The Case of Hir-Waris', *Journal of Regional History*, IV (1983), 1-6.

————, 'Ramdaspur to Amritsar: From a Town to a City', *Studies in Urban History* (ed. J.S. Grewal & Indu Banga), Guru Nanak Dev University, Amritsar, 1974, 1-18.

————, 'The Qazi in the Pargana', *Studies in Local and Regional History* (ed. J.S. Grewal), Guru Nanak Dev University, Amritsar, 1974, 1-36.

————, 'The Sikh Movement : A Historical Note', *Dissent, Protest and Reform in Indian Civilization* (ed. S.C. Malik), Indian Institute of Advanced Study, Simla, 1977, 159-66.

Grover, B.R., 'Presidential Address : Medieval Indian Section', *Proceedings Indian History Congress*, Calicut 1976, 1-36.

————, 'Relationship between the Sovereign State (the Mughals & Afghans) and Panjab Hill Chiefs during the 17th and 18th centuries (A Case Study of Chamba Chieftainship based on Bhuri Singh Museum, Chamba Documents)', *Proceedings Punjab History Conference*, Patiala, 1983, 94-102.

Irfan Habib, 'Monetary System and Prices', *The Cambridge Economic History of India* (ed. Tapan Raychaudhuri & Irfan Habib), Vol. I, Cambridge University Press, Cambridge, 1982, 360-81.

Johal, Daljinder Singh, 'Literary Evidence on Social Structure in the Punjab (1750-1850)', *Journal of Regional History*, II (1980), 51-70.

Maclagan, Lieut R., 'Fragments of the History of Mooltan, the Derajat and Bahawalpur from Persian MSS', *Journal of the Asiatic Society of Bengal*, Vol. XVIII, Part II (1848), 559-72.

Nurul Hasan, S., 'Three Studies of Zamindari System', *Medieval India-A Miscellany*, Vol. I, Aligarh Muslim University, Aligarh, 1969, 233-39.

————, 'Presidential Address', *Proceedings Punjab History Conference*, Patiala, 1965, 73-81.

Raychaudhuri, Tapan, 'Inland Trade', *The Cambridge Economic History of India* (ed. Tapan Raychaudhuri & Irfan Habib), Vol. I, Cambridge University Press, Cambridge, 1982, 325-59.

Rodgers, C.J., 'On the Coins of the Sikhs', *Journal of the Asiatic Society of Bengal*, Vol. I, Part I (1881), 71-93.

————, 'Some Coins of Ranjit Deo, King of Jammu a Hundred Years Ago', *Journal of the Asiatic Society of Bengal*, Vol. LIV, Part I (1885), 60- 66.

————, 'The Coins of Ahmad Shah Abdali', *Journal of the Asiatic Society of Bengal*, Vol. LIV, Part I (1885), 67-78.

Sachdeva, Veena, 'Administration under the Bhangi Chiefs', *Proceedings Punjab History Conference*, Patiala, 1982, 94-105.

————, 'Jāgīrdāri System in the Punjab (Late Eighteenth Century)', *Journal of Regional History*, Vol. V (1984), 1-13.

———, 'Subjugation of the Bhangis', *Maharaja Ranjit Singh and His Times* (ed. J.S. Grewal & Indu Banga), Guru Nanak Dev University, Amritsar, 1980, 79-86.

———, 'The Non-Sikh Chiefs of the Punjab Plains and Maharaja Ranjit Singh', *Journal of Regional History*, Vol. II (1981), 1-11.

———, 'The Religious Men as Chiefs in the Late 18th Century Punjab', *Proceedings Punjab History Conference*, Patiala, 1985, 178-83.

Satish Chandra, 'Presidential Address', *Proceedings Punjab History Conference*, Patiala, 1972, 16-25.

———, 'Some Aspects of Indian Village Society in Northern India during the 18th Century - The Position and Role of the Khud Kasht and Pāhi Kāsht', *The Indian Historical Review*, Vol. I, No. I (1974), 57-64.

Sharma, Radha, 'Agrarian Structure in the Districts of Amritsar, and Lahore, in the Early Nineteenth Century', *Maharaja Ranjit Singh And His Times* (ed. J.S. Grewal & Indu Banga), Guru Nanak Dev University, Amritsar, 1980, 169-76.

IX. THESES/DISSERTATIONS

Grewal, Reeta, 'Polity, Economy and Urbanization: Early Nineteenth Century Punjab', M. Phil. Dissertation, Guru Nanak Dev University, Amritsar, 1983.

Sachdeva, Veena, 'The Rule of the Bhangis (1765-1810)', M. Phil. Dissertation, Guru Nanak Dev University, Amritsar, 1981.

Sulakhan Singh, 'The Udasis under Sikh Rule (1750-1850)', Ph.D. Thesis, Guru Nanak Dev University, Amritsar, 1985.

Wadhwa, Kumari Asha, 'Vaishnava Bhakti in the Punjab (1600-1850 A.D.)', M.Phil. Dissertation, Guru Nanak Dev University, Amritsar, 1981.

INDEX